Le Recueil des inscriptions

ESTIENNE JODELLE

Le Recueil des inscriptions

1558

A LITERARY AND ICONOGRAPHICAL EXEGESIS

Victor E. Graham and W. McAllister Johnson

University of Toronto Press

Printed in the United States of America
for University of Toronto Press
Toronto and Buffalo

ISBN 0-8020-1752-5
Microfiche ISBN 0-8020-0088-6
LC 79-163818

This book has been published with the
help of a grant from the Humanities Research Council of Canada,
using funds provided by the Canada Council.

PREFACE

In our separate studies of literary and artistic manifestations in sixteenth-century France, we each came to the conclusion some time ago that collaboration on interdisciplinary projects was now likely to yield more valuable results than independent research in more narrowly restricted fields. For this reason, we decided to follow such an approach in a re-examination of some of the works of the members of the Pléiade, a group of poets almost as much involved in artistic as in poetic endeavours. Our first joint effort was a brief article on relations between Ronsard and the architect and sculptor responsible for decorating the inner façade of the *Cour carrée* of the Louvre ('Ronsard et la *Renommée* du Louvre,' *Bibliothèque d'Humanisme et Renaissance*, XXX (1968), pp. 7–17). We then turned our attention to Jodelle, who in his own person combined both literary and inconographical interests in a quite remarkable way. We have further similar studies in mind through which we hope to shed more light on other aspects of the activities of the Pléiade between 1550 and 1585.

One of the most productive features of this collaboration has been that there was never any sharp division of labour since we very quickly discovered in our researches that the answers to certain problems in iconography were to be found in literary sources, whereas the explanation of not a few passages in prose and poetry became clear only when they were related to artistic phenomena. The most rewarding period of investigation of this kind was the summer of 1969 which we spent at the Bibliothèque Nationale in Paris. Here, daily consultations and investigations into little explored areas led to many interesting and significant discoveries. We are particularly grateful to the Canada Council for awarding us grants which made possible this research.

We would like to thank especially the following members of the staff of the Bibliothèque Nationale for their generous assistance: in the Cabinet des Estampes, Monsieur Jean Adhémar and his associates; in the Réserve des Imprimés, Madame Veyrin-Forrer and Madame Basanoff; in the Cabinet des

Manuscrits, Mademoiselle Concasty; in the Cabinet des Médailles, Mademoiselle Jacquiot; and in the Département de la Musique, Monsieur François Lesure. In the Salle des Catalogues Monsieur Peyraube was a constant help in bibliographical matters.

In addition, we would like to thank most warmly Mademoiselle Bacou, Cabinet des Dessins (Louvre) for her helpful interest. Miss Dorothy Thickett also very kindly aided us in many ways in procuring materials from the British Museum.

Finally, we would like to express our gratitude and admiration to our friend and colleague, Professor D.F.S. Thomson, for his stylish translations of Jodelle's sometimes obscure Latin into elegant English.

University of Toronto — VEG
August 1971 — WMcAJ

CONTENTS

PART I

INTRODUCTION

As a member of the Pléiade, Estienne Jodelle (1532–73) is best known as the author of the tragedy *Cléopâtre captive* (1552), which is generally regarded as the starting point for the classical theatre in France.[1] He also composed at least one other tragedy, *Didon se sacrifiant* (1555), and a comedy, *Eugène* (1552), which may or may not be the same play as one called *La Rencontre*, also referred to by his contemporaries.[2]

Jodelle is a very curious figure whose career has only recently been investigated in a scholarly way.[3] He was much admired by his contemporaries for his erudition and his creative powers, but during his lifetime he published almost nothing. His three plays and some poetry were collected into a single volume put out posthumously by his friend Charles de La Mothe in 1574, with the promise that there would be a number of others which actually never appeared.[4]

Jodelle frequently contributed the usual type of laudatory poem to volumes written by his friends,[5] but the only book which he published personally was the *Recueil des inscriptions* (1558), here reproduced along with textual notes and adduced illustrations. Because of its significance, it is all the more surprising

1 Cf. Raymond Lebègue, *La Tragédie française de la Renaissance*, Brussels, 1944, p. 30. There are modern editions of the play by F. Gohin (Paris, Garnier, 1926) and L. Bryce Ellis (Philadelphia, University of Pennsylvania, Series in Romance Languages and Literatures, Extra Series No. 9, Pennsylvania University Press, 1946).

2 Cf. Victor E. Graham, 'Jodelle's "Eugène, ou la Rencontre" Again,' *Renaissance News*, XIV (1961), pp. 161–4.

3 See E.H. Balmas, *Un Poeta del Rinascimento Francese, Etienne Jodelle*, Florence, Olschki, 1962.

4 *Les Œuvres et meslanges poetiques*, Paris, N. Chesneau et M. Pattison, 1574. See especially the preface by La Mothe.

5 Cf. Etienne Jodelle, *Œuvres complètes* I, ed. E.H. Balmas, NRF Gallimard, 1965, pp. 77–158, etc.

that this important work has never before been edited or reprinted in its entirety.[6]

The *Recueil des inscriptions* is an elegant in quarto of some 48 folios.[7] The numbered foliation is preceded by the title-page and its verso with the *Extraict du Privilege*, *Estiene Jodelle à ses amis S.* (a 2^r–a 3^v), *Le Livre à la France* (a 4^r), and the *In librum elegia* (a 4^v). The justificatory text of the *Recueil* follows (fols. 1^r–28^v), after which appears the *faux titre* and the text of the *Christianorum nostri temporis heroum, et heroinarum icones* (fols. 29^r–40^v), *Ad Claud. Kerquifinanum* (fols. 41^r–42^v), and *A sa Muse* (fols. 43^r–44^r).

The circumstances surrounding the composition of the *Recueil des inscriptions* are explained by Jodelle in some detail. The occasion was the recapture of Calais from the English, a triumph widely celebrated in poetry and in song.[8]

6 Balmas includes most of the material from the *Recueil des inscriptions* in his edition of the *Œuvres complètes*, but he splits it up among the following sections: *Le Poète chez les hommes* (Vol. I, pp. 126–8); *Le Poète à la cour* (Vol. I, pp. 166–9, 185–203); *Le Poète dramatique* (Vol. II, pp. 217–56); *Le Poète satirique* (Vol. II, pp. 287–9). Cf. p. 9.

7 An error in the foliation after folio 20 results in the doubling of folio numbers 25–8, but not the text itself, which therefore does not alter the folio count.

We have incorporated without further note the only *fautes survenues en l'impression* listed on the final folio: LETHI: LOETHI (p. 96); *Qu'est encores ici cil qui ma toison porte: Que font encore ici ceux qui ma toison portent* (p. 110).

Copies of the volume are to be found in the following libraries (the list does not pretend to be complete): Bibliothèque Nationale (with a second copy in the Collection Rothschild), Arsenal, Ste Geneviève, Bordeaux; British Museum; Toronto; Harvard, Johns Hopkins, Wayne State. The only textual variant seems to be the correction in some copies of GBNIVM to GENIVM (p. 81) made sometime during the course of the printing.

8 Cf. V.-L. Saulnier, 'Les Poètes de la prise de Calais,' *Bulletin du Bibliophile et du Bibliothécaire* (1949), pp. 270–4. To the 27 works listed by Saulnier one may add the following: *Discours de la prinse de Calais* 23 a. Paris, L'Homme, 23 b. Tours, I. Rousset, 23 c. Paris, E. Denise, 23 d. Paris, A l'enseigne de l'éléphant, 27 a. *La Réduction de Calais au royaume de France*, Claude Micard, 1558, 28. *La Prinse de la ville et chateau de Guines*, Rouen, F. Valentin et R. Petit, 1558, 29. François Habert, *Le Dieugard de la*

The fortress had fallen to the Duc de Guise on 8 January 1558,[9] and when the king advised the municipal council of Paris that he would dine with them on Thursday, 17 February, the day after the Duc de Guise was due to return to the capital from Picardy, it was decided to provide a suitable reception for the monarch and his victorious general.[10]

The king's command had been given on 8 February, and steps were immediately taken to send for 'les rotisseurs, m^e^ d'hostel, paintres et autres ouvriers necessaires pour faire les aprestz dud. festin et banquet.' It was also decided to employ workmen 'pour aller partout où ilz pourroient pour querir du lierre,' and to send out selected invitations 'pour faire une semonce des Dames de Paris pour assister aud. festin.'[11]

It was apparently only decided on 14 February to include some sort of entertainment after the banquet, and it was at this point that Jodelle appeared before the members of the city council,[12] though it seems highly probable that the painters and other artisans had been working under his direction in the meantime.

There has been a good deal of discussion as to whether Jodelle offered his services or was invited to assume the responsibility for co-ordinating all aspects of the entertainment.[13] There is no good reason, however, to doubt the

Ville de Paris à Monseigneur de Guise . . . à son retour de Calais, Paris, d'Attaignant, 1558, 30. Jacques Du Plessis, *Hymne triumphal sur la reduction du Conté d'Oye en l'obeissance du Roy . . .* Paris, Federic Morel, 1558.

9 Henry was in residence at the Louvre when the news reached him on the day after the event, and its impact may be imagined from the description of how he, 'le landemain lundi ensuivant alla, acompaigné de la Royne et les Dames de sa Compaignée, les cent Gentilzhommes et plusieurs Evesques, faire chanter le *Te Deum laudamus* à la Saincte Chappelle, où led. S^gr^ oyst la Saincte Messe à deulx genoulx en grande devotion; puis alla baiser toutes les Sainctes Reliques, en remerciant Dieu de lad. Victoire.' Cf. *Histoire générale de Paris. Registres des délibérations du Bureau de l'Hôtel de Ville de Paris*, t. IV, p. 517.

10 Ibid., t. IV, 520–4.

11 Ibid., p. 520.

12 Ibid., p. 522.

13 Cf. Henri Chamard, *Histoire de la Pléiade*, II, pp. 293–6 and Jodelle, *Œuvres*, ed. Marty-Laveaux, pp. xxix-xxxiv.

accuracy of the poet's own version of the circumstances, since the wording of the request, as he gives it, is almost identical with that which appears in the *Registres des délibérations du Bureau de l'Hôtel de Ville de Paris*.[14]

There is, of course, the problem of time. Whether Jodelle began his preparations shortly after 8 February or on 14 February, to devise such an elaborate scheme of decoration and have it executed, and to compose in such a short time two *mascarades* (one with long poems)[15] which would have to be memorized and rehearsed, would seem to be an almost impossible task.

Fortunately, there is a good deal of evidence testifying as to Jodelle's virtuosity under such circumstances. Charles de La Mothe, in his preface to the *Œuvres* of 1574 says: 'Nous luy avons veu en sa premiere adolescence composer et escrire en une seule nuict, par gageure, cinq cens bons vers Latins, sur le sujet que promptement on luy bailloit.' Jodelle himself, in the dedicatory epistle to Claude Colet's translation of *Amadis de Gaulle*, Book IX, writes: 'Tant que voyant un jour sortir de ses mains le neufiesme d'Amadis, prest à mettre sur la presse, je luy dictay une ode Françoise de gayeté de cueur, et sus le pié, comme j'ay de coustume.'[16]

Charles de La Mothe also pays tribute to Jodelle's versatility: 'Il estoit grand Architecte, docte en la peinture, et Sculpture, et de tout il discouroit avec tel jugement, comme s'il eust esté accompli de toutes cognoissances.' Less modestly, Jodelle himself notes:

> Je suis dedans Paris encor que j'en sois loing,
> Où je desseine, et taille, et charpente et massonne,
> Je brode, je pourtray, je couppe, je façonne,
> Je cizele, je grave, émaillant, et dorant,
> Je griffonne, je peins, dorant et colorant,

14 *Registres des délibérations du Bureau de l'Hôtel de Ville de Paris*, t. IV, p. 520. ('Led. seigneur [Henry II] leur dist . . . qu'il voulloit aller soupper avec eulx en leur Hostel de Ville jeudi prochain, qui est le jeudi gras.') Cf. p. 72.

15 Cf. pp. 103–15.

16 For the poem in question, cf. Jodelle, *Œuvres complètes*, ed. Balmas, I, pp. 88–91.

> Je tapisse, j'assieds, je festonne et decore,
> Je musique, je sonne, et poëtise encore . . .[17]

Given the context, this passage may be purely fanciful, but at least it indicates Jodelle's wide interests in handicrafts and the fine arts.

It was quite another matter, of course, to direct others in the execution of such a project, and this is Jodelle's main defence in what he considered to be an unmitigated disaster: 'J'ose dire que je me fei quasi de tous mestiers, et assés heureusement, comme on pourra voir par ce recueil, si l'execution eust esté telle que l'ordonnance.'[18]

This, indeed, was Jodelle's main reason for publishing the *Recueil des inscriptions*. He wanted both friends and detractors to know about all the problems he had encountered in working out plans for the reception so that they would understand the reasons for the failure and better appreciate the closely integrated concept he had in mind.[19]

In selecting a unifying theme for the decoration and the entertainment, Jodelle says that he first considered a Christian one in order to reinforce the idea of a monarch *Treschrestien* who, with his predecessors, 'pour quelque grande victoire qu'ils sceussent avoir, n'avoir jamais triomphé.'[20] A Christian

17 'Epithalame de Madame Marguerite' in Jodelle, *Œuvres complètes*, ed. Balmas, I, p. 176.

18 Cf. p. 75.

19 Cf. Balmas, *Etienne Jodelle*, p. 380. The plaquette was likely composed in April and May 1558, set in type in June (the *privilège* is dated 11 June) and offered for sale that summer.

20 i.e. in the antique mode (cf. p. 72). Of course the suitable equivalent of the triumphal entry – around which the mythological accoutrements and *mystères* seem to have evolved – had been the processional of thanksgiving to Notre-Dame de Paris culminating in a *Te Deum*. (Cf. Josèphe Chartrou, *Les entrées solennelles et triomphales à la Renaissance 1484–1551*, Paris, Presses Universitaires Françaises, 1928, recently supplemented by Bernard Guenée et Françoise Lehoux, *Les entrées royales françaises de 1328 à 1515*, Paris, CNRS, 1968.) Most Valois entries were based upon the concept of a Roman emperor, not only in terms of a Trojan descent but in the superposition of an antique upon the contemporary city and rather conscious attempts at 'antique' painting upon

theme would have pleased the poet and painter, Nicolas Denisot, who was constantly urging his friends among the Pléiade to turn away from pagan inspiration,[21] but it is doubtful that Jodelle was really serious. Far more scope was allowed him by the classics – as he says, 'l'antiquité admirée d'un chacun, et aucunement recherchée par moy, tant en tous mes autres ouvrages qu'en ces miennes petites inventions.'[22]

Even if we presume that Jodelle actually had more than three days in which to prepare his decorations and entertainments, it is equally obvious that the set-pieces rely on events relating to the taking of the Trois-Evêchés in 1552 and whatever of his previous incidental verse could be accommodated to the circumstance.[23] Similarly, while Ronsard and Dorat provided in the space of a fortnight the programme for the Parisian entry of 1571, the *topos* which would be printed in the *Franciade* scarcely a year later had been evolving fitfully since the *Ode de la Paix* of 1550.[24]

A fundamental point is thus established: one follows a great example most faithfully by its modification or even turning away from it altogether; but the example is great simply by having created a new type. Whether it was created from familiar, even popular, elements is of little consequence and no doubt contributed to its ultimate authority. Once created, however, a type merely

triumphal arches and other decors. (Cf. Frances A. Yates, 'Antoine Caron's Paintings for Triumphal Arches,' *Journal of the Warburg and Courtauld Institutes*, XIV (1951), pp. 132–4.)

The full measure of difference between the *Recueil des inscriptions* and the commonplaces of the entries may be seen in Denise Gluck, 'Les entrées provinciales de Henri II,' *l'Information d'histoire de l'art*, X (1965), pp. 215–18. That the theme of triumph was limited to the iconography of the celebrations may be seen from Jodelle's comment that, despite general rejoicing, 'ayant doncques dressé et fait dresser tout ce que j'avois projecté, le Roy sur les quatre heures du jour que j'ay dit, *sans aucune pompe* arriva avecques toute sa compagnie en la maison de la ville . . .' (Cf. p. 76).

21 Cf. Clément Jugé, *Nicolas Denisot du Mans*, Paris, 1907, p. 79 *et seq.*

22 Cf. p. 76.

23 Cf. p. 74.

24 Cf. the introduction to the *Franciade*, Ronsard, *Œuvres complètes*, ed. Laumonier (STFM), XVI[1].

repeated creates nothing new and proportionately less that is memorable. In the process, the idea of the exemplar itself is destroyed. Thus the historical continuum necessary for the understanding of the reference points of an elaborated conceit would be meaningless had there been no intervening developments. Even the events from Metz to Calais would have had less impact without the disaster of Saint-Quentin.[25] Of this Jodelle is aware if for no other reason than the *Recueil*'s printing as an apologia. Accepting the basic conceits, he rather self-consciously underscores the novelty of his undertaking in terms which reveal his sources and their application.

As a pendant to the *Recueil des inscriptions*, Jodelle included in the second half of the volume which he published in 1558 a collection of 'images' entitled *Christianorum nostri temporis heroum, et heroinarum icones*.[26] In addition to these 64 Icones, however, there is also a long elegy in Latin (166 verses) addressed to Madame Marguerite (to whom this section is dedicated), an inscription to Europe (*Lugentis et laceræ Europæ*), as well as the Latin elegy to Claude de Kerquefinen and the poem, *A sa Muse*.

Balmas questions the unity of this part of the work, which is why he decided to separate the various items under rather arbitrary sub-headings. (Cf. p. 4 n. 6.)[27] This procedure may have suited his purposes in establishing a rationale for a complete edition of Jodelle's extant poetry, but it utterly destroys the identity of the one volume published by the poet himself and further overlooks the many links between the two halves of the book which help to explain why Jodelle combined them as he did.

25 For the sequence of historical events and Jodelle's references to them, see pp. 98–100.

26 This form of reference is more or less repeated in the early lines of Jodelle's 'INSCRIPTION POUR UNE STRUCTURE ENTREPRISE PAR LA ROINE MERE DU ROY,' which is to be dated between 1561 and 1568 owing to the mention of both Charles IX and Elisabeth de Valois as reigning monarchs. (Cf. Jodelle, *Œuvres complètes*, ed. Balmas, I, pp. 486–7), This inscription clearly shows the evolution of the genre as well as Jodelle's attempt at a vernacular parallel similar to the D. D. VIRTVTI ET VICTORIÆ of the *Recueil*. (Cf. pp. 77–8.)

27 Cf. Jodelle, *Œuvres complètes*, ed. Balmas, I, p. 470.

A closer examination reveals that, while the Icones may be considered in and of themselves or in their relation to the entire *Recueil*, they must of necessity be studied in relation to conceptual structures which are not to be found in the volume. The most obvious analogy to draw is that of the author-portraits, which are usually considered *icones sive effigies* in the narrow sense of the word. One rather suspects that the traditional and etymologically sanctioned French usage of the word *iconographie* as the equivalent of 'portrait' (at the other extreme, as anything having to do with images or imagery) has resulted in the idea that the portrait is something added to a volume. The use of such a terminology naturally minimizes the intent, even the very existence of the portrait, as anything but a physiognomical likeness. Nor does it enquire whether, even in a limited sense or for a limited period, the portrait is part of a greater structure reposing upon all the *pièces liminaires*, whether in themselves or in relation to the main text.[28]

The problem of the Icones is really that of general iconography, which is to say the study of intrinsic relations of subject matter in connection with the form it has assumed. It is rather more an interpretive pursuit than the collection and classification of material, which is its perquisite but which, in turn, relies upon the proper identification and description of component parts. Jodelle has provided us with both the structure (i.e. the printed *Recueil* and Icones, whether considered together or separately) and his own interpretations – and these do not seem merely a literary *ekphrasis*. His lengthy justification of procedures, moreover, emphasizes his consciousness of their very novelty and we, as were his contemporary readers, are invited to discover those proportional correspondences 'et de l'epistre, et de l'oraison, et de l'histoire'[29] which he would surely have intended to rejoice 'l'œil, l'oreille, et l'entendement.'

Indeed, the chronological and dynastic (by implication, Imperial) procession of the 64 Icones is adequate testimony of this intent whether or not

28 This problem will be clarified in a study on the portraits of Ronsard and Cassandre in the *Amours* of 1552–3.

29 Cf. p. 67.

each or any of the separate Icones was in truth accompanied by some recognizable likeness. By placing them in a sequence established by precedent and understandable ulterior motives, Jodelle has related them to those printed portrait galleries of historical or contemporary figures which derive from the collections of Paolo Giovio of Como (1521) and which were reissued throughout the century.[30] It is to these illustrious and accessible precedents of 'images' in close proximity to an explanatory text or direct relation to a more abbreviated legend that we must look for orientation. Jodelle has merely placed them in a higher, more allusive literary style. In context, they are characterized by a brevity which can only be called emblematic in its ability to conflate an image with a structure capable of the greatest extension and evocative possibilities on the one hand, and the greatest reductive powers into a single image or category on the other.

To begin with, the Icones may well have been thought of as part of the decorative scheme of the banquet hall. In the description of the decorations Jodelle gave only a summary and royal enumeration of devices proposed without any indication of the total number, which nonetheless must have been rather extensive.[31] Those mentioned specifically are Henry II, Catherine de' Medici, the Dauphin, and Madame Marguerite, but in the *Registres des délibérations* the names of Diane de Poitiers, the Duc de Guise, and the Cardinal de

30 Paul Ortwin Rave, 'Paolo Giovio und die Bildnisritenbücher des Humanismus,' *Jahrbuch der Berliner Museen*, I (1959), pp. 119–54, with bibliography and abundant representative illustration. Many of these series were dependent upon actual works of art, even to the woodcuts of the second edition (1568) of Vasari. (Cf. Wolfram Prinz, *Vasaris Sammlung von Künstlerbildnissen*, Florence, 1966.) If the Icones actually had visual counterparts, it would be nearly impossible to determine prototypes for those not described in detail. This may be suggested by referring to the title of the most complete and original French publication of like nature, André Thevet's *Les vrais pourtraits et vies des hommes illustres grecz, latins, et payens, recueilliz de leurs tableaux, livres, medailles antiques et modernes* (Paris, 1584).

31 Cf. p. 83.

Lorraine are also cited.[32] From the point of view of the unity of the collection, the most significant icon is the one for Henry II (p. 156) which is drawn from the *Pyramide* of the Cardinal de Lorraine (p. 98). One could also mention the Latin elegies to Madame Marguerite and Claude de Kerquefinen, both of which deal with the same themes which prompted publication of the *Recueil* – the poet's efforts to please, the lack of appreciation by certain elements of his public, and personal despair concerning his unhappy plight. The mood expressed is very close indeed to that of the introductory epistle and the poem, *In librum elegia*, which set the tone for the apologia.

In short, it is clear that the book, as Jodelle published it, has an organic unity which stands up to the closest scrutiny and which reveals, the more one studies it, an increasingly complex texture of cross-references.

THE ICONES

In many ways, the 64 Icones are the most interesting part of Jodelle's book. They were obviously not all composed between 8 February and 17 February 1558, and indeed those in honour of the seven Electors of the Holy Roman Empire (pp. 191–5) would seem clearly to have been composed at the time when Henry II was actively campaigning for nomination as Emperor. (See especially Icon LIX.)

The distribution of the Icones is significant. Jodelle begins with Francis I, his two wives (Claude and Eleanor), his sister (Marguerite de Navarre), and his deceased children (Francis, Charles, and Madeleine, but not Louise and Charlotte, who died in infancy). For each of these there is a separate Icon except for Francis and Charles, who are combined in one probably because Henry II heartily disliked them both. (Cf. p. 147.)

32 *Registres des délibérations du Bureau de l'Hôtel de Ville de Paris*, t. IV, p. 523. One additional name quoted which does not appear in the Icones is that of 'le garde des sceaux' – Michel de l'Hospital.

For Henry himself, Jodelle composed no fewer than seven Icones. The net effect is very well described by Balmas:

> La figure du roi en sort auréolée d'un prestige incomparable, d'une dignité vraiment romaine. Roi heureux (car il dispose de l'appui de Fortune), roi fort, car il aime le métier des armes, roi victorieux, pour lequel on dresse des pyramides (symboliques) et dont on doit dès maintenant prévoir l'apothéose et l'inscription funéraire.[33]

The choice of the number seven is not hard to rationalize. To begin with, it was the number of perfection and is usually thought to refer to the seven gifts of the Holy Spirit. The Electors of the Holy Roman Empire (to which Henry aspired) were seven in number, by analogy with the seven-branched candelabra of the Apocalypse. Francis I had had seven children and the living children of Henry also numbered seven (cf. Icon XXVII). In short, seven was considered an auspicious royal number and it was thus used in many public functions and receptions.[34]

After Henry, the immediate members of his family were each honoured with Icones as follows: his wife, Catherine de' Medici (2), the Dauphin (2), Marie Stuart (2), Charles, Edward, Hercule, Elisabeth, Claudia, Marguerite (one each plus one Icon for the three princesses and one for the seven children together).

Jodelle then introduced 3 Icones addressed to his patroness, Madame Marguerite, and added tributes as follows for other important figures of the day: Antoine de Bourbon (2), Jeanne d'Albret (2), Charles de Lorraine (1), the Duc de Guise (2), the Cardinal de Lorraine (3), Anne de Montmorency (2),

33 Etienne Jodelle, *Œuvres complètes*, ed. Balmas, I, p. 472.

34 Cf. especially André Valladier, *Labyrinthe royal de l'Hercule Gaulois triomphant*, Avignon, 1601, p. 3 and Robert E. Hallowell, 'The Rôle of French Writers in the Royal Entries of Marie de' Medici in 1600,' *Studies in Philology*, LXVI (1969), p. 188.

Odet de Châtillon (2), Diane de Poitiers (2), Gaspard de Coligny (1), Jacques d'Albon (1), Jean de Cossé (1), and Paul de Thermes (1).

Finally, he appended Icones for a number of foreign dignitaries: Pope Paul IV, Charles V, Ferdinand I, Philip II, Mary Tudor, the Seven Electors (Maximilian of Bohemia, the Archbishops of Mainz, Cologne, and Trèves, the Duke of Saxony, the Marquis of Brandenburg, and the Count Palatine), the Duke of Ferrara, and Cosimo de' Medici.

Throughout, Jodelle follows the order of protocol strictly. The only personages apart from the king to whom he devotes more than two Icones are Madame Marguerite and the Cardinal de Lorraine, both protectors and patrons of the poet. Other important individuals have two Icones each but lesser ones (including Henry II's very young children) have only one. All this is logical and carefully thought out, and there do not appear to be any obvious omissions or errors despite Jodelle's statement that 'the rest of the Images of both men and women, which I shall compose and publish in due order, are lacking: for at this time I was able only to publish with several omissions, and in a confused arrangement for the most part, even those Images that I had in my possession' (p. 186).

For the justification of the Icones, Jodelle seizes upon a telling simile in the casting of medals 'lesquelles comme chacun sçait, ne se jectent pas si tost en moulle que les medalles de ces princes [de l'Europe].'[35] He then invites the readers of these two treatises

> de les laisser couler avecques si peu de faveur qu'ils meritent, comme une chose legere et meslée. Ce que seullement vous monstrera assez la prose dont j'ay usé en mes *descriptions*, *confondant*,[36] *comme je pense tout ensemble le style*, *et de l'epistre*, *et de l'oraison*, *et de l'histoire:* combien que j'espere bien de vous faire un jour juger, qu'en tous ces genres d'escrire Dieu ne m'a point degarni de jugement. Je croy bien aussi, que *l'ortho-*

35 Cf. p. 66. For the historical significance of this simile see pp. 32–3.

36 Jodelle uses the sense of the Latin *confundo:* to pour together, mingle, mix or blend.

> *graphe confuse vous decouvrira une pareille meslange, et que les allusions et repetitions frequentes*, qui seront trouvées dedans mes vers, montreront de prime face quelque affectation. L'une de ces choses a esté ainsi faite pour le peu de resolution de nostre langue en ce point là, et les autres pour l'ornement et la vraye beauté des inscriptions, *ce que vous ne verrés pas en mes œuvres continués de longue alaine*.[37]

By this passage Jodelle explicitly discredits, which would be unusual for any author, his unpublished longer works, even to the *petit œuvre* of some 600 heroic Latin verses which was the Cardinal de Lorraine's *Pyramide*. This is done to the benefit of these more concise 'meslanges' which he expects to have a *prima facie* effect upon the reader by reason of beauty, ornament, or content.

The Icones were obviously designed to be used as inscriptions, but it is questionable how many spectators would have been able to read and understand them. Both Ronsard and Du Bellay, who copied Jodelle's idea, preferred to compose similar tributes in French using decasyllabic quatrains (with the rhyme scheme ABBA for Du Bellay, ABBA and ABAB for Ronsard).

Du Bellay's *Inscriptions* were composed for the tournament held on the occasion of the double marriage of Elisabeth of France and Philip of Spain and Madame Marguerite and the Duke of Savoy.[38] Ronsard's *XXIIII Inscriptions* were written for the same celebrations where they were intended to be used 'en la Comedie qu'on esperoit representer en la maison de Guise, par le commandement de Monseigneur le Reverendissime Cardinal de Lorraine.'[39] It was at the tournament, of course, that Henry II was mortally wounded, so that the *Comedie* in the Hôtel de Guise was not actually presented.[40]

37 Cf. p. 67. Italics have been introduced in quotations in order to draw attention to significant elements.

38 See Du Bellay, *Œuvres poétiques*, ed. Chamard, VI, pp. 53–67.

39 See Ronsard, *Œuvres complètes*, ed. Laumonier (STFM), IX, pp. 193–201.

40 Elisabeth of France and Philip of Spain were married 22 June 1559. The tournament in which Henry II was wounded was held 1 July and Madame Marguerite and the Duke of Savoy were married on the evening of 9 July, just before Henry's death the following day.

Both Du Bellay and Ronsard honoured almost exactly the same list of dignitaries[41] and there are many similarities between certain of their poems. There are fewer resemblances with Jodelle's Icones, no doubt because the form and language were different. There are a few, however, and they are sufficiently close to make it clear that Ronsard and Du Bellay were quite familiar with Jodelle's text. (Cf. pp. 160 and 170.)

The form used by Jodelle for the Latin Icones is a tristich of epic hexameters. This is not a traditional classical form but it may have been derived from the lost *Imagines illustrium virorum* of Varro.

Again, despite the introduction of the word *Christianorum* into the title, the emphasis in the Icones is on classical mythology: Hecuba, Hercules, Mars, Cæsar, Alexander, Augustus, Neptune, Minerva, Achilles, Ulysses, etc. There are a few historical allusions as well as conventional references to Destiny, Virtue, Honour, and so forth. There are also some plays on words and, in the case of the Icones addressed to the Electors of the Holy Roman Empire, allusions to their traditional functions.

The problem of the illustration in the *Recueil* and the Icones is particularly perplexing. Millard Meiss, although availing himself of primarily quattrocento examples, has remarked that 'Artists themselves crowded the boundaries between paleography and epigraphy by introducing into paintings the simulated epigraph.'[42] In the *Recueil* the inscriptions are intimately connected with images of specific iconographical context which are 'explained' immediately in the text. And the inscription giving the programme of the banqueting hall

41 Henry II, Catherine de' Medici, Philip of Spain, Elisabeth of France, the Dauphin and the Dauphine (Marie Stuart), the Duke of Savoy and Madame Marguerite, Charles, Duke of Lorraine and his Duchess (Claude de France), the dowager Duchess of Lorraine, the Cardinal of Lorraine and the Duc de Guise. Ronsard also added the Duchess of Guise and the dowager Duchess of Guise and, in addition, both poets wrote inscriptions to 'La Paix' and 'Le Mariage.'

42 Millard Meiss, 'Towards a More Comprehensive Renaissance Paleography,' *Art Bulletin*, XLII (1960), p. 98. Cf. also John Sparrow, *Visible Words. A Study of Inscriptions in and as Books and Works of Art*, Cambridge University Press, 1969.

was 'si bien escrit, et en si grands caracteres, qu'il se pouvoit facilement lire de la table du Roy.'[43] We may still be sure, however, in maintaining that general attention was not directed towards the inscription, but rather at its accompanying paintings and the entertainments.

For the Icones, on the other hand, the majuscule inscriptions certainly can exist without images altogether.[44] Nor is the album illustrated by woodblocks, itself a time-consuming and costly process and no doubt scarcely able to be effected by the time of publication.[45] Are we then to assume that the italicized descriptions are mainly for retrospective identification even though they may occasionally be incorrect?[46] In any case, the few Icones providing elements suitable to the isolation of actual types all pertain to Henry II;[47] alternatively, of *imprese*,[48] which makes a very small proportion of the whole.

Of the first category, only one (IX) has a secure artistic prototype, and only one (XI) a restricted variety of known types. Yet another (XII) is based on a literary effort, and its companion (XIII) on a common conceit later developed only by Henry's progeny.[49] Only one (VIII) refers to a type popularized by engravings, and only one (X) is by 'some artist' but does not correspond to any known type. In the first place, its description, *in aulæo variis floribus ambulantis*, gives no element which would have been considered significant of itself by contemporaries and provides instead a minor descriptive detail. Or so it would be unless this is a composition elaborated upon a passage in the *Recueil* describing the significance of the month of January for the taking of Calais. Here one appreciated 'contre l'ordre acoustumé des années un beau Printens au

43 Cf. p. 98.

44 Cf. pp. 52, 98, and especially 160.

45 Cf. pp. 35–6. The major entries of Henry's reign – Lyon, 1548; Paris, 1549; Rouen, 1550 – were without exception luxuriously illustrated, but are of a different character than the *Recueil des inscriptions*.

46 Cf. Icones XLIX, LVI.

47 Icones VIII, IX, X, XI, XII, XIII.

48 Icones XXIII, XXIX, XXX, XXXIX, XLIV, and the second *mascarade*. Cf. p. 122.

49 That of Charles IX and Michel de l'Hospital as Alexander and his preceptor Aristotle, in 1564. (Cf. J.G. Espiner-Scott, *Claude Fauchet, sa vie, son œuvre*, Paris, Droz, 1938, pp. 25 *et seq.*)

meilleu de l'hyver: Quand à moy [Jodelle] j'ose affermer estant pour lors au chams avoir veu sortir les herbes nouvelles, et tous autres indices du renouveau.'[50] The second category of *imprese* refers mainly to printed and illustrated sources, so Jodelle's vagueness about the preceding Icon may simply indicate that the innumerable Icones were manufactured by mere artisans assembled for the task. This would presumably have left the painter Baptiste to do what he could of the more complex scenes required to establish the iconographical structure of the Grande Salle.[51]

Jodelle's statement that he intends to compose and publish more Icones in due order, and his repeated references to re-use of material make it likely that not only did the Icones precede any portraits, but that only a few of them could be capable of supporting known artistic examples or any but the more generalized of allegorical exegeses. In the latter respect only, much the same may be said of the descriptions in the *Recueil*, all of which are detailed enough to invite speculation, but none of which is of an exactitude to permit a sure identification or retrieval. The example of 'Alexandre tout tel que nous le pouvons retirer des medailles antiques, baisant et accollant une Royne figurée en Amazone, de mesme sorte aussi que les antiques nous l'ont montré'[52] is not restrictive enough to be of help, and the scene seems interchangeable in all but name to the popular views of Mars and Venus than anything else.[53] In two instances, that of the V.V.V. emblem[54] and of the Battle of Actium,[55] Jodelle flatters his audience by accompanying his nonetheless ample descriptions with a 'chacun sçait assés,' which is not beyond belief.

Thus the printing of the *Recueil* and the accompanying Icones served to clear up the visual distractions and confusion which made the taut structure of

50 Cf. p. 89.
51 Cf. p. 92.
52 Cf. p. 94.
53 One engraving from the court circle and dating from the 1540s would have been of similar character, the *Apelles with Alexander and Campaspe* by the Master L.D. at Fontainebleau. (Cf. Henri Zerner, *Ecole de Fontainebleau. Gravures*, Paris, 1969, cat. 51.)
54 Save for the substitution of the VVV for a 'minotaure,' a likely source would have been Alciati's Emb. XII, *Non vulganda consilia* (ed. 1549, p. 33). Cf. p. 90.
55 Cf. p. 97.

the event less apparent to all. The clarification of the iconographical programme must then be analysed in relation to contemporary (and thus accessible) *lieux communs*, and prefaced by a consideration of common iconographical procedures.

Iconography[56] is perhaps one of the few completely fascinating intellectual pursuits remaining in this epoch of dismal and ungracious pragmatism. It is also one of the potentially most dangerous in that it is a highly speculative discipline where a surabundance or imbalance of component parts may prove utterly disastrous on all accounts. Once a *vue d'ensemble* is advanced, everyone proceeds to examine it at leisure. Something is added here, something suppressed elsewhere, and in the process the integrity of the ensemble may be seriously endangered without any viable alternative being proposed in what may not be any more than a series of learned digressions which, if illuminating, may be somewhat peripheral to the subject at hand. This is the nature of classic or general iconography, constructed from a multiplicity of individual cases and attempting to come to some conclusions which may be aphoristically expressed so as to cover most instances.

A convenient analogy is that of the reader of the full orchestral score at the piano. Here one must instantly take in an enormous quantity of staves, determine the melodic line, separate the harmonies, and regulate the transpositions of certain instruments into the G clef. All of this is done concurrently while the score is played in tempo with its phrase and expression marks observed. Here too the analogy ceases, for the purpose of iconography is to establish a judicious, often intuitively-based, structure capable of elaboration or of documentary verification rather than to strive for that illusory sense of completeness which is but rarely achieved at a given moment in time and, moreover, is humanly impossible in the historical disciplines. In sum, this means that while

56 Cf. particularly the subtle translation of Bernard Tessèydre of the *Essais d'iconologie* (Paris, NRF Gallimard, 1967) containing the new preface, pp. 3–5, with Erwin Panofsky's final considerations as to the preferability of the word iconography to describe at least part of our exegetical method.

the experienced score reader may devote his whole attention to critical interpretation, the iconographer spends an unconscionably large portion of his time in building his score at the very moment he is engaged in its interpretation.[57] If his work has been well conceived and executed, his proposed iconographical programme will be capable of supporting a number of nuances or precisions (no matter how diverse) without losing its essential validity or modifying its inherent structure and proportions.[58] And the enormity of this responsibility may be imagined when a specific import may be carried by the most generalized of conventions, or a motif invested with meanings not originally its own. As a result, the relation of cause and effect is not nearly as variable or as significant as matters of status and relationship within a highly structured system of images.

No amount of recurring to an 'Iconographer's Emergency Kit' will then provide more than a series of (presumably) correctly identified exemplars in some sort of defined historical or literary context. And if an argument is constructed upon such lexica, it is only fitting that the conclusions will be as worthy as the sources. Each case was, we know, created for a specific time, place, and circumstance.[59] And within certain and easily definable norms of variance, each case exists in an historical continuum which, if properly researched, explains not only its origins but, should one find distasteful the

57 Just as Panofsky's rising hierarchy of layers of subject matter – simple motifs, images of definable significance, intrinsic meaning – are separable for pedagogical purposes. These are in reality one and the same process since a recognized intrinsic meaning may lead us inadvertently back through the other ('lower') categories, resulting either in a reidentification or reinterpretation of simple motifs and images or else the eventual nuancing of an accepted intrinsic meaning.

58 Cf. the synopsis of the decorations and entertainments, pp. 42–60.

59 Jodelle's dilemma arose from the fact that, in accepting the charge of the Procureur du Roy to execute within such a short space of time those accoutrements suitable to the reception of the king, he had not anticipated that 'je me deusse soucier d'autres charges que d'inventer quelques belles masquarades, ou parlantes, ou muetes, *qui estans accommodées aus tens, aus lieus, et aus choses, peussent donner quelque agreable plaisir à la compaignie*.' (Cf. p. 75.)

prospect of independent 'direction' in such abstract entities as images, at least their 'drift.'

One should never lose sight of the fact that both artists and authors of the Renaissance were forced to extrapolate from data restricted in both number and quality. Their thematic developments will of necessity be subject to problems of transmission,[60] comprehension,[61] timeliness,[62] and of an intent whose implications may not be as easily or as correctly perceived by contemporaries as by their successors. Some means of control are clearly in order if we are to place the individual cases within a less problematical structure, and any contemporary testimony of some intelligence (much less any literary value) reduces almost in geometric ratio the probabilities of error. Hence the importance of the *Recueil* and the Icones as Jodelle's personal account of the programmes of 17 February 1558. The album, simply because it is an apologia, is exceptionally rich in kind and in quantity of such details as would otherwise have been lost to posterity. We would never have possessed them had the events been an unqualified success in Jodelle's own eyes.[63]

For these reasons we rejected from the beginning any idea of a critical edition as it is ordinarily comprehended. We are convinced (as was Jodelle) that the *Recueil des inscriptions* does not pose the problems of a purely literary effort. In point of view of method, the album is virtually unique in that it is an iconographical laboratory which instructs us exemplar by exemplar of the

60 Cf. Icones XLIV, XLIX.

61 The 'HOC HERCVLE DIGNÆ' conceit at the entrance would have been meaningless without a knowledge of its appropriation from the Emperor Charles V. (Cf. p. 79.)

62 For example, the elaborate allusions to Philip II and Mary Tudor (Icones LIV and LV and pp. 93–7) could only have been made between their marriage in July of 1554 and her death in November of 1558, only a few months after the printing of the *Recueil*. The selection of the Virgilian *aurea œtas* theme for Henry II made almost obligatory a reference to Actium, but it would have been taxing to attempt to place Elizabeth in the same iconography.

63 Cf. the repeated references to *necessité*, *desastre* in Jodelle's preface (pp. 63–7) and *Le Livre à la France* (p. 68, vv. 10, 14), as well as the opportune theme of Vicissitude.

working procedures of one of the more important literary figures of the French Renaissance. Whether considered in relation to literature or art (and the distinctions are often arbitrary), iconography and style are not merely manipulations of externals but the study of causal forces. When one also introduces qualitative limitations into the discussion, it becomes the more obvious that the problems behind artistic creation are often of more importance and interest than what has been created. Thus, while we would be the last to claim that our reconstitution of Jodelle's method is faultless,[64] or that it might even have been representative, we do ask that the implications of our exposition be carefully considered.

The *Recueil* as a physical object is but a presentation of texts, notwithstanding which we have adduced a rather considerable illustration. In justifying this, we have resorted to extraordinary measures, foremost among which is a self-imposed restriction to printed sources prior to 1558. This decision is defensible on three counts: first, in that there are few motifs or events for which we have not been able to provide an exact reference; then, in the sense of *actualité* upon which the iconographical programme is based; and finally, by the fact that the decade 1550–60 was for France a prodigious epoch in the creation of sources which soon became standard references and were widely reprinted later. It is not likely that many manuscript sources adding substantially to our knowledge of the events of 1558 will be unearthed. Nor should we be obliged to await their coming since it was the *Recueil* which was generally

64 Despite malicious talk, Jodelle twice insists that, with the exception of verses originally cut from the first *mascarade*, he has added nothing that was not originally present (cf. pp. 118 and 120). He maintains that he no longer possessed at time of writing the originals of the Latin verses accompanying the figures (presumably those of the *Recueil* iconography rather than the Icones) and preferred 'sur le champ user du changement que du travail de les recouvrer' (cf. p. 65), but this may in any event correspond to the type of ordering of circumstantial verse prior to general publication which is widely recorded in literary history.

known and influential, not the more ephemeral considerations which went into its making.[65]

The illustrations have been selected with the above criteria in mind in order to situate firmly Jodelle's conceits at some point along a line of development and thereby to suggest both their fugitive and continuing nature. Here too, the problems of proportion are such that not everyone will agree with the choice and distribution of elements. For this we ask the reader's indulgence since what appears can only be suggestive rather than exhaustive and, as such, may pose more problems for future study than are presently answered. We have nonetheless attempted to fix guidelines which are as applicable to literature as to iconography: these necessarily revolve around the universal problem of *lieux communs* versus their particular applications.

This concern is paralleled in our choice of documentation, for to establish a hand-list of plaquettes relating to the taking of Calais[66] is a bibliographical exercise, while discussing their contents in relation to the *Recueil* means we cannot avoid mention of Ronsard and Du Bellay as primary poets of the period and, like Jodelle, sometime members of the Pléiade. Rather than an accumulation of references of similar character, we have emphasized whenever possible Jodelle's own poetry in the hope of placing the *Recueil* in some meaningful relation to his entire literary production. This procedure has provided ample reward in demonstrating its genesis while continuing to maintain the integrity of the album as a work severely limited in scope.

SELECTION OF SUPPORTING TEXTS AND ILLUSTRATIONS

The nature of the *Recueil des inscriptions* is such that its unity can only be appreciated by what might at first seem to be excessive cross-referencing. In harmony with this observation, we have not risked the disruption of its

65 For these, see *Registres des Délibérations du Bureau de l'Hôtel de Ville de Paris*, t. IV, pp. 515, 517–24.

66 Cf. p. 4, n. 8.

delicate equilibrium by the complete analysis of any one theme in a single place, but have demonstrated its particular applications in various sections of the album and invited tacit comparison.

All the same, the reader needs some explanation for the choice and use of adduced texts and illustrations as well as the rather summary indications concerning the underlying themes of the *Recueil*, which are not necessarily apparent in the first or even following readings. We are all too mindful that a brief explication of the *idées reçues* to which Jodelle had more or less direct access cannot hope to give an adequate idea of their actual complexity, much less their genealogy. To document them properly would require a separate study, involving in each case almost endless citations and obfuscations which, in the using, Jodelle reduced to the bare bones – in order again to elaborate upon them in creating the *Recueil*. We may arouse some sense of frustration in the reader in briefly resurrecting them, but to let them lie would be to merit a certain and richly deserved censure.

Failing then a treatment which would be out of all proportion to the *Recueil* itself, we hope to have achieved a passable compromise in setting forth our reasons for utilizing several types of documentation in the explication of the album. In so doing, an attempt has been made to situate these individual cases properly within the century's intellectual production. They are of the following kinds, each indicated by a numbered sub-section below: 1 the choice of one Alciati edition and gloss to explain the imagery; 2 the origins and evolution of the *Pietate et Iustitia* impresa prior to its exclusive appropriation by Charles IX; 3 the *ex utroque Cæsar* symbol and its implications; and 4 the unexpected conjunction in the *Recueil* of Guillaume Rouillé's *Promptuaire des medalles* of 1553 and the drawings for Antoine Caron's *Histoire Françoyse de nostre temps*, executed after 1562.

1 EMBLEMES / D'ALCIAT / de nouueau Trãslatez en / Frãçois vers pour vers / iouxte les Latins. / *Ordonnez en lieux cõmuns, auec / briefues expositions, & Figu- / res nouuelles appropriées / aux derniers Emblemes.* / A LYON CHEZ GVIL / ROVILLE, 1549.

Certain of these decisions were relatively straightforward, notably the selection of Alciati's *emblemata* in the Lyon edition of 1549 shared by the publisher Guillaume Rouillé and his printer Macé Bonhomme.[67] The numbering of the emblems is that later established by the Plantin editions of 1571 *et seq.* which, with the commentary of the Dijonnais Claude Mignault (Claudius Minos), became the standard collection of diverse texts relating to a given emblem. Thus our citations give the emblem's standard numbering and Latin title followed by the pagination of this particular edition, e.g. Emb. CLXXX *Eloquentia fortitudine præstantior* (ed. 1549, pp. 221–2).

Since this edition reappeared in 1558[68] it was doubly accessible, and its woodblocks are among the most sophisticated of the Lyonnais productions which established mid-century standards of excellence. Its early vernacular translation by Barthélemy Aneau (†1561) is perhaps less important than the lesser-known commentary on the use and definition of the emblem,[69] and those accompanying glosses which, notwithstanding several barbed contemporary allusions, are still in the discursive tradition of general humanistic thought on iconography.

Aneau joined forces with Maurice Scève and Guillaume Du Choul for the Lyon Entry of 1548,[70] and also published the *Picta Pœsis* of 1552[71] and the *Trois premiers livres de la Metamorphose d'Ovide* with Rouillé in 1556.[72] His 1549 Alciati is then of considerable importance in comprehending contemporary iconography through manuals, in which the organically-developing research

67 Baudrier, *Bibliographie lyonnaise*, IX (1912), p. 158. Cf. Henry Green, *Andrea Alciati and His Books of Emblems*, London, Trübner, 1872.

68 Ibid., p. 251.

69 Preface, pp. 5–13. See more recently Hessel Miedema, 'The Term *Emblema* in Alciati,' *Journal of the Warburg and Courtauld Institutes*, XXXI (1968), pp. 234–50.

70 Baudrier, *Bibliographie lyonnaise*, IX, pp. 161–5. Cf. *La Magnificence de la superbe et triumphante entreé* . . ., ed. G. Guigue, Lyon, 1927, p. 149 and V.-L. Saulnier, *Maurice Scève*, Paris, Klincksieck, 1948–9.

71 Baudrier, X, pp. 225 and 227. Reprinted in 1556, 1563, and 1564.

72 Baudrier, IX, pp. 236–7.

and writing of a single *sourcier* is responsible over the years for a vast diffusion of subject matter and approach.

2 The *Pietate et Iustitia* impresa

The creation of symbols is not easily effected in even the most favourable of circumstances. What seems to be the result of spontaneous generation at a given point in time is more likely to have been the forcible assimilation and convergence of intractable entities only lately given a memorable expression. This process may be more consciously retrospective in nature, employing the processes of nuance and emphasis, a fortuitous selection or suppression of detail. At times the true antecedents may have so descended into commonplaces that they are unknown in their original form and context. And only every so often do we find ample justification for the conscious falsifying of an ascendance – and with it the realization of the presence of a hitherto unrecognized thematic touchstone. Such is the case with the *Pietate et Iustitia*, usually considered only as an *impresa* of Charles IX (1561–74), which presents far vaster implications for French historical and religious thought than its seeming simplicity would lead one to believe at first glance.

This conceit exists in a bewildering variety of types occurring on everything up to and including printer's marks[73] which we cannot here hope to catalogue or explain satisfactorily. One substantive change had already taken place within Charles' own reign, for an order was given on 16 October 1570 for the reworking by goldsmiths of the present intended for his Parisian entry, which had been anticipated since 1562.[74] The terms of work are explicit: 'reffaire et remectre les coullonnes qui sont à present torces, droictes, et y

73 Philippe Renouard, *Les marques typographiques parisiennes des XVe et XVIe siècles*, Paris, Champion, 1926, s.v. Federic I Morel, Nicolas Nivelle, Guillaume II Nyverd. The *impresa is* presumably by Michel de l'Hospital.

74 After delays in 1561 occasioned as much by politics as by weather, an entry 'sans aucune solennité' came off on 6 April 1562 (*Registres des délibérations du Bureau de l'Hôtel de Ville de Paris*, t. v, p. 120, n. 1). The full celebration resulted from Charles' marriage with Elisabeth d'Autriche on 26 November 1570 and clearly took a different form than that which could have been anticipated a decade earlier.

mectre les devises telles qu'elles sont à present.'[75] It is possible that, even if the entwined columns persist as types after the introduction of the straightened ones, some allusion is made to the declaration of Charles' majority on 21 August 1563.[76]

Charles' entry into Paris (6 March 1571) was then accompanied by an abundance of imperial symbolism and by what one may call the definitive allusions to the *Pietate et Iustitia* motif.[77] Foremost among these was the arch of the Porte aux Peintres, commemorating Charles' filial piety by an iconography modelled on the deification of the Emperor Severus: an urn containing Henry's ashes was rapt by an eagle from the sorrowing children who united to raise it. To one side of this central motif was Hercules strangling Antæus and, to the other, a Henry resplendent in coronation robes reaching out towards two gigantic columns (fig. 1), under the first of which were several books signifying Religion and, alternatively, a large eye as a radiant sun to represent Justice. The explanatory distich ran: 'Affin de maintenir son royaume prospere / Ces colonnes soustient, ainsi qu'a faict son pere,' and reduced into manageable form the declaration of the city fathers that 'par lesquelles deux coulonnes le feu Roy Henry, son pere, et ses predecesseurs Roys se sont maintenuz; et aussy sans telz appuiz ung royaulme ne peut prosperer, ne longtemps durer; que, à leur exemple, nostre Roy a embrassé la Religion et Justice, lesquelles pour plus honorer il porte en ses devises.'[78] It is rare that one possesses both the notarized drawing and a woodcut after the completed work. Here the former (fig. 2) shows how a formal iconographical

75 Ibid., t. VI, pp. 244–5.

76 One of the columns is silver and one gold, as in Simon Bouquet's coloured presentation copy of his *Bref et sommaire recueil* (1572) to Catherine de' Medici (British Museum, C 33.m.1) and the arms of the manuscript of Jean du Tillet's *Recueil des Rois de France* of 1566. (Cf. E. Quentin-Bauchart, *La bibliothèque de Fontainebleau et les livres des derniers Valois à la Bibliothèque nationale 1515–1589*, Paris, 1891, p. 161.)

77 Cf. Frances A. Yates, 'Poètes et artistes dans les entrées de Charles IX et de sa reine à Paris en 1571,' *Les Fêtes de la Renaissance*, I, Paris, CNRS, 1956, pp. 61–84.

78 *Registres des délibérations de l'Hôtel de Ville de Paris*, t. VI, pp. 270–1. The Porte aux Peintres was traditionally associated with the City of Paris.

symmetry devoted to Hercules had been destroyed in order to insert the *Pietate et Iustitia* reference.[79]

Further on, in the perspective painting placed at the Chatelet, were personifications with the tristich:

IUSTITIA ET PIETAS, VETERUM CUSTODIA REGUM,
MAIESTATIS HABENT ANTE ALTA PALATIA SEDEM,
STIPANTES REGALE LATUS, VI TUTIUS OMNI.[80]

Thus, far from being merely a circumstantial allusion to the Catholic and Huguenot conflicts in the decade 1560–70 which culminated in St Bartholomew's Massacre (fig. 14), the *Pietate et Iustitia* conceit was painstakingly developed to emphasize the peculiar character and privileges of the French monarchy as a whole.

We find it on the Arc de Bourgneuf during the Lyon Entry of 1548, at the precise moment of Henry's renewal of the Ordre de St Michel,[81] and perhaps more pertinently in Robert Gaguin's *Compendium de origine et gestis Francorum* (fig. 3) with the inscription 'H[a]ec sunt francorum celebranda insignia regum / Qu[ae] demissa polo sustinet alma fides.'[82] The wide circulation of this source, along with Estienne Pasquier's reference to the testimony of Procopius and Agathius that, of all princes of the provinces of the Empire, Justice had been primary among the Gauls,[83] may even help to explain the choice, truly symbolic rather than merely historical, of Francus as the hero of Ronsard's epic poem.

79 Stockholm, Nationalmuseum (Coll. Cronstedt 190). The *Registres des délibérations du Bureau de l'Hôtel de Ville de Paris*, t. VI, p. 241 maintain that 'du costé droict de la premiere façade sera ung Hercullin qui de ses mains fortes estouffera des serpens,' which well underscores the mutations in programme that could arise on like occasions.

80 Ibid., p. 276.

81 *La Magnificence de la superbe et triumphante entrée* . . ., ed. G. Guigue, Lyon, 1927, pp. 31–4 (illus.). Cf. p. 101.

82 We illustrate among many editions that of 1515 chez G. du Pré, fol. $_2$B6^v.

83 *Les Recherches de la France*, Paris, 1560, ch. 2, fol. 12v°. Miss Dorothy Thickett has kindly verified the earliest appearance of this passage. If the

3 The *ex utroque Cæsar* emblem

Despite the unquestioning citation by writers of Francis I as 'Père des Arts et Lettres (– des Arts et Sciences),' we know of no comprehensive study of the origins and development of this theme. Such an attempt would be well worth the trouble since Francis really possessed no iconography except this epithet. It is explicitly commemorated in Rosso Fiorentino's fresco of '*L'Ignorance chassée*' (fig. 5) in the first bay of the Francis I Gallery at Fontainebleau in 1534–6[84] and reserved for the highest, or theological, category of images in *Achillis Bocchii Bonon. Symbolicarum quæstionum libri quinque*, Bologna, 1555 (fig. 6).[85] Under Henry II the theme of the Virgilian *aurea ætas* was developed from the time of the Lyon Entry of 1548 and was passed on to Francis II;[86] indeed each of his surviving sons employed *imprese* more or less directly dependent upon this *topos*.[87]

Erwin Panofsky once attempted to trace the application of the *ex utroque Cæsar* emblem, which was originally conceived in the highest generality of

Iustitia aspect of the French monarchy is thus accounted for, the synoptical illustration in Gaguin with its associated SS. Denis and Rémi finds a more pictorial expression in a succeeding woodcut (fig. 4) devoted to *Fides* on fol. vi. A sequential narrative in two parts depicts the Conversion of Clovis and appropriate references to the *Sainte Ampoule*, *oriflamme*, and *écu de France*, further showing Clovis' triumph in battle, to which was popularly attributed the cry 'Mon[t]-joye Sainct Denys' occurring on $_2$B6^v. Cf. Marc Bloch, *Les rois thaumaturges*, Paris, Colin, 1923, pp. 135 and 231 *et seq.*

84 Cf. Icon I. The theme is repeated under Catherine de' Medici and Charles IX as 'La remise du livre et de l'épée' of the *Suite d'Arthémise*, Louvre, Inv. RF 29752^4.

85 Although printed at Bologna, the *privilège* was given by Henry II at Blois on 29 January 1555 and the *achevé d'imprimer* is of 5 April 1555, so Bocchius' work, divided into books with a descending hierarchy of intermixed symbols from the theological, physical, moral, and philological spheres, is to be considered under French patronage.

86 Cf. W. McAllister Johnson, 'A "Biface" Medal of Henry II?,' *Journal of the Warburg and Courtauld Institutes*, XXX (1967), p. 403, n. 18.

87 Cf. p. 85, n. 47 and Icones XVI–XVII.

humanistic thought, to Francis I.[88] We illustrate as fig. 7 the woodcut appearing in Gabriel Symeoni's *Les devises ou emblemes heroiques et morales*, Lyon, G. Rouillé, 1559 and its gloss (pp. 16–17):

POUR UN GRAND SEIGNEUR

Un grand Seigneur me demanda un jour, quelle Devise il pourroit porter pour donner à entendre au monde qu'il avoit grande envie, et cherchoit tous les moyens d'estre encore plus grand et puissant que les autres. Parquoy je luy en baillay une d'un Empereur armé avec sa couronne de laurier en la teste, tenant d'une main un livre, et de l'autre un espée, et luy estant debout sus un globe de la terre avec ces parolles: EX VTROQVE CÆSAR. Voulant signifier que par le moyen des lettres et des armes, et estant tousjours debout, et prest à entendre ses affaires, Iule Cesar devint Seigneur de tout le Monde.

The recipient has not been identified, but would have been highly placed. Moreover, despite the commonplace of comparisons with Cæsar, Panofsky later adduced a text relating to Cicero and Justinian, noting that 'the humanism of the Renaissance transformed the original contrast between *arma* and *leges*, arms and law, into a contrast between *arma* and *literæ*, arms and learning.'[89]

In 1579, Jean de Foigny published at Reims a curious little tract written by Nicolas Boucher and translated from the Latin by Jacques Tigeou. Called *La conjonction des lettres et des armes des deux tresillustres princes Lorrains Charles Cardinal de Lorrain . . . et François Duc de Guyse*, it is entirely developed from this theme and celebrates the two brothers, who appear prominently in the

88 Dora and Erwin Panofsky, *Pandora's Box*, 2nd ed. rev., New York, 1965, p. 38 *et seq.*

89 Ibid., p. 39, n. 10. One tentative observation based on the mention here of the substitution of tablets for an opened codex in certain versions: could this be a 'clarification' of the original humanistic *arma/leges* duo which, by the use of the Mosaic Tablets and the Twelve Tables, became somehow developed into the *Pietate et Iustitia* impresa of Charles IX?

Recueil (Icones XXXVI–XL). On 3ᵛ, Tigeou quotes *Ciceron au premier livre des Offices*:

> Les Armes faut qu'à la Toge concedent,
> Et les Lauriers à l'eloquence cedent.

> Parquoy il y a en plusieurs personnages, qui au temps de paix et de guerre se sont acquis grande louange et gloire par l'une des deux: Mais qui ait excellé en toutes les deux, entre bien peu ne s'en trouve de celebre et renommé, que Iules Cesar, lequelz ilz ont effigié tenant une espée d'une main, et un livre de l'autre, non pour autre chose, sinon pour declarer et donner à congnoistre, que toute sa grandeur procede de la conionction des Lettres et des Armes.[90]

This provides us with a fairly secure source for the conceit, and leads to a further observation derived from a bizarre printed book which could have been of use, whether as source for some of the *Recueil*'s iconography or as parallel. This is the *Cesar renouvellé par les observations militaires du S. Gabriel Symeon[i]*, dedicated to the Dauphin François and published by V. Sertenas in 1558.[91]

Symeoni justifies his reworking of Cæsar and Sallustius by commenting that, if both Alexander (for the Greeks) and Cæsar (for the Latins) achieved world dominion, 'non seulement ne s'arresterent à leur science acquise ... mais tous deux furent ordinairement accompagnez d'hommes sçavans, en l'observation des histoires grecques et latines,' going on to cite Cicero as preceptor of Cæsar and Pompey.[92] A Ciceronian source for the *ex utroque*

90 One notices the possibilities of convergence between this emblem and the Gallic Hercules (Icon VIII) as well as the dual duties of the monarch in peace and war (Icon XV).

91 Cf. T. Renucci, *Un aventurier des lettres, Gabriel Symeoni, Florentin (1509–1570?)*, Paris, Didier, 1943. The *privilège* is of 23 November and the *achevé d'imprimer* of 2 December 1557, in enough time to have been known to Jodelle.

92 Cf. fols. aijʳ-aijᵛ.

Cæsar emblem has thus been independently confirmed by two sources, but there is more, on the title-page itself (fig. 8). Contrary to general procedures, Symeoni's works as a whole do not bear the ordinary printer's marks of their publishers,[93] but rather an emblem for which he alone is responsible. Thus an entire study is to be done on Symeoni's marks in connection with the content of his plaquettes.[94] Implicitly referring to his preface to the Dauphin, Symeoni has placed a version of the *ex utroque Cæsar* emblem – a Nike supported by a globe (in turn supported by a book) who advances to the left with an enserpented sword in her left hand and a diadem of laurel with two banderoles in her right.

Most writers even aware of Symeoni rather casually dismiss him as an eccentric pamphleteer. Yet his relations with the antiquarian Du Choul, his position as an emblematist, the knowledge that he continually proclaimed an unheeded thesis (at least by action) of Imperial destiny for France, and particularly that he was a compatriot of Catherine de' Medici indicate that his writings are perhaps more relevant to an understanding of the decade 1550–60 than many standard sources.

4 The *Promptuaire des medalles* and the *Histoire françoyse de nostre temps*

The *Christianorum nostri temporis heroum, et heroinarum icones* of the *Recueil*[95] have no illustrations. It is only for the royal series of Henry II that we may isolate specific types which would have had enough currency to permit the Icones and their tristichs to be generally comprehended.[96]

Any consideration of the 64 Icones as a series related to historical galleries of printed portraits brings us to a further discussion of the most likely prototype: Guillaume I Rouillé's *Premiere (-seconde) partie du promptuaire des medalles* of 1553.[97] This was in reality not one but three issues, each in a different

93 For Sertenas, cf. Philippe Renouard, *Les marques typographiques parisiennes des XVe et XVIe siècles*, Paris, Champion, 1926, cat. 1038 *et seq.*

94 Cf. Icon XVII and p. 86, n. 48 for instances relating to Francis II and Mme Marguerite.

95 Cf. pp. 127–97.

96 See above, p. 17.

97 See above, p. 24.

language with a separate dedication, although pagination and text (insofar as translation permitted) were identical.[98]

The cutting of the portrait medallions was early attributed to Georges Reverdy by La Croix du Maine (1584), although his signed title-page in the second part does not assure his authorship of the over 800 unsigned woodcuts, which are, moreover, of uneven quality. It is equally obvious that the models are of variable historicity and competence, the better ones in the historical sequence following the Nativity (Part Two) being attributed to Corneille de Lyon, and most if not all of the Old Testament sequence in Part One being based upon free adaptations of ancient coinage. The accompanying texts are purely narrative in character, and some attempt is made to provide a factual *précis* of the reign or person under consideration. Since its form is closer to that of the Icones, we illustrate as figure 9 the medallion of Henry II which finds its place on the last page of the book (247^{v}), but which appears with the portrait of Catherine de' Medici and their joint histories as well (246).[99]

One need not dwell on the knowledge that such texts were considered reliable enough to furnish the basis for works of art with historical references. On 13 April 1551 Pierre Bontemps contracted with Philibert Delorme to do the bas-reliefs of the tomb of Francis I for Saint-Denis and thus:

98 Baudrier, *Bibliographie lyonnaise*, IX, pp. 204–7. Issued with a joint *privilège* of 18 June 1553 for ten years, the Latin edition is dedicated to Henry II, the Italian to Catherine de' Medici, and the French (this version presumably by Charles Fontaine) to Mme Marguerite; the Latin version only was reprinted in 1578, ibid., p. 368.

99 The opposite approach to that of the *Promptuaire*, with verses but no images and therefore closer to the Icones, may be seen in a like album by an eminent historian, Guillaume Paradin's *Epigrammata. Accessit Francorum Reges series* . . . , Lyon, A. Gryphius, 1581, among whose epigrams on the 59 kings of France that of Henry II (p. 71) is typical:

THEVTONAS, ac Thuscos ex servitute resolui,
  Senseruntque meam Rhenus, et Arnus opem.
Inque fidem Caletos, post secula bina reduxi:
  Quod dudum Reges non potuere novem.

> eslever et esliger les histoires de la deffaicte des Suisses selon le texte des annalles et cronicques de France . . . [et] en laquelle frise seront faiz, insculptez, entaillez et eslevez lesd. histoires [i.e. scenes] en basse taille . . . rempliz et garniz de chevalliers, gens de pied, artillerie, enseignes, estendars, trompettes, clerons, tabours, phifres, municions, camps, pavillons, bagaiges, villes, chasteaulx *et autres choses aprochans et suyvans la vérité historial de lad. cronicque* . . .[100]

This is to say that such reconstitution of scenes or people from the past necessarily comprehended for the Renaissance a certain artistic licence in disposition – and consequently of style. In such efforts there would be present verifiable elements or details upon which the authority of the image depended, a process which may be said to have prevailed up to the advent of photographic journalism.[101] Jodelle simply casts these historical events or epithets into a compact tristich form and relies upon their allusive characteristics to underscore their circumstantial usage. A prior knowledge of the individual elements is assumed.

There is a tendency in the early printed book (most easily verifiable in the albums of *emblemata*) for the illustrations soon to become overtly pictorialized rather than to present the requisite elements in a void. This is most often represented by the paper itself and results in a patently two-dimensional image of black on white.[102] Our vocabulary is as yet insufficient to describe the function and effect of even the illustrated sources common to the fifteenth and sixteenth centuries, and the task would be yet more difficult if one took into consideration the number of truly abortive or, alternatively, merely unsuccessfully realized attempts to provide new sources or to refine older ones. In most cases, the problems may lie in the attempts made to portray more of the

100 Maurice Roy, *Artistes et monuments de la Renaissance en France*, I (Paris, Champion, 1929), p. 174.

101 The best-known example of this process is Alfred Franklin, *Les grandes scènes historiques du XVIe siècle, reproduction fac-similé du recueil de J. Tortorel et J. Perrissin* (c. 1570). Paris, Fischbacher, 1886.

102 For the importance of this description, see below, p. 35, n. 103 and p. 38.

external world than could be known from sight alone. In the same way, between the synoptical format and prose of the *Promptuaire* on the one hand and the emblematical poetry of the Icones, we have a basis for the projects which would have made general the same banal conceits or events in ever more elaborate manner.

One counts oneself fortunate in this period to possess even woodcut images; because of its almost prohibitive expense, copper-engraving became the rule in deluxe editions only around 1580. A more likely parallel is then the *Histoire françoyse de nostre temps*[103] drawn up at the order of the apothecary Nicolas Houel (†1587)[104] who was also responsible for the cartoons of the

103 The publication of the drawings by Jules Guiffrey under the title *Les dessins de l'histoire des Rois de France* (Paris, Champion, 1920) does some violence to the actual title, which is modelled on Guillame Paradin's *Continuation de l'histoire de nostre temps . . .* (Baudrier, *Bibliographie lyonnaise*, IX, p. 226) of 1556. A full citation from the title-page of the series (RF 29722, fig. 10) will be useful in further discussion:

> L'HISTOIRE / FRANÇOYSE DE NOSTRE TEMPS, / Comprenant en brief les faictz & / Gestes du grand ROY / FRANÇOYS premier, / de HENRY / second, de FRANÇOYS / second, & / de CHARLES ixe; ROYS / de FRANCE. / PLVS VN PETIT RECVEIL DE / leurs Genealogies, & lignées, auec les Figures & Pourtraictz / des plus illustres ROYS de FRANCE & Hommes / verteux de la maison de MEDICI. Le tout par / Cartons de peincture de blanc & noir, Façonnez par les / plus excellentz Peinctres de FRANCE, ET d'ITALIE, / Ausquelz ont esté adioustez plusieurs Sonnetz pour / l'intelligence de l'HISTOIRE. Par Nicolas Houel, Parisien. / A la ROYNE de FRANCE Mere du ROY./

Houel's *Abrégé de l'Histoire des Français, contenant la vie de chacun roi de France avec leurs visages et ressemblances et la description des batailles qu'ils ont données* has not come down to us. Its descriptive title alone would suggest that it was not the text for the *Histoire françoyse* but rather more on the order of the *Promptuaire*.

104 Cf. J. Guiffrey, 'Nicolas Houel, apothicaire parisien, fondateur de la maison de la Charité chrétienne et premier auteur de la tenture d'Artémise,' *Mémoires de la Société de l'Histoire de Paris et de l'Ile-de-France*, XXV (1898), pp. 179–270. Houel and Pierre Quthe (painted by François Clouet in 1562) seem to have been

Suite d'Arthémise[105] commemorating the widowhood of Catherine de' Medici. Both sequences were for the most part executed by the artist Antoine Caron after 1562[106] and must in any case be regarded as mutually dependent in genesis and intent.

For subjects of *actualité* these rather uniformly sized compositions[107] are curiously generalized, with usually four vignettes discreetly alluding to or repeating the iconography of the main scene. They are disarmingly simple for the mind's eye to grasp and are not at all like the charming and abundant invention of which Caron could be capable in his posthumously engraved illustrations for the *Imagines* of Philostratus.[108] One appreciates in this case his ability to create an impression from what is in reality 'très peu de fonds,' and this must parallel his undertaking to effect a normalization in the execution.[109] For the *Suite d'Arthémise* this is thought to result from their use as tapestry

friendly rivals in the field of public philanthropy, but it is not clear how they financed such efforts and whether their initiatives went unaided. Cf. Henri Stein, 'Le peintre François Clouet et l'apothicaire Pierre Quthe,' ibid., XXXVI (1909), p. 227.

105 Reproduction and discussion in Maurice Fenaille, *Etat général des tapisseries de la Manufacture des Gobelins depuis son origine jusqu'à nos jours, 1600–1900*, I[1] (Paris, 1923), pp. 103–212. Two additional Houel commissions, this time relating to Henry III and Louise de Lorraine, are preserved. (Cf. Frances A. Yates, 'Dramatic and Religious Processions in Paris in the late Sixteenth Century,' *Annales Musicologiques*, II (1954), pp. 215–70).

106 See Jean Ehrmann, *Antoine Caron, peintre à la cour des Valois, 1521–1599* (Geneva, Droz, 1955).

107 Averaging 410 × 555 mm, pen and brown ink, brown wash with white heightenings over pencil.

108 See W. McAllister Johnson, '*Prolegomena* to the *Images ou Tableaux de Platte Peinture . . .*,' *Gazette des Beaux-Arts*, s. 6, LXXIII (1969), pp. 277–304.

109 The known sheets for the *Histoire françoyse* seem almost solely the work of Caron (see below, p. 40, n. 119), yet we have three versions alone (one his) of the 'Assemblée des Etats' for the *Suite d'Arthémise* (cf. Sylvie Béguin, 'La Suite d'Arthémise,' *l'Œil*, nº 38 (1958), pp. 34–5 [illus.] and 36). This surely indicates a troubled history for the commission and some initial confusion or haste on the part of the patron.

cartoons;[110] no particular intent has been attributed to the *Histoire françoyse.*

In reality, the compositions of the latter fall into three categories: 1 the title-pages based on themes or *imprese* 2 the 'profane triptychs' modelled on the frescoes and surrounds of the Francis I Gallery at Fontainebleau 3 the few with the so-called 'tapestry border' and disposition, which is used almost exclusively in the *Suite d'Arthémise.*[111] The triptych compositions would make strange tapestries indeed in scale and distribution of elements.[112] That the

110 J. Guiffrey, 'Nicolas Houel . . . etc.' *Mémoires de la Société de l'Histoire de Paris et de l'Ile-de-France*, XXV (1898), p. 189. It should be noted that these notations, which have not been transcribed, are nonetheless on the large sheets of paper on which the drawings are laid down, not on the drawings themselves, which could be significant for our argument.

111 Plate references to J. Guiffrey, *Les dessins de l'histoire des Rois de France*, 1920, here appear for the first time with the inventory numbers of the drawings in the Cabinet des Dessins of the Louvre, and are reproduced with the kind authorization of Mlle Roseline Bacou. A sample notation is RF 29271 [G XXVI], a drawing which is in reality part of the *Suite d'Arthémise.*

1 *Title-pages:* RF 29722 ([G I] and fig. 10), 29716 ([G IV] and fig. 11), 29717 ([G XXVII] and fig. 12), 29752^{14} ([G XVII] and fig. 13) and 29752^{18} ([G XXVIII] and fig. 14).

2 *Triptychs:* RF 29713 ([G XVIII] and fig. 15), 29718 ([G XII]), 29719 [G III], 29720 [G IX], 29723 [G XIII], 29724 ([G XIX] Icon XXVII and fig. 16), 29725 [G XXIII], 29726 [G XIV], 29727 [G VI], 29728 ([G XI] and fig. 17), 29752^{8} ([G II] and fig. 18), 29752^{9} [G V], 29752^{10} [G VII], 29752^{11} [G VIII], 29752^{12} [G X], 29752^{13} [G XV] and 29752^{19} ([G XVI] and fig. 19).

3 *Tapestries:* RF 29714 ([G XXII] and fig. 20), 29715 [G XXV], 29752^{15} [G XXI], 29752^{16} [G XX] and 29752^{17} [G XXIV].

The title-pages are laws unto themselves, but this is not the case with the triptychs and tapestries, which have standing ovals at the side borders. Were one to suppress the architectural disposition and the pairs of personifications of the triptychs there would be little difference except the size of the central scene.

112 Like dispositions to those of the triptychs occur in suites of subjects found in the drawings of the engraver Etienne Delaune (fl. 1557/61–1576). Cf. Ilaria Toesca, 'Quelques dessins attribués a Etienne Delaune,' *La Revue des Arts*, X (1960), pp. 254–9.

'tapestry' border need not carry conviction may be seen in comparing certain albums of *bois populaires* in the Cabinet des Estampes of the Bibliothèque Nationale in Paris.[113]

In this conclusion lies the full realization of the importance of Maurice Fenaille's attempt to use the calligraphed sonnets placed on the verso of the drawings in the *Suite d'Arthémise* (also attempted by Guiffrey for the *Histoire françoyse*) as indications of the sequence of compositions. Altogether the same procedure is employed in the larger or smaller suites of biblical subjects in the above-mentioned albums of popular imagery from the 1570s and following. This is to say that one has a picture album with an abbreviated text on the verso of each composition which refers to the scene following; while the text itself may be copious, it presents a catchword which appears prominently on the abbreviated poetic text accompanying the succeeding image.[114] Prominent as well are the plaques or cartouches which contain only a summary inscription and an indication of the 'nails' fastening the label to the picture (figs. 22 and 25). The only substantive question remaining is whether the compositions were intended for multiplication and, if so, for reproduction in the original scale or in a more reduced format. The regular format of the cartoons, the consistent compositional schemes, the express mention that we are dealing with 'cartons de peincture de blanc et noir' – all these imply copper-engraving in exact scale.[115] The logical alternative would be a precious collection of drawings

113 Rés. Ed. 5g and Rés. Ra. 15a++, the latter of which contains later reductions of compositions in the former album.

114 In just as many instances where the recto only was printed (or where recto and verso were two different compositions forming part of a pictorial series), all more extended texts were altogether dispensed with.

115 Cf. above, p. 34, n. 102. The title may even imply two complementary works in different formats, e.g. a text and an album. On the other hand, a curious discrepancy is present in all the title-pages of the *Histoire françoyse* in the form of small sheets of paper with the important inscriptions or titles which are laid down over the corresponding part of the drawing. In instances which can be easily verified the inscriptions are the same, so the major pre-occupation seems to have been the replacement of a cursive or italic script with an epigraphic majuscule.

which could exist alone but which were created in view of eventual engraving.

The *Histoire françoyse* is then an official commemoration of the Valois and Medici dynasties, whose arms surmount each composition, and, like the *Suite d'Arthémise*, makes sense only in relation to Catherine de' Medici. Consequently even Houel's personal idea of a retrospective homage would have been forced into a deadeningly conservative mould. Only Caron's genius in developing simple concepts stamps these productions as ineffably French and much more masterpieces than the festival pictures for which he is known.

This fact is most obvious in the title-pages relating to *imprese*,[116] which contrast sharply with the woodcut reductions in octavo of Claude Paradin's *Devises heroïques* of 1551 by which they were more widely known.[117] Jodelle avails himself of the advantages of a literary presentation for like elements in the Icones, but the number of acceptable conceits within the royal circle was doubtless restricted. This (and Houel's access to Catherine's art collections) resulted in a 'fonds commun' for artists and poets, so we should not be surprised to find in Icon XIII

HENRICI
æternæ memoriæ, ut hoc aliquando regali
tumulo insculpatur
CÆSAR ALEXANDRI QVOD FLEVIT IMAGINE VISA,
HOC TANTVM IVBET ELATOS MEA FLERE NEPOTES,
QVÆ VEL ALEXANDRO GEMITVM EXTORSISSET IMAGO.

a parallel which is exact in elements and presentation to one of the title-pages for the *Histoire françoyse*.[118]

116 Cf. pp. 84–5.
117 This edition was not available to us, so we have used that of 1557. (Cf. figs. 21, 29.)
118 Cf. p. 156 and fig. 13. From a preserved letter to Lord Burghley thought to date in October 1571, it is evident that Houel offered to Elizabeth I the totality of an art collection which, by his own admission, had been some twenty-five years in the making. His enumeration is by

Some writers have suggested that emblematics and, more particularly, illustration, are not really art at all, which may be truc in the narrowest sense of the word. Yet they may be understood as the stimuli existing almost *in vacuo* which may be transmuted into new forms by those descriptive variables usually agglomerated under the word 'style'. Even then, style and iconography do not go their separate ways but instead complement each other not only at the outset of previously unanticipated needs but also once the (even mistaken) implications of the subject have been fully comprehended. Hence the feeling of the present writers that only an iconographical analysis dependent upon a broadly-based series of studies can hope to provide a fuller understanding of such meta-literary works as the *Recueil des inscriptions*.

A final word by way of hypothesis. The title-page of the *Histoire françoyse* expressly mentions that the cartoons were done by the most excellent painters of both France and Italy, a characterization also appearing in Houel's dedication of the *Suite d'Arthémise*.[119] It has heretofore been possible to identify with certainty only the artists Caron and Niccolò dell'Abbate even if several other hands of varying quality were involved at some time in the genesis of the two suites. If Me Baptiste was important enough to execute decorations for Jodelle's banqueting hall in 1558, and if he is the same Baptiste Pellerin whose works were posthumously to illustrate verses of Ronsard by 1579 (fig. 22),[120]

categories, so we cannot say whether the *Histoire françoyse* or the *Suite d'Arthémise* were included or reserved; surely no great efforts to extend the suites would have been undertaken after this time, which corresponds to the paucity of known materials from the reigns of Francis II and Charles IX. Cf. Gustave Lebel, 'Une lettre oubliée de Nicolas Houel,' *Bulletin de la Société de l'histoire de l'art français* (1923), pp. 40–4.

119 J. Guiffrey, 'Nicolas Houel . . . etc.,' *Mémoires de la Societé de l'Histoire de Paris et de l'Ile-de-France*, XXV (1898), p. 187, 'par cartons de peinture de blanc et de noir, qui sont de mon invention, et delivrez de la main des mellieurs ouvriers du monde, avec l'exposition d'un sonnet à chacune histoire pour la clere et facile intelligence d'icelle.' (Cf. above, p. 34, n. 102.)

120 Cf. p. 92, n. 71. This would develop a suggestion first made by S. Béguin, 'La Suite d'Arthémise,' *L'Œil*, nº 38 (1958), p. 36.

then it is not impossible that, as an artist of consequence, he could have participated in the commissions of the Parisian Houel. One strong and coherent hand is identifiable in two drawings from the *Histoire françoyse* and five from the *Suite d'Arthémise*.[121] Unless we are mistaken, this hand is similar to certain *bois populaires* (fig. 25) published in the Rue Montorgueil, the place of origin of our *Portraits* of Calais and of Guignes (figs. 23 and 24) and the centre of mass production of images in Paris.[122] A like number of coincidences invites future consideration.

All this is a far cry from the *Promptuaire des medalles* and the dreary illustrations of the *Annales et Chroniques* which were so generalized that they were interchangeable in all, including name. The problems of interpenetration of models and genres, provided one may demonstrate the mode of transmission, are such as to affright the hesitant researcher in this troubled and fascinating epoch. It is the unexpected source which sheds most light upon familiar ground rather than the manipulation of extant texts so as to display neglected meanings. Even in its day the thread of Ariadne would have been difficult to follow, and faced with heroic but unappreciated efforts Jodelle would certainly have agreed with Ronsard's 1572 preface to the *Franciade*:

> Un list ce livre pour aprendre,
> L'autre le list comme envieux:
> Il est aisé de me reprendre
> Mais malaisé de faire mieux.

> Tu excuseras les fautes de l'imprimeur: car tous les yeux d'Argus n'y verroient assez clair, mesme en la premiere impression.[123]

121 Respectively, Louvre, RF 29723 and 29728 (fig. 17) (cf. above, p. 37, n. 111) and BN Est Rés. Ad. 105 gr. in folio, fols. 13^r, 23^r, 24^r (fig. 26), 33^r, 36^r.

122 Cf. p. 38. See Jean Adhémar, 'La rue Montorgueil et la formation d'un groupe d'imagiers parisiens au XVIème siècle,' *Le Vieux Papier*, XXI (1951), pp. 25–34.

123 *Œuvres complètes*, ed. Laumonier (STFM), XVI^I, pp. 11–12, where Ronsard even employs the image of the vendor used by Jodelle in the *Ad D. Margaritam Francicam*. (Cf. pp. 137–8.)

SYNOPSIS OF THE DECORATIONS AND ENTERTAINMENTS

We may in any case reconstruct a coherent iconographical profile from the details mentioned in the *Recueil* alone (fig. A). These may be divided into two complementary but physically distinct entities – the prologue beginning at the arcade of the entrance to the Hôtel de Ville up to and including the very door of the Grande Salle, and the decorations contained in that room itself. To this may be appended the two *mascarades* which elaborate conceits apparent in both prior entities.

The initial problem was to make do with the minimum materials required to set up the general iconographical programme; for this, Jodelle contrived a series of inscriptions (accompanied or not by figures) to be seen sequentially as the royal party ascended the stairs to the banqueting hall set up in the Grande Salle.

In the arcade above the building's entrance, Jodelle had had painted 'force trophées à l'antique, des armes, et enseignes ennemies'[124] in the middle of which was a recumbant oval surrounded by laurel with *pourtraits* of Calais and Guignes at one and the other end,[125] and between them a long Latin inscription in honour of Henry II and François de Guise.[126] Below the arcade but above the frieze of the portal, Jodelle had feigned in gold lettering on black marble the inscription REGI PIISS [imo] PII CIVES surmounting a Latin tristich.[127] On each side of the arcade was a Doric column 'dont les deus pieds costoyent deus lettres d'or H H et au meilleu des deus escrit en lettres d'argent HOC HERVCLE DIGNÆ.'[128] It was intended that the two columns be each surmounted with a silvered crescent, but this plan was abandoned because of lack of time. Jodelle does not enlighten us as to the other decorations, including those of laurel, since they were probably not very important. No matter, for the essential was there to serve as a prologue to what was to follow, 'decouvrant dedans l'inscription les merites, dedans les trois vers l'excuse du triomphe,

124 Cf. p. 76.
125 Cf. p. 76.
126 Cf. pp. 77–8.
127 Cf. p. 78.
128 Cf. pp. 78–9.

FIGURE A

Portal III

VOTVM

SIC RAPIDAS AQVILAS, SIC FVLMINEOS LEOPARDOS
GALLIA CALCET OVANS, ILLAM QVOQVE MOBILE LAVRV
TEMPVS, ET ARMIFVGA MVNDVM DIGNETVR OLIVA.

Stairwell

GRADATIM
GRADATIM
GRADATIM
[GRADATIM]

Portal II

VICISSITVDO

NE PROPERA, NVMENQVE VIDE, VISVMQVE VERERE,
AC GENIVM METIRE TVVM, NAMQVE OMNIA LEGI
SVPPOSVIT NOSTRÆ, NOSTRA QVI LEGE SOLVTVS.

REGI PIISS. PII CIVES.

HOC	NON POMPA, NON ROMVLEIS TE CVRRIBVS ALTVM	HOC
H HERCVLE H	ACCIPIMVS, FACTIS CVM SIT SPES REGIA MAIOR,	H HERCVLE H
DIGNÆ	SPE QVOQVE MAIORES, QVORVM EST TVA LAVREA, DIVI.	DIGNÆ

DD.

VIRTVTI ET VICTORIÆ. S.

D. HENRICO REGI PRÆCLARISSIMAR.
RERVM IN VNIVERSA TVM GALL. TVM ITAL.
TERRA MARIQ. BENE AC FELICITER GESTARVM
ERGO TRIVMPHVM PVBL. DIGNAMQ. SVIS FACTIS
ET LAVREAM ET MEMORIAM MERENTI RENVENTI SED
IN POSTERVM EXPECTANTI. OB FORTISS. ET VETVTISS.
NOSTRORVM CALETVM CIVITATEM NVPER A FRANCISCO LOTHA-
RINGO GVISIORVM PRINCIPE GLORIOSISS. OMNI INGENIO OB-
SESSAM MOX OMNI MARTE EXPVGNATAM AC PERENNI VOTO CVM A
CC ET X AN. BRITANNORVM SERVITVTEM PATERETVR SVÆ GALL.
RESTITVTAM. OB GVINAS OMNIB. ET VI ET VIRIB. CAPTAS,
SOLOQ. AD ÆQVATAS. OB HAMMENSEM PAGVM QVI HOSTIVM
METV DERELICTVS FVERAT RECEPTVM. OB LIBERATAM
DENIQVE AB OMNIB. BRITAN. GALL. HOC INTERIM
AD PRIMAM ILLAM INSPERATÆ REI COMMENDA-
TIONEM ET IN VOSTRVM O DD VIRTVS ET VIC-
TORIA FAVOREM EX VOTO ET DEBITO VRBS.
P D CONS. ST. IODELIVS PAR. PPP

Portrait de Calais [fig. 23] (left) — Portrait de Guignes [fig. 24] (right)

A Suggested disposition of inscriptions from the entrance of the Hôtel de Ville to and including the portal of the banqueting hall. May be read sequentially from the bottom of the page.

dedans les colonnes l'esperance future, j'ay taché de donner quelque merque à la souvenance des hommes.'[129]

Jodelle therein introduces the concept of epigraphical evidence as an *aide-mémoire*, a theme taken up in both the banqueting hall and the second *mascarade*, and further elaborated in the Icones.[130] This care could scarcely have been appreciated by Henry and his entourage, who arrived promptly at four o'clock in a downpour,[131] though it may have announced inadvertently the theme of VICISSITVDO with its tristich and image, placed on the second portal.[132]

After passing through this portal, the king and his retinue continued to mount the stairs leading to the banqueting hall. The stairwell contained tapestries, festoons, and the arms of the king and of the city of Paris, among which was interspersed several times the motto GRADATIM, 'escrite tousjours dedans une ovalle couchée, et entourée d'un compartiment semé de couronnes, *montrant qu'on ne va point autrement aus victoires que par degrez*, et qu'en les voulant trop haster on se precipite soymesme.'[133] This charming pun needed no further development and served as a transition between the VICISSITVDO portal and the third, or VOTVM, portal through which one entered the hall. Here was 'une autre figure enrichie de mesme sorte que la premiere [i.e. Vicissitudo] et *ainsi qu'estoient mesme toutes les autres que je diray*'[134] – a France armed and triumphant, amidst broken columns and captured standards, with enleashed eagles and leopards symbolizing Spain and England. The tristich accompany-

129 Cf. p. 80.
130 Cf. pp. 143–97.
131 'et plouvoit si fort allors qu'il fut contrainct se mettre dedans une coche. En descendant de laquelle coche, l'artillerye qui estoit en la place de Greve sonnoit si fort et faisoit si grand bruyt que les haquenées qui menoient lad. coche eurent peur et cuyderent faire choir le Roy en descendant d'icelle' (*Registres des délibérations du Bureau de l'Hôtel de Ville de Paris*, t. IV, p. 523).
132 Cf. p. 81.
133 Cf. p. 81.
134 Cf. p. 81. Such a normalization no doubt permitted the artisans to complete the essentials of the iconography in due course while giving the effect of stylistic and conceptual consistency.

FIGURE B

VICISSITVDO

Image:

une Deesse
tenant une couronne de
laurier en l'une de ses mains,
et une chaisne de fer en l'autre,
ayant le Soleil et la Lune aus
deux costés d'icelle et
poussant une sphere
du pié.

NE PROPERA, NUMENQVE VIDE, VISVMQVE VERERE,
AC GENIVM METIRE TVVM, NAMQVE OMNIA LEGI
SVPPOSVIT NOSTRÆ, NOSTRA QVI LEGE SOLVTVS.

B Reconstitution of format for those inscriptions accompanied by images of the second and third portals and of the banqueting hall. The texts specify 'un grand compartiment entouré de son chapeau de triomphe,' which does not necessarily assure a standing rather than the recumbant oval here used because of a disposition of elements (*inscriptio, image, subscriptio*) significantly common to contemporary emblem books. Particularly applicable to the device GRADATIM (fig. A) 'tousjours dedans une ovalle couchée, et entourée d'un compartiment semé de couronnes.'

C Suggested disposition of major elements of the banqueting hall iconography, not to scale. The high table was directly under the D. LETICIÆ and close enough to the EX. D. CAROLI LOTHARINGI PYRAMIDE that the latter, encompassed in a six-foot square 'se pouvoit facilement lire de la table du Roy.'

ing the motto VOTVM expressed the hope for the universal peace that would be Henry's doing[135] and the format of motto, image, and tristich permitted an easy and logical transition into the transformed Grande Salle (figs. B, C).

Nor may we doubt Jodelle's description of the Grande Salle and its iconography[136] since it seems but an abbreviated version of the official account of the banqueting hall:

> acoustrée de lierre par hault en forme de plancher,[137] et y avoit force chappeaulx de triumphe . . . Lad. salle estoit tappissée de la tappysserye de lad. Ville, et natée par le bas avec le theatre où estoit la table du Roy qui estoit plus hault que l'aire de lad. salle de trois marches de degres; y avoit chandeliers faicts exprès, painctz des coulleurs du Roy, penduz au plancher pour mettre grande quantité de flambeaux.
>
> Mes. Srs ordonnerent que ung eschaffault fut fait en lad. Salle pour mettre aucuns de leurs amys.[138]

This passage clarifies several important details. First, that our reconstruction must allow for a certain number of black and white chandeliers, despite the curious usage of the word *plancher*. Moreover, that the tapestries spoken of in this room and elsewhere[139] were the ordinary property of the city and could not be said to have contributed directly to the circumstantial iconography. Rather were they intended to ornament the bare walls and, more importantly

135 Cf. p. 82, plaintively echoed by Du Bellay in the *Regrets* of 1558, *Œuvres poétiques*, ed. Chamard (STFM), II, p. 202.

136 Cf. p. 83.

137 Evidently a false ceiling, perhaps on the order of that at the banquet offered Elisabeth d'Autriche in the Episcopal Palace on 30 March 1571: 'lequel estoit d'une fine toille blanche de lin sur compartimens de feuilles de liarre en quadrature, enrichiz d'or cliquant, parmy lesquelz estoient plusieurs rozases d'or eslevées, chiffres, devises et armoiries, tant de ladicte dame que de la Ville.' (Cf. *Registres des délibérations du Bureau se l'Hôtel de Ville de Paris*, t. VI, p. 311.) The appearance of these elements would be requisite in any decor of like nature.

138 Ibid., t. IV, pp. 522–3.

139 Cf. pp. 80, 98.

FIGURE C

ARGO	D. LETICIÆ	ARGO
CÆLOQVE	TV DEA, BACCHVS, AMOR, LVDISQVE, EPVLISQVE, IOCISQVE,	CÆLOQVE
SOLOQVE	HEROVM MEMORES GRATA VICE MERGITE CVRAS,	SOLOQVE
SALOQVE	PRÆLIA MNEMOSYNE NON POCVLA REGIA CVRET.	SALOQVE

IAM NON RESPEXIT VTRINQVE

QVI BIFRONS FVERAM, GALLIS SVM GALLICVS VNA
FRONTE DEVS, CÆLVMQVE MEA DVM CLAVE RESOLVI,
VIDI INCVMBENTEM GALLIS TOTVM ACRIBVS ANNVM.

NOVO SVA SALVA PICARDIA PERSEO

CAVTIBVS ANDROMEDEN PERSEVS, CETOQVE MARINO
ERIPVIT, MONSTRIS TV ME ME HENRICE MARINIS,
ESQVE TIBI, SI NOS PHINEVS PETAT, ALTERA GORGON.

CESSIT NATVRA FAVORI

NON CONIVRATI VENIVNT AD CLASSICA TANTVM
ÆOLIDÆ, VERVM GELIDO SOL SYDERE VERNANS
FVNDIT INASSVETOS ARVISQVE ARMISQVE CALORES.

DAT INIQVA SVPERBIA PŒNAS

LATONÆ NIOBE TIBI SESE O GALLIA PRÆFERT
ANGLIA, PROLE TVMENS, PHŒBVM, PHŒBENQVE LACESSENS,
SIC SAXVM GENITRIX, FIVNTQVE CADAVERA NATI.

ARRIPIAM VIGILET LICET

VELLVS AB INSOMNI LOTHARENE DRACONE TVLISTI,
CARMINIBVS NEC SVNT FERA LVMINA VICTA, NEC HERBIS,
INGENIVM, MARTEMQVE VOCES NISI CARMEN, ET HERBAS.

RES IMPAR SED FATA EADEM

VLTIMA TE MACEDO REGINA CVPIVIT AMAZON,
ANGLICA CÆSAREVM CVPIIT REGINA PHILIPPVM,
VTRAQVE SIC REGINA SVI MANET VLTIMA REGNI.

TER HOC FELICITER ACTVM

CÆSARIS HOC, CÆSAR DEMAS TIBI, GVISIUS ADDAT,
NAM VENIT, VIDIT, VICIT SIMVL ISTE, TVOSQVE
DVM QVOQVE VINCEBANT, VICTO IAM CÆSARE VICIT.

ET LECTI ET LETHI CONSORS

IN FVRIAS FVRIATA PARES CLEOPATRA MARITVM
ISTA TRAHIT, LICET ABSIT AMOR, TIMOR ADSIT, ET HORROR,
AVGVSTIQVE MEO REDEANT SVB PRINCIPE REGNA.

EX. D. CAROLI LOTHARINGI PYRAMIDE
A STEPH. IODELIO DESCRIPTA

SCOTIA TVTA SVIS, ACCEPTA BOLONIA, METÆ,
ET RHENI PAVOR ATTONITI, FVSVSQVE PER VMBRAS
CÆSAR, ET HINC VICTÆ TVRMIS REDEVNTIBVS VRBES,
MOX QVOQVE DEFENSÆ LOTHARENI GLORIA METÆ,
INSTAVRATÆ ACIES, VRBESQVE ÆDESQVE SORORIS
CÆSAREÆ, RENTINA TIBI PALMA ADDITA GVISI,
AC SI QVA IN BELGIS QVÆSITA TROPHŒA SVPERSVNT:
HAS INTER PALMAS PARMA, ET MIRANDVLA, SENÆ,
CORSICAQVE, ET TOTIES DECEPTVS IN ALPIBVS HOSTIS:
NVNC QVOQVE QVOD RELIQVIS POTIVS FATALE CALETVM,
QVÆQVE FEROX POTIOR FATALI GVINA CALETO,
HÆC SVNT QVAE REGEM LAVRV RES LAVDE CORONANT.

for the season, to provide warmth. And finally, that a scaffolding was added upon request at some unspecified place in the room, which undoubtedly contributed to the general encumberment and the great affluence of uninvited or disobedient guests.[140]

As to the distribution of the iconographical motifs, we must first imagine Henry's table as being elevated on a platform some three steps above the regular floor level. This is qualified as being '*du costé des fenestres*, à l'endroit où se devoit soir le Roy'[141] and where '*ce front de salle* estoit orné de ces trois figures'[142] that is, the D. LETICIÆ[143] in the centre with, on either side, an identical composition of the ARGO.[144]

'*Au bas de la salle, qui estoit le costé par où l'on devoit servir*,[145] outre la tapisserie et le lierre qui le decoroient, dedans un grand et spatieus quarre de la longueur d'une toise, estoient escrits douze vers comprenans toutes les choses que le Roy a faites depuis son avenement à la couronne, le tout allant d'ordre, et le tout si bien escrit, et en si grands caracteres, qu'il se pouvoit facilement lire de la table du Roy.'[146] This extract was taken from the *Pyramide* of the Cardinal de Lorraine.[147]

Thus, on the major axis are established those structural and presumably unvarying aspects of the royal presence. A purely factual enumeration of Henry's deeds from the moment of his accession to the taking of Calais appears

140 *Registres des délibérations du Bureau de l'Hôtel de Ville de Paris*, t. IV, p. 523. Cf. p. 118.

141 Cf. p. 86.

142 Cf. p. 87.

143 Cf. p. 86.

144 Cf. p. 87. The Argo from the Paris entry of 1549 will be synonymous with the state or Paris itself in all festivals in the capital. Cf. Antoinette Huon, 'Le thème du Prince dans les entrées parisiennes au XVIe siècle,' *Les Fêtes de la Renaissance*, I (Paris, CNRS, 1956), p. 26.

145 A precious detail, as the direction from which the table service came was also probably that from which 'ceulx qui devoient jouer la comedie entrerent dedans la Salle à grande force, et commencerent à chanter; mais ilz estoient enrouez, et n'en fut pas tenu grand compte.' (Cf. *Registres des délibérations du Bureau de l'Hôtel de Ville de Paris*, t. IV, p. 523.)

146 Cf. p. 98.

147 Cf. p. 100.

as an inscription of 'permanent' nature. Opposite it is a reference to the very banquet which is now taking place to commemorate all those events as one (viz. Calais), not only as a general but more particularly a Parisian celebration. PRÆLIA MNEMOSYNE NON POCVLA REGIA CVRET is first replied to by the very insignia of Paris, the vessel Argo, and also by its accompanying device CÆLOQVE SOLOQVE SALOQVE, which literally sets the stage for the first *mascarade*, of the Argonauts, which is to follow.[148] The inscription, best seen from the superior position of Henry's own table[149] and existing in splendid isolation on a wall otherwise devoid of ornament, is then posterity's record of this moment.

We then have the curious spectacle of the monarch attending, perhaps more subtly than in a *comédie* or ballet in which he actively participates, his own deification. He is the fulcrum of the iconography, both historically and in his own person. It may be expected that the remainder of the motifs will proceed in a predetermined manner on either side of the axis determined by his very glance.

It is scarcely surprising to note that 'premierement du costé droit, au premier intervalle respondant encores sur la table du Roy [i.e. the platform]'[150] was the IANO GALLICO. This established a standard form which was followed in all the remaining pictures: a device above (IAM NON RESPEXIT VTRINQVE) and a tristich below the image described, whether or not it depicted one or more figures.[151] Therefore, no doubt is left as to the interpretation of *du costé droit* as meaning to Henry's right, for the dexter side was tradition-

148 Cf. pp. 103–15. The same idea is expressed in the first few lines of the inscription DD. VIRTVTI ET VICTORIÆ and in the last line of its accompanying tristich (SPE QVOQVE MAIORES etc.).

149 A procedure not unlike that at the triumphal entries, where only the king and his immediate entourage would be able to see, and in the proper sequence, the entirety of the decorations, *mystères*, and speaking or mute *figurants*. This is to say that these festivities must be considered not in terms of the spectators, but rather in terms of the personages around whom the iconographies are constructed.

150 Cf. p. 88.

151 Icones V, XXVI, XXVII.

ally the more favourable. In any case, the choice of Janus to lead off the programme is as appropriate as incontrovertible, since Jodelle maintains, 'J'avois voulu montrer par ceste peinture, combien le mois de Janvier nous a esté favorable . . . La figure que l'on voyoit *au prochain espace d'après* suivoit d'assés bonne grace la premiere pour exprimer ceste faveur du tens.'[152] Here was the sign of Aquarius with the device CESSIT NATVRA FAVORI and its explanatory verse.[153]

This explanation accounts for one side of what may be termed the circumstantial iconography, and Jodelle takes pains to assure us of the orientation of the wall opposite. '*Vis à vis de ces deus dernieres figures, dedans les deus premiers espaces que faisoient les Croissants de l'autre costé*, j'en avois fait assoir deus autres, qui suivoient le mesme argument de ceste nouvelle et heureuse conqueste [de Calais].'[154] The crescents of which he speaks were those large ones of ivy hanging from the frieze surmounting the tapestries down toward the floor, crescents entwined together in such a way that they might be coupled at top and bottom, where they crossed by means of black taffeta bonds. On these were written in silver letters the motto IVNGVNTVR, 'soit pour autant que la rencontre des deus fait un rond, ou soit pour l'alliance du Roy et du Grand seigneur, qui portent tous deus le croissant.[155] It would seem that, in either case, the pairs of images were rather closely spaced. On the opposite side, then, appeared Jason and the Golden Fleece with the device ARRIPIAM VIGILET LICET[156] followed by a presumed banner of Julius Cæsar with its V.V.V. and device TER HOC FELICITER ACTVM.[157]

It was evidently only at the time of printing that Jodelle took it upon himself to provide a brilliant variation upon this latter theme, thereby showing his literary facility. He thus changed the TER to QVATER and added below the banner an enchained Fortune.[158] This alternative makes even more emphatic a rather hyperbolic conceit, and is indicative of the ease with which such cir-

152 Cf. p. 88.
153 Cf. p. 89.
154 Cf. p. 89.
155 Cf. p. 86.
156 Cf. p. 90.
157 Cf. pp. 90–1.
158 Cf. p. 91.

cumstantial allusions could be successfully modified. Here the nuancing is even more subtle in that no express mention is made of François de Guise.

This happy afterthought was nonetheless prompted by more practical considerations relating to the disposition of the room, and thus of its decorations:

> J'ay ajousté ceci de gayeté de cueur, comme j'ajousteray *quatre autres figures qui estoient deja toutes ordonnées, et dont les compartimens estoient faits*, ainsi que me sont tesmoins ceus qui estoient avecque moy *et mesmement Baptiste* excellent peintre qui les faisoit, et *qui en avoit receu l'ordonnance dès le soir de devant*: Mais l'arrivée du Roy nous pressa de si près, qu' encores que le peintre fist une admirable diligence, *il fut impossible d'en faire tant: et fusmes contraints de nous contenter de ces quatres premières, pour les intervalles des croissants, dont les deus premiers qui en estoient remplis contenoient autant d'espace de la salle, que faisoit le lieu où l'on devoit couvrir*[159] *pour le Roy.*[160]

Whereas the four previous elements had been in the spaces enclosed by the crescents, the other four were to be included in the intervals between them. Into the bargain, the latter provided specific allusive footnotes to the main iconographical text supplied by the sequence of crescents. It is noteworthy that Jodelle devotes an inordinate amount of explanation to these last subjects to make absolutely sure that they will not be vulgarly or maliciously misunderstood,[161] and his care is all the more requisite in that they deal with England either as a sovereign power or in the person of Mary Tudor. He also exercises admirable discretion (which is as well an indirect testimony to the coherence of his iconographical programme) by including in the printed *Recueil* only those motifs actually executed. He further invites his readers to verify his assertion by accepting the oral testimony of his co-workers, most particularly that of the painter Baptiste. This invitation would scarcely be

159 i.e. where the table was to be set. (Cf. p. 48.)

160 Cf. p. 92.

161 Cf. pp. 92–7.

accepted by the general reader in any case, and would become impossible to confirm with the passage of time, so Jodelle's word would stand in the normal course of events. Nonetheless, he inadvertently gives himself away by lamenting the difficulties of working with 'une entrée assés estroite, et dedans une salle qui n'est pas des plus spatieuses'[162] in such a way that we are not at all sure that there were in truth additional motifs planned which could not be accommodated under the circumstances. The important thing is that the iconography is both complete and entirely comprehensible as it is described.

These last four motifs, of secondary nature insofar as they relate to the major set-piece, develop at some length the individual cases and parallels implicit in the general iconographical structure. Jodelle merely lists them in sequence from first to last without further details as to their placement beyond, of course, their subsidiary relation to the crescents. They nevertheless fall into two distinct subject groupings, the first pertaining to England (historical facts) and the second to her rulers (prophecies developed from these facts), so we shall not be far wrong in distributing them in like manner to the right and left of Henry.

First would be Perseus and Andromeda with the device NOVO SVA SALVA PICARDIA PERSEO showing 'combien la Picardie estoit heureuse d'avoir un tel Roy pour son prince,'[163] and followed by Niobe and her children (DAT INIQVE SVPERBIA PŒNAS). 'L'orgueil d'Angleterre si bien rabaissé par ceste peinture, estoit suivi de la destinée du mesme païs.'[164] Here Jodelle begins to equivocate as he realizes that any inconsiderate fusion of contemporaries into a classical frame of reference may well result in the selection of an obvious, but quite inappropriate, referent. The device RES IMPAR SED FATA EADEM which accompanies Alexander and Thalestris embracing is intended to forestall any unseemly haste in interpreting the final two compositions and to express Jodelle's very real dilemma as an iconographer.

162 Cf. p. 118.
163 Cf. p. 93.
164 Cf. p. 94.

> Pour autant qu'on pourroit trouver quelques choses, en ceste figure qui du tout ne s'accommoderoient point, je luy ay fait porter la devise d'en haut qui est telle, *que les choses estans differentes*, le destin est de mesme.[165]

No competent historian would fault Jodelle on method. Nor indeed would any contemporary iconographer whose success depended upon the persistence of received images or themes and a consolidation of past innovations to provide a secure point of reference for the future. That which was intended – whether a detail or, less probably, the recessive structure itself[166] – may seem in retrospect to have been trivial or misplaced, but *toutes proportions gardées*, all of this was correspondingly less apparent, even less relevant, to his contemporaries.

Perhaps more pertinently, any elevated form of political allegory in this period required a certain delicacy of expression, failing which the equilibrium of traditional iconographical procedures would have been destroyed in a tasteless broadside.

Jodelle minimizes rather than exploits to the full those anti-English sentiments which could be expected from the victory at Calais, and this restraint gives his work the timeless character of any work of redeeming literary value. He frankly concedes that the image of Alexander and Thalestris is an inappropriate parallel to Philip II and Mary Tudor, since the latter couple were lawfully joined by Church ritual. But this does not prevent him from using the conceit of legitimacy as the basis for the final motif of Anthony and Cleopatra at Actium (ET LECTI ET LETHI CONSORS).[167] In doing so, he anticipates the succession of Octavian to the Empire and can return to the subject of Henry II who, as a result of Calais, would bring 'tout un monde sous sa monarchie, ramenant encores ici l'heureus et paisible siecle d'Auguste.'[168]

165 i.e., the events being different, their destiny is *the same*. (Cf. p. 95.)

166 If the Guise victories from Metz to Calais provide Jodelle's scenario, the recapture of Boulogne from the English a decade earlier would still have been remembered.

167 Cf. p. 96.

168 Cf. pp. 97–8.

One need not dwell at length on the fact that the two medals which Giovanni Antonio de Rossi (fig. 27 A, B) struck for the event bear the legend MAIORA SEQVENTVR,[169] nor that the laurel diadem Jodelle imagined for Henry was to bear two verses (MAGNA TIBI CAPTO CONCESSIT CVRA CALETO and CINGE COMAS, SIMILES IANVS ET ANNVS ERVNT), both referring us obliquely back to the Inscription facing Henry and to the Gallic Janus to his immediate right.[170] Could anyone now remain unconvinced that a convention was a liberating rather than a confining force, or that a vast superstructure could be built from an excessively limited number of conceits, endlessly elaborated?

As a citizen of the City of Paris and a subject of the king, Jodelle was well aware of the diplomatic implications of any immoderate or inconsiderate reference. His justification for this reticence is all the more revealing for the very clarity of its formulation:

> Car j'aye esté d'avis de tout tens que c'estoit le plus sotement fait qu'on sçauroit faire, d'injurier par escrit les Princes qui nous sont ennemis, principallement aus choses qui sont controuvées, ou qui touchent tellement leur honneur, que nos Princes mesmes s'en doivent facher. *Quand aus legeres attaintes, aus veritables reproches, aus propheties et aus promesses qu'on se fait à soymesme, cela est permis de l'ennemi à l'ennemi.*[171]

This 'escape clause' totally absolves Jodelle of any personal responsibility. He is, after all, relying upon events of common knowledge, whether his sources be printed or simple hearsay. His French nationality enables him to use them with detachment, and his conflation of the Amazon queen Thalestris with Mary Tudor (. . . VTRAQVE SIC REGINA SVI MANET VLTIMA REGNI) is simply 'ce que les Anglois mesmes sçavent avoir esté prophetizé de ceste

169 Alfred Armand, *Les médailleurs italiens des quinzième et seizième siècles*, 2e ed. (Paris, 1883), I, p. 243. (Cf. pp. 73–4 and 95.)

170 Cf. pp. 123–4. The legends for the diadem were not in fact executed.

171 Cf. p. 95.

Royne cy.'[172] It would be difficult to adduce at a distance of some 400 years a polemic which Jodelle could have known with certainty. Whether his iconography be received or created, it nonetheless relies upon concepts which could quickly escape their parochial bonds and become generalized.

With the Inscription EX D. CAROLI LOTHARINGI PYRAMIDE, A STEPH. IODELIO DESCRIPTA,[173] the enumeration of the banqueting hall decorations is complete and Jodelle turns to accounting for the entertainments, which included the so-called failure of the first, or speaking, *mascarade*.[174]

Jodelle first excuses himself by inviting those persons of quality in the realm who had themselves been spectators and would most likely have access to the *Recueil*, to accede to his request in its reading and, 'après avoir à l'imitation des dieus, *receu la volonté pour le fait, et l'ordonnance pour l'execution*, ne souffrir plus dore en avant, que les calomnies des envieus tachent à me faire demeurer sus la teste ce que je ne meritay jamais.'[175] He goes one step further than the author excusing himself for typographic errors and with some pride implies that not only was it impossible to execute his inventions in the time given[176] but also that it was surely difficult to carry them off at all.[177]

172 Cf. p. 96 and Icon LV. This comment can only refer to the first of the two compositions devoted to Bloody Mary, for Jodelle continues 'encore donnerois-je volontiers ceste loy, combien que je ne l'aye pas observée, que toutes telles choses se fissent par souhaits et imprecations seullement, comme je l'avois fait dans la figure suivante *qui devoit estre la derniere de toutes*.' This conveniently introduces the Anthony and Cleopatra simile leading to historical results which 'chacun sçait assés' and further reinforces the preceding two compositions of Jason and Niobe, where the taking of Picardy results in the humiliation of England. We are obviously involved in a process of insinuation between historical and allegorical parallels of the highest sophistication.

173 Cf. p. 98.

174 Cf. p. 103 *et seq*.

175 Cf. p. 124.

176 Cf. pp. 75, 79–80: 'j'ose dire que je me fei quasi de tous mestiers, et assés heureusement, comme on pourra voir par ce recueil, si l'execution eust esté telle que l'ordonnance'; 'Je ne parle point ici . . . de tout autre ornement d'entre les deus portes, un peu mieus devisé que mis en œuvre . . .'

177 Cf. p. 88: 'mais chacun sçait que la main des ouvriers ne peut suivre l'abondance de mes inventions.'

Even if he would readily admit that his verses for the first *mascarade* were far from ideal, owing to their hasty composition, some on the very day of performance, Jodelle assumes that they would have been at least effective had it not been for the confusion and lack of initiative on the part of those assisting him. The artisans had presumably first produced *clochers* instead of *rochers*, so that the conceit of Orpheus charming inanimate objects by his music was reduced to a shambles.[178] Since Jodelle mentions only two pages later that the entrance of the Argonauts with their ship and the rocks added to the press and confusion, this may well be an elaborate justification of his qualities vis-à-vis those of his collaborators. It is, moreover, the only cited example of the type of philologically-based error which is common to absurd iconographies in any case, so we do not really need to accept it at face value. What is of note is the care expended on props which would be used only for the extent of the musical composition sung 'comme si ce fust esté la vois de quelques Satyres ou quelques Nimphes cachées au dedans'[179] in reply to the summons from Orpheus which opens the *mascarade*.

The first *mascarade* was by far the more elaborate of the two, consisting of some fourteen persons, 'a sçavoir *celles qui ont parlé avecq' dix autres Argonautes*[180] tous habillés à la matelote antique de blanc et de noir, qui sont les couleurs du Roy, nous en fismes entrer *une autre qui ne parloit point*,[181] que j'avois devisée

178 Cf. p. 117, n. 119.

179 Cf. p. 103.

180 The four speaking roles were Minerve, Jason (-Jodelle), Argon, and Mopsus. In his three-part justification for taking a role himself, Jodelle intimates that 'cinq ou siz gentils hommes miens amis furent des Argonautes muets, qui autrement n'en eussent point esté.' (Cf. p. 118.)

181 Despite his excuses for the presentation and execution of everything, Jodelle is conscious that 'quand on se fust du tout arresté, sans en prononcer un seul vers, que la chose n'eust pas esté moins louable à cause de l'invention, *veu que coustumierement toutes telles mascarades sont muetes* . . . (et) je ne m'en deusse aucunement soucier, ni penser que la gloire de mes autres inventions en fust amoindrie, *veu que c'est une chose qui ne fait seullement que passer pour un leger plaisir*.' (Cf. p. 120.) This popular impression is explicitly disavowed by Jodelle early on in the *Recueil* when

en telle sorte que *la premiere ayant esté des couleurs du Roy, ceste ci seroit des couleurs de la Royne qui sont blanc et verd.*'[182] Thus at the first entry, Orpheus sang two *sixains* whose refrain, 'Suivés (-Chantés) rochers, et avecq' vostre Orphée / Adorés moy *d'un grand Roy le Trophée*,'[183] prepares for the entrance of the vessel Argo, built by Minerva 'du bois de la forest parlante, qui est la cause qu'elle parloit, et qu'elle estoit prophete ... pour le [Henry II] conseiller et lui prophetiser ses heurs et ses malheurs.'[184] This was to be carried on the shoulders of the Argonaut maskers (as an allusion to the 'support' of the city of Paris) just as the Argonauts of old had carried it through the Libyan desert. To this invocation, the *rochers* replied in like measure that they were,

> Raviz, abstraits, mourants d'ouir Orphée,
> Et plus encore d'ouir un tel Trophée . . .
> O trois trois fois trois fois heureus Trophée.[185]

The speaking characters then took over for the remainder of the spectacle to deliver, each in turn, his *harangue*, the structure of which is of exceptional clarity despite differences in length and a change to Alexandrine verse. Each speaker (i.e. Minerve,[186] Jason (-Jodelle),[187] Argon,[188] Mopsus,[189] and – to close the *mascarade* as Orpheus and the *rochers* had opened it, Jason (-Jodelle) once again) is announced by a catchword or introductory *précis*, and in his

he mentions, 'affin que les peuples ou ennemies ou estrangers ne pensent point que ce que je decriray ci-après ait esté fait pour autre chose que pour un leger passetens, sans aulcune forme ou de gloire ou de triomphe' that the king himself had arranged to be in Paris for compelling political reasons as well as to take advantage of the pleasures of the season. (Cf. p. 72.)

182 Cf. p. 121.

183 Cf. p. 104, vv. 5–6, 11–12.

184 Cf. p. 103.

185 Cf. p. 104, vv. 5–6, 12.

186 Cf. pp. 105–8, especially vv. 67–71, of which vv. 67–8 are but a reworking of the previous decasyllabic refrains of Orpheus and the *rochers*.

187 Cf. pp. 108–11, especially vv. 61–2 and 67–8.

188 Cf. p. 111, especially vv. 1 and 12–14.

189 Cf. pp. 112–14, especially vv. 1–2.

declamation replies colloquially to the preceding speaker. It seems probable that the *mascarade* could have been understood by anyone present, provided of course that he were listening. Finally, Jason makes a direct address to the king which interprets Mopsus' prophecy in the light of the now familiar image of the ship of state[190] conducting Henry and his pantheon, 'Par tout où il plaira à ta grand Majesté / Singler d'un voile plain de la prosperité.[191]

With these words, Jodelle's participation as an author actively declaiming and interpreting his own verse ceases as the (now mute) second *mascarade* begins. As the preceding entertainment had dealt with the conceit CÆLOQVE SOLOQVE SALOQVE in relation to the Argo, so is the primary figure of the following *mascarade* (Mnemosyne-Memoire) taken from the decorations appearing behind Henry.[192]

In Memoire's entourage were personifications of Vertu and Victoire, each of whom would have been identifiable at a glance by the descending hierarchy of motifs strewn on their costumes in the antique mode: the serpents of eternity,[193] stars,[194] and trophies.[195] Accompanying them were to have been 'trois enfans *nuds*, comme si ce fussent esté de petits Amours ou de petits Jesus'[196] of which two were to have baskets of flowers and of eggs blown and filled with perfumes to cast about the room. The remaining cupid was to be entrusted with a basket full of floral diadems arranged in order of their intended presentation and appropriate to the qualities of each recipient. Most of them relate to personal devices or conceits developed elsewhere in the *Recueil*:

190 Cf. pp. 114–15.
191 Cf. p. 115, vv. 31–2.
192 Cf. p. 87.
193 The ordinary attribute, derived from Horapollo, *Hieroglyphica*, Venice, 1505¹, and widely circulated.
194 Perhaps something on the order of the four cardinal virtues 'representées par quatre filles vestues de bleu celeste, ayans leurs robes chargées d'estoiles d'or bruny: faisant entendre la perfection de ceux qui accompagnent et suyvent la vertu' illustrated in Baltasar de Beaujoyeulx, *Balet Comique de La Royne*, 1582, ed. G.A. Caula, Turin, 1965, p. 41.
195 One remarks the clear progression from abstract to concrete entities.
196 Cf. pp. 121–2 (Jeus in the original).

laurel: for the king (Phœbus);[197] palm fronds for the queen;[198] olive for Madame Marguerite (Pallas);[199] poplar for François de Guise (Hercules);[200] ivy for the Cardinal de Lorraine (his *Pyramide*);[201] and laurel or flowers for Diane de Poitiers since she may appropriate the attributes of her brother Phœbus-Apollo or of her nymphs.[202] Monsieur, Monsieur de Lorraine, la Reine d'Ecosse, and Mesdames were to receive myrtle, the crown of love,[203] all of which were to be offered by Vertu and witnessed by Victoire and Memoire. 'Ce present fait la Vertu avecques une harangue convenable à cela'[204] was to invite Henry to dance while her companions did likewise with two other princes, one of whom was probably François de Guise. This would be the signal for the general dancing which customarily ended such festivities.

This *mascarade* was also troubled, first by the fact that the natural foliage required for the diadems was not to be found and could only be imitated. Even then, only Henry's diadem was actually completed, but so late that Jodelle could not add to it the commemorative verses he had intended.[205] More injurious to the general effect was that a travesty was made of Jodelle's own mythological travesty in that the Parisians apparently either refused or forgot to have their children appear in the nude.[206] Notwithstanding these *contretemps*,

197 Cf. p. 83, n. 45 and p. 122.
198 Cf. p. 122 'laquelle elle porte mesme en l'une de ses devises,' but which does not belong to any of Catherine de' Medici's devices known to us.
199 Cf. Icon XXVIII and p. 122.
200 Cf. Icon XXXVI and p. 122.
201 Cf. pp. 100 and 122.
202 Cf. Icon XLV and p. 122.
203 Cf. Icon XXVII and p. 122. Francis II, aged 14 years, and Mary Stuart (Icones XVI and XVIII) were married 24 April 1558, whereas Claude de France, aged 11 years and Charles de Lorraine (Icones XXIV and XXXV) were married in early 1559. Of the remaining immediate members of the royal family, Charles IX, Henry III, and Hercule-François (Icones XX, XXI, and XXII) were respectively eight, seven, and four years of age, and Elisabeth and Marguerite (Icones XXIII and XXV) were twelve and six.
204 Cf. p. 122.
205 Cf. pp. 123–4.
206 Cf. p. 123: 'au lieu d'enfans nuds, les Parisiens mirent de leurs enfans vestus et bien peu deguisés, tellement que les ailes et les trousses que devoient avoir ces Amours, demeurerent au peintre.'

all went well enough that Jodelle considered the invited guests were not really dissatisfied with this spectacle.

Thus, as he did throughout the book, Jodelle pleads his case and his artistic standards winningly, and he concludes by emphasizing to his readers and to France the reciprocal nature of such an undertaking as the *Recueil des Inscriptions*:

> Voila comme je pense, tout ce qui se peut recueillir de tout le labeur que j'avois pris pour penser me montrer, en une si belle occasion, curieus de l'honneur de mon païs, et affectionné au service de mon Prince . . . la bonté de tes Princes, ne doit esperer de nous une moindre recompanse, que l'accroissement de leur gloire, la commodité de leur vie, et l'immortalité de leur renommée.[207]

207 Cf. pp. 124, 126.

PART II

LE RECUEIL DES INSCRIPTIONS, FIGURES, DEVISES, ET MASQUARADES,

ordonnées en l'hostel de ville à Paris,
le Jeudi 17. de Fevrier. 1558.

Autres Inscriptions en vers Heroïques Latins,
pour les images des Princes de la Chrestienté.
par Estiene Jodelle Parisien

A PARIS
Chez André Wechel, à l'enseigne du Cheval volant,
rue S. Jean de Beauvais.
1558.
Avec privilege du Roy.

EXTRAICT DU PRIVILEGE

Par lettres patentes du Roy il est permis à André Wechel, imprimeur et libraire juré en l'Université de Paris, d'imprimer et vendre ce livre intitulé, Le recueil des inscriptions, figures, devises, et masquarades, ordonnées en l'hostel de ville a Paris, le Jeudi 17. de Fevrier. 1558. Et autres inscriptions en vers Heroïques Latins pour les images des Princes de la Chrestienté Par Estiene Jodelle Parisien avec inhibitions et defences à tous autres imprimeurs, et marchans, de non imprimer ny vendre en ce Royaume ledict livre de dix ans après la premiere impression parachevée, sur peine de confiscation, et de mille livres parisis d'amende. Ensemble a ledict seigneur voulu, qu'en inserant le contenu de ses lettres patentes, ou l'extraict d'icelles, à la fin ou au commancement dudict livre, elles soyent tenues pour suffisamment signifiées, et venues à la notice et cognoissance de tous libraires et imprimeurs, tout ainsy, que si lesdictes lettres leur avoyent particulierement et expressement esté monstrées et signifiées: comme appert plus amplement par lesdictes lettres patentes, données a Reims l'unziesme de Juing 1557.[1] Signées par le Roy, le seigneur de Villemor, maistre des requestes ordinaire de l'hostel, present.

ESTIENE JODELLE A SES AMIS. S.

N'ayant point encore bien connu (mes Amis) que c'estoit des amités de nostre tens, j'eusse pensé avant le desastre que vous sçavés m'estre survenu, que donnant un tel tiltre à une epistre mienne j'eusse bien escrit à un plus grand nombre que je ne fay, et que lui adressant la moindre chose qu'il eust peu souhaiter de moy, j'eusse bien autrement senti, combien les œuvres de ceus qui sont aimés, sont agreables à ceus qui les aiment. Mais d'un costé, le grand nombre d'adversaires et le peu d'amis qui se sont decouvers en mon malheur,

1 The date should read 1558. Cf. E. Balmas, *Etienne Jodelle*, p. 381, n. 83; Jodelle *Œuvres*, ed. Balmas, I, p. 468; II, p. 219.

d'un autre costé, la commune et naturelle jalouzie que je voy en nostre nation, me font au vray connoistre le contraire de l'une et de l'autre esperance. Toutesfois sçachant que je ne suis pas tant haï du ciel, que je n'aye encores quelques amis en la terre, j'ay bien voulu envoyer à ce peu qui m'en reste ce petit livre, que je n'estimerois du tout rien au pris de ce qu'on attend de moy, n'estoit que ce n'est pas peu de fait, que par le moyen de son bon droit et la juste deffence de ses amis, remetre un tort devant les yeus de ceus qui se font contraires sans occasion. Vous asseurant de ce que vous avés tousjours connu en moy, qui est d'avoir l'envie de bien faire si grande et si haute, que si je n'eusse veu que vos prieres (tant quelques uns d'entre vous m'ont esté bons) et les calomnies de nos ignorans me contraignoient à ce faire, j'eusse tousjours tenu mon thresor fermé à tout le monde selon ma coustume, ou je vous eusse bien envoyé des pieces de plus grand pris. Mais puisque une necessité a pris telle puissance sus ma deliberation, je ne veus point entierement desesperer du bien qui me pourroit venir de ceci, estant assés certain que le malheur a bien souvent acoustumé d'engendrer un bon heur, et que des petits et chetifs commencemens, on voit souventesfois sortir les choses plus louables et plus parfaites. J'en ay maintenant mile raisons et mile exemples au bout de ma plume, si je voulois, comme on dit en se raillant, alambiquer dedans une familiere epistre, les secrets et les belles quintes essences de la Nature, ou tirer avecque je ne sçay quelle friandise affectée, la moüelle des profondes et abondantes histoires.[2] Si est ce que si j'escrivois à ce propos tout ce qu'on pourroit alleguer, je ne ferois pas taire tous ces larrons de merites, qui diront aussi tost que ce petit livre viendra dedans leurs mains, qu'après tant de magnifiques promesses que je puis avoir faites, après la grande et longue expectation que l'on a eüe de mes ouvrages, au lieu des montaignes d'or selon le proverbe des Pedants, je fay sortir une souris. J'auray bien la patience d'escouter un peu ces mignons, pour

2 The references to 'quintes essences' and 'moüelle' seem to be drawn directly from Rabelais' prologue to *Gargantua*. The commentary to Ronsard's *Amours* of 1553, p. 211 states: 'La meilleure et plus pure partie. Si tu veus entendre plus amplement que c'est a dire, quinte essence, voi un livre apellé, le Ciel des Filosofes.'

avoir bien tost le plaisir, de les voir eusmesmes se dementir. Il me semble encores, mes amis, que j'en voy venir d'autres, qui un peu plus resolus, et faisans semblant d'estre curieus de mon honneur, me viendront prescher, et moy, et vous s'ils vous connoissent pour tels que je vous estime, disans que le blame, la honte, et l'accusation que j'ay encourue en l'execution d'une chose, qui est contenue en ce recueil, me devoit garder de faire refreschir ma playe, par la seconde publication de ma faute. Ceus qui s'adresseront à nous avecques ce faus visage, me presentans une si douce poison, ne rapporteront aussi de moy autre chose, qu'une douce priere au lieu d'une rigoureuse response: laquelle est telle, que s'ils m'aiment seullement la moitié d'autant qu'ils disent, ils me facent ce seul bien, de faire la lecture entiere de ce que je vous presente, et lors je m'asseure qu'ils auront beaucoup plus d'envie que de pitié. Si quelques uns plus malins, font venir leurs propos jusques à vos aureilles, disans que toutes les choses que j'ay recueillies, n'estoient pas toutes telles que je les veus faire croire, asseurés les et leur jurés pour l'amour de moy, après le serment que je vous en fay par nostre amitié, que je n'ay voulu mentir en rien, et que je n'ay ajousté aucune chose, fors le retranchement que premierement j'avois fait en la Masquarade premiere, et peut estre huit ou dix vers d'avantage. Bien est-il vray qu'aus vers latins, qui servoient d'inscriptions aus figures, j'ay peu changer neuf ou dix mots, mais ce n'a pas esté pour ce que les autres qui y estoient ne fussent aussi bons, mais ç'a esté pour autant que n'ayant point l'original, et ne les pouvant pas trouver tous tels qu'ils estoient dedans ma memoire, j'ay mieus aimé sur le champ user du changement que du travail de les recouvrer. Et s'ils sont tant obstinés contre ma cause, qu'ils ne vous veulent point prendre pour garants, qui cherchent les tesmoings qui l'ayans veu à l'œil, leur pourront faire une plus seure foy, du nombre desquels ont esté quelques uns d'entre vous. S'ils repliquent qu'encores qu'il fust ainsi, si est-ce que l'on ne sçauroit tant faire, que l'on ne croye que j'y ay beaucoup ajousté et corrigé, veu que j'ay esté si long temps avant que d'en metre le recueil en lumiere. Je vous suplie de ne les payer point d'autre monnoye, sinon de cela que la plus grand part d'entre vous a connu. Qui est que je me trouvay quelque espace de temps si faché, si depit, si resveur, et si pesant, que tant s'en fault que je peusse guerir la piquure du scorpion par le scorpion mesme, que tous les instrumens de mes malheurs, qui sont les livres, les papiers, et les plumes, me puoient de telle sorte, que peu s'en fallut que je n'en fisse un beau petit sacrifice dans mon feu. Mesmement que deslors que je commençay à me recueillir un peu moymesme, et vouloir faire un recueil de tout cela, par qui injustement je pensois m'estre perdu, je demeuray quelques jours malade d'une fievre tierce: laquelle encore qu'elle peust venir d'une extreme colere, n'avoit point tant sa cause de cela que de mon desastre acoustumé, qui quasi ne me permet point d'estre connu d'autre que de moy: et qui toutes les fois que je veus m'efforcer à l'encontre, comme vous verrés plus à plain dedans ce petit ramas, ou bien ront mon entreprise, ou bien la couronnant d'une honte non esperée, et non meritée, ne me permet pas seullement le moyen de faire mes excuses: que di-je excuses? ains la juste poursuite de la louange et de la recompanse, qui me fuyans allors qu'elles se sont plus presentées, ne me laissent payer d'autre chose, que de la vanité d'un agreable labeur. Vous pourrés bien encores dire deux autres causes de ce retardement, l'une est que combien que ceci eust esté bien plus tost imprimé, ni l'imprimeur, ni vousmesmes, ni moy, n'avons point esté d'avis, de faire sortir telle chose en ces jours saints et devots, ains plus tost attendre la rejouissance commune d'après Pasques.[3] La seconde est que voyant la court sejourner à Fontenebleau,[4] j'ay bien voulu attendre son retour à Paris, affin que ceux qui m'avoient condamné sans voir mes pieces, fussent les premiers judges de mon innocence. Outre que ces causes sont asséz suffisantes, j'en ay encores une qui fait plus pour moy, qui est l'addition d'un second livret que j'ay mis avecque le premier, pour les raisons que vous lirés autre part. Ce petit labeur dont je vous parle, ce sont quelques inscriptions des princes de l'Europe, lesquelles comme chacun sçait, ne se jectent pas si tost en moulle que les

3 In 1558 Lent began on 2 March and Easter was celebrated 10 April.

4 According to Eugène Thoison, *Les Séjours des rois de France dans le Gâtinais*, Paris, Picard, 1888, p. 51, the court was at Fontainebleau (with excursions in the neighbourhood no doubt) on the following dates: 3, 4, 8, 10, 12, 13, 15–17, 19, 21, 26, 28, and 29 March and 1, 4, 7, and 13 April.

medalles de ces princes, si d'avanture l'ouvrier ne me resembloit, qui ay tousjours eu ce meschant heur de faire les choses aussi facilement et aussi bien, comme je les fay malheureusement. Je ne vous useray point ici ni de recommendation, ni d'excuse des deux ouvrages, je vous prieray encores moins, de les faire plus grands envers ceus qui vous en parleront que je ne les estime, mais plus tost de les laisser couler avecques si peu de faveur qu'ils meritent, comme une chose legere et meslée. Ce que seullement vous monstrera assez la prose dont j'ay usé en mes descriptions, confondant comme je pense tout ensemble le style, et de l'epistre, et de l'oraison, et de l'histoire: combien que j'espere bien de vous faire un jour juger, qu'en tous ces genres d'escrire Dieu ne m'a point degarni de jugement. Je croy bien aussi, que l'orthographe confuse vous decouvrira une pareille meslange, et que les allusions et repetitions frequentes, qui seront trouvées dedans mes vers, montreront de prime face quelque affectation. L'une de ces choses a esté ainsi faite pour le peu de resolution de nostre langue en ce point là, et les autres pour l'ornement et la vraye beauté des inscriptions, ce que vous ne verrés pas en mes œuvres continués de longue alaine: desquels je vous promets ouvrir la bonde le plus tost que je pourray, vous asseurant que je ne m'en senti jamais tant picqué qu'à ceste heure. Si donques tant en ceus là qu'en cetui ci vous pensés voir quelques fautes, je vous prie de m'estre si benins, que de penser, et faire penser aus autres, que la faute vient d'autre part que de moy, ou bien de derober quelque chose à la severité de vostre bon jugement, pour le donner à nostre amitié. Quand à moy je vous promets que tant en vos labeurs, qu'aus labeurs d'autrui, je me montreray dorenavant tel, que vous aurés juste occasion d'un contentement et d'une perpetuelle recommandation de moy, qui suis vostre à tout jamais. A Dieu.

LE LIVRE A LA FRANCE[5]
Sonet.

Si mon pere a taché de payer le devoir,
Dont l'obligoit à toy la loy de sa naissance,
En s'efforçeant d'aider à chasser l'Ignorance,[6]
Sur qui le Ciel lui donne et vouloir et pouvoir:
Si travaillant pour toy sans fin et sans espoir,
Il pense son service estre sa recompanse:[7]
Je te pri fay ce bien, fay lui ce bien ô France,
De vouloir son enfant et recevoir et voir.
Si l'on dit que je vien farder par mes harangues
Son desastre, les yeus condamneront les langues.
Si l'on dit qu'on en doit estre plus irrité,
Veu que je ne suis rien au pris de ton attente,
Je le sçay bien, mais las que ceci te contente,
Qu'on laisse le devoir pour la necessité.

5 Essentially a reduction of the missive, *Estiene Jodelle à ses amis s.*, immediately preceding (here pp. 63–7). Jodelle forsakes, or rather circumvents, the personal apologia by having his book address France concerning its father's efforts on France's behalf. The words *desastre* and *necessité* are retained to emphasize Jodelle's hope that 'les yeus condamneront les langues' once his own justification is printed.

6 Jodelle rather belatedly insinuates himself into Du Bellay's footsteps ('Prosphonematique au roy treschrestien Henry II,' *Œuvres poétiques* ed. H. Chamard (STFM), III, p. 70, vv. 139–44 and 'La Musagnœomachie,' ibid., IV, pp. 3–26) in celebrating the battle against 'le vil monstre Ignorance.' This theme is intimately connected to the popular *ex utroque Cæsar* emblem (cf. introduction, pp. 29–32) and received its earliest and most brilliant treatment in Rosso Fiorentino's fresco at Fontainebleau in 1535–6. See Dora and Erwin Panofsky, 'The Iconography of the *Galerie François Ier* at Fontainebleau,' *Gazette des Beaux-Arts*, s. 6, LII (1958), pp. 119–20 (fig. 5).

7 These two lines are echoed almost verbatim when Jodelle more familiarly addresses a sympathetic Muse in his *Chapitre*, pp. 204–6, vv. 13, 55–60.

Estiene Jodelle à ses amis. S.

IN LIBRUM ELEGIA[8]

Infœlix quales Naso iubet esse libellos,
  Quos patriæ gelido mittit ab axe suæ,
Regia te talem, cum sis liber exulis, Aula
  Cerneret, exilium ni mihi dulce foret,
Ni quoque sponte mea, non iussu Numinis exul,
  Semotus Clario redderer usque Deo.
Ergo cultus abi, auratis quoque cornibus audax,
  Sis licet ingenii pars prope nulla mei.
Nec tener invidiæ timeas examen edacis,
  Nam multum quod te vindicet agmen erit:
Iamque cothurnatum potui revocasse Sophoclem,
  Smyrnæum, Siculum, Threïciumque senem,
Lætus Aristophanes, et amatrix umbra Philetæ,
  Thebanæque aderit pulsor et ipse lyræ.
His quondam cessit Livor, cedetque vocatis,
  Dum vivus nostra quilibet arte redit.
Quid si Pelides hos inter, et acer Ulysses,
  Alcidesque, et quos hi cecinere iuvent?
Ac sic Bellonæ me me natum artibus aptent,
  Regibus invitis Regibus ut placeam?
Sed tu vade prior, bene si successerit, illi
  Grandia dona ferent, nulla venena ferent:
Sic sequar, et Reges repetam, sic spretus Apollo
  Qui comes exilii, forsan honoris erit.

IODELIUS.

8 For a translation of Jodelle's opening elegy to his book, see p. 70.

ELEGY TO HIS BOOK

Such books as Ovid in misfortune bids his own to be – the books he sends to his own country from the frozen North[9] – such a book would the royal court believe you to be, inasmuch as you are an exile's work – were it not that exile is pleasant to me, and were it not also that, being removed afar off by my own choice, not driven into exile at the bidding of any god, I have ever been restored to Apollo.[10] Depart, then, in your finery, brazen in the very gilding of your clasps,[11] even though you be but the smallest part of my talent. Nor need you, young and tender as you are, fear the censure of mordant ill-will, for there will be a host of friends to defend you; already I have succeeded in calling back buskined Sophocles and the Man of Smyrna[12] and the Sicilian[13] and the Ancient of Thrace;[14] while merry Aristophanes and the ghost of the lover Philetas,[15] and the player of Theban lyre[16] himself will come to your support. To these, malice did formerly yield; and yield she will once more when they are summoned, as long as any of them is recalled to life by my skill. And what if Peleus' son,[17] and fierce Ulysses, and Alcides,[18] and other heroes whom these poets sang, should also lend aid – and so make me fit for the arts of war,[19] and thus able to find favour with my 'Kings,' even against the will of kings? But you must go before, and if your cause should prosper, they will bring generous gifts, and no bane: so shall I follow you and rehearse my 'Kings,' and thus perchance my despised Apollo[20] – now my companion in exile – shall in time be my companion in honour.

Jodelle.

9 The *Tristia* and *Ex Ponto*, written during Ovid's banishment on the shores of the Black Sea.
10 i.e. as god of poetry; hence 'to poetry' (literally 'to the Clarian god'; Claros was an Anatolian shrine of Apollo)
11 Lit. 'horns.'
12 Homer
13 Theocritus
14 Orpheus
15 Of Cos; traditionally the father of elegiac love-poetry
16 Amphion
17 Achilles
18 Heracles
19 Lit. 'of Bellona' – goddess of war
20 i.e. my verse

LE RECUEIL DES INSCRIPTIONS, FIGURES, DEVISES, ET MASQUARADES

ordonnées en l'hostel de ville à Paris le Jeudi 17 de Febvrier 1558.

Après l'heureuse et memorable conqueste faite au mois de Janvier sur l'ennemi, le Roy estant de retour de sa conté d'Oye nouvellement remise en son obeissance,[21] delibera de sejourner à Paris jusqu'au commencement de Quaresme,[22] tant pour les plaisirs qu'on y pouvoit trouver en telle saison, que pour faire gratifier à son peuple l'heur de ses dernieres victoires, la prosperité de son voiage, et la delivrance de toutes nos premieres craintes. Durant ce tens doncques, ne voulant en rien imiter l'insolence des temeraires Princes en leurs prosperes avantures, et se temperant beaucoup mieus en son heur que n'avoit

21 After the recapture of Calais (8 January 1558) and the fortress of Guignes (20 January 1558), along with the adjacent county of Oye, Henry II personally visited the area. Preparations for his entry into Calais were necessarily rather sketchy but the following inscriptions were set up in the city: *Sur la grande porte de Calais à l'entrée du Roy.* Henr[icus] II. Rex Christianiss. [imus] Philippi antecessoris temporibus ab Anglis occupatam Excellentissimo Principe Francisco à Lotharingia Duce Guysio pare et magno Camerario Francie [Franciæ] pro rege et cum copiis agente, recuperavit, octavo Idus Januarii 1557 [i.e. 1558] et regni sui undecimo, ab obsidione die quarta. *Sur la porte du Logis des Marchans.* Excellentissimi principis Francisci à Lotharingia Ducis Guysiæ, paris et magni camerarii franciæ posterorumq-[ue] virtuti, hanc domum dedit dicavitq[ue] Regis liberalitas in urbis recuperatæ memoriam eo pro rege et cum copiis agente, octavo Idus Januarii 1557 [1558]. Cf. BN ms. fr. 22560, fol. 145.

22 i.e. 2 March 1558

fait paravant son ennemi, se contenta de mille louables passetens assés acoustumés à sa Majesté: en mesurant si bien et son allegresse et celle de sa Court, 1v°
avecque la reconnoissance de ce qui est de plus hault, qu'il n'a point eu moins de louange de vaincre dedans soy la folle coustume des vaincueurs, que d'avoir en ceste victoire plus vaincu que de coustume. Or, affin que les peuples ou ennemis ou estrangers ne pensent point que ce que je decriray ci-après ait esté fait pour autre chose que pour un leger passetens, sans aulcune forme ou de gloire ou de triomphe: ainsi que sa Majesté passoit le plus joyeusement qu'il estoit possible ces jours les plus delectables de l'année, il s'avisa de mander au Prevost des marchants, et Eschevins de Paris qu'il iroit souper en leur maison de Ville le Jeudi gras ensuivant, qui seroit le jour d'après que monseigneur le Duc de Guise arriveroit de Picardie,[23] où il achevoit pour lors, de donner tel ordre que les hautaines esperances de l'Espaignol ont occasion de s'en rabaisser à bon-droit. Je croy certainement que messieurs de la Ville, qui de tout tens se sont montrés prompts et devots envers leurs Princes, et qui, à mon avis, (si d'aventure on n'i estoit bien trompé) auront tousjours en leurs entreprises plus grand besoin de bonne conduite que de bon vouloir, eussent volontiers fait en l'honneur d'un si grand Roy l'appareil d'un triomphe à l'antique:[24] mais peut estre qu'ils considererent, au moins les plus avisés d'entre eus, toutes les choses qui pouvoient empescher l'effect d'un si superbe dessein. Leur Roy premierement porter le nom de Treschrestien, et que la gloire des Chrestiens ne peut 2r°
estre sinon qu'en leur Dieu, qui tenant les victoires en sa main s'en reserve les triomphes:[25] Les feus Roys Treschrestiens pour quelque grande victoire qu'ils sceussent avoir, n'avoir jamais triomphé: La fin de la bravade estre bien souvent le rabaissement, la queüe de la joye la douleur, et les grandes pompes d'un Prince l'occasion à son ennemi de bien faire: Le Roy Philipes avoir esté lors averti du siege de Calais qu'il faisoit un magnifique tournoy, pensant du tout tenir la Fortune au poin, et ne prevoyant point qu'elle sçait encore mieus tournoyer que lui. Mesmement que quand ils auroient dressé tous les apprests

23 See introduction, p. 5.

24 See introduction, pp. 7–8.

25 Cf. Du Bellay, 'Hymne au Roy sur la prinse de Callais,' vv. 71–6 *Œuvres* ed. Chamard (STFM), vi^{1}, pp. 24–5.

d'un tel triomphe, il estoit certain que sa Majesté autant moderée aus fortunes heureuses, qu'asseurée aus fortunes adverses,[26] n'accepteroit jamais une gloire qui ne tournast en l'honneur de celui seul, qui faisant vaincre les Roys leur commande de plus tost triompher de soymesme et des vices de leurs subjects, que des despouilles et captivités de leurs ennemis. Et aussi que quand le Roy ne refuseroit point tel honneur, ils auroient faute et de tens et de gens pour conduire telle entreprise à quelque agreable et admirable issue, et l'issue à une perdurable memoire. Si toutes ces choses furent pensées, je ne doute point qu'elles ne persuadassent facilement aus Parisiens, que pour recevoir un si grand Roy, il se falloit simplement contenter d'un festin,
2v° adjoustans comme il est à croire, à toutes ces causes la despence, non pas tant pour l'egard qu'ils avoient en l'espargne, que pour ce que la nourriture de la plus part de ceus qui gouvernent la ville est telle, qu'il faut necessairement que les choses belles et grandes les estonnent, n'ayans point d'autre mouvement, ni d'autre regle que le jugement d'un sens commun, la frugalité vulgaire, la simple bonté, et le rude exemple de leurs predecesseurs. Sur quoy, je diray ce mot en passant, qu'on se doit bien garder de metre les affaires qui peuvent tirer quelque memoire après soy, entre les mains de ceus qui sont du peuple, qui pourautant que la Police suit tousjours l'Œconomie, pensent tout ainsi mesnager leur ville que leur maison. Il n'i aura peut estre pas un, ni des nostres, ni des estrangers, qui regardant la grandeur du Roy, la grandeur de la victoire, la grandeur de Paris, ne s'emerveille, encore qu'on voulust laisser le triomphe qu'on ne deliberoit pour le moins mille gentillesscs aucunement dignes de ces trois : et veu que monseigneur de Guise devoit arriver le jour de devant, qu'on devoit bien songer à honorer d'une autre sorte l'arrivée d'un si vaillant et victorieux Prince : lequel contre les dernieres de faveurs de la guerre, contre l'importunité de l'hyver, contre l'arrogance de l'ennemi, contre l'esperance d'un chacun, s'estoit porté si fort, qu'il avoit emporté en moins de dix jours[27] la ville, qui depuis ccx ans[28] avoit servi de regret et frayeur à nos peres, de vollerie

26 Cf. p. 9.

27 The siege lasted from 1 January to 8 January 1558 (new style).

28 Calais had been captured by the English on 3 August 1347.

à la France, de mere nourrice aus Anglois, et mesme (s'il faut ainsi parler) servoit encore d'espouvantail à nostre vaillance. Lequel outre une si brave et glorieuse prise, avoit peu de jours après forcé[29] le fort de Guignes, jugé pour lors inexpugnable, par ceus mesmes qui nous avoient tant obstinément sous-tenus. Et lequel, pour dire en brief, ayant en si peu de tens contraint les Anglois de s'en retourner honteusement cacher en leur coin, raportoit un tel merite, qu'en entrant dans la ville (j'apelle ainsi Paris sans lui donner queue) il ne pouvoit esperer moins que les couronnes publiques, les applaudissemens du peuple, et la seconde partie du triomphe Royal. Or quant à ceus qui pourroient avoir tel esbahissement, je ne leur fay ni autre excuse, ni autre responce, m'asseurant que s'ils sont Chrestiens, ce que j'ay dit par ci devant, les peut assés contenter. Et aussi que je ne puis maintenir que ma ville ait esté si mal curieuse et de l'honneur de son Prince, et de son honneur, qu'après avoir un peu songé, elle n'aperceust bien qu'il falloit pour le moins festoyer un Roy de quelques autres choses que de viandes. Ce qui fit que quatre jours seullement devant le jour du festin, le procureur du Roy d'icelle, un des plus honnestes et metables[30] hommes que j'aye sceu voir en leur compaignie, sçachant que j'estois né de Paris, et que Dieu m'avoit donné quelque peu de prompitude d'esprit pour secourir à une chose si hastée, me vint prier au nom de tous eus, que si j'avois quelque Tragedie, ou Comedie, qui peust estre apprise entre ci et là, je la baillasse pour estre recitée devant le Roy, et qu'ainsi je ferois service à mon Prince, et honneur à mon païs. Je fi responce que j'avois, et des Tragedies et des Comedies, les unes achevées, les autres pendues au croc, dont la plus part m'avoit esté commandée par la Royne et par Madame seur du Roy, sans que les troubles du tens eussent encore permis d'en voir rien, et que j'attendois tousjours une meilleure occasion que n'est ce tens tumultueus et miserable pour les faire metre sur le theatre, adjoustant ce petit mot assés poëtiquement dit, que ceste année la Fortune avoit trop tragiquement joué dedans ce grand echaufaut de la Gaule sans faire encore par les fauls spectacles reseigner les veritables playes. Mais bien si on me vouloit prometre de me

3r°

3v°

29 See p. 5.

30 i.e. agréables

croire et de me soulager, que je ferois bien des choses, lesquelles estans bien conduites, ne raporteroient point moins de grace que l'un de ces deus poëmes. Je ne pensois en faisant telles promesses que je me deusse soucier d'autres charges que d'inventer quelques belles masquarades, ou parlantes, ou muetes, qui estans accommodées aus tens, aus lieus, et aus choses, peussent donner quelque agreable plaisir à la compaignie: Mais l'amour de mon païs, la priere qu'on m'avoit faite, l'envie que j'avois de plaire tant au Roy comme à la maison de Guise à laquelle je me suis tousjours humblement voué, et la faute
4r° d'appareil et de conseil que je voiois en telle necessité, me firent tellement prandre charge sur charge, que j'appelle en tesmoins tous ceus qui m'ont veu en un tel embrouillement, s'il est possible de croire qu'en si peu d'espace un seul esprit ait peu soustenir et tel fais et telle facherie. Car allant dès l'heure à la maison de ville et n'i trouvant aucun ornement qui peust estre remerquable, j'ose dire que je me fei quasi de tous mestiers, et assés heureusement, comme on pourra voir par ce recueil, si l'execution eust esté telle que l'ordonnance. Combien que si tout eust esté bien veu le jour du festin, on eust cogneu qu'avecques un labeur desesperé, j'avois mis tel ordre à tout, qu'il ne restoit quasi rien qu'il n'allast comme je l'entendois, et comme on le pouvoit esperer de moy, fors les deus masquarades d'après souper, lesquelles, à cause qu'on n'avoit point fait les choses comme je les avois dites, et à cause aussi de la multitude, du desordre, et de la confusion, furent si mal menées, que moy-mesme, qui à mon grand regret faisois l'une des personnes,[31] epris quasi d'une rage de voir si mal porter devant mon Roy la chose où il m'alloit de l'honneur, demeuray quasi tout tel, (s'il faut qu'ainsi je parle) que si la Minerve qui marchoit devant moy m'eust transformé en pierre par le regard de sa Meduse. Mais combien que j'en aye porté et porte encore un tel regret, que je ne le puis autrement nommer que desespoir, non pas tant pour la faute que pour voir
4v° que Dieu m'a fait naistre si malheureusement, que de toutes choses que j'ay bien faictes, ou que j'eusse peu bien faire en ma vie, je n'en sceu jamais avoir l'usage, vivant presque en ce monde tout tel qu'un Tantale aus enfers, s'il faut

31 Jason. Cf. p. 118.

ici parler encore de fable: qui est ce toutesfois qui en ceci n'estimera ceus impitoyables qui avecques leurs brocards publiques, leurs secretes reproches, et leurs injustes injures ne m'ont point pardonné d'avantage que si j'eusse esté coupable du plus grand crime de lese majesté? Mais je parleray de tout ceci en son lieu, et me semble deja que j'ay trop longuement discouru avant que de venir au recueil que je delibere de faire, qui peut estre, estant bien leu, si la France n'est la plus facheuse maratre du monde, encore que je me tienne moymesme grandement coupable, me pourra bien apporter au lieu des haynes, mespris, et calomnies, le pardon et la grace des grands, la louange des doctes, l'admiration des estrangers, l'excuse de nostre peuple, la repentance des maldisans, et le crevecueur de l'envie. Ayant doncques (pour venir au point) dressé et fait dresser tout ce que j'avois projecté, le Roy sur les quatre heures du jour que j'ay dit, sans aucune pompe arriva avecques toute sa compagnie en la maison de la ville, devant laquelle on lui fit seullement une salue de l'artillerie avecques quelque escopterie qui s'accordant fort bien à l'affluance du peuple, au bruit des tabourins, et au son des trompetes, donnoit un tesmoingnage publiq de l'allegresse que recevoient tous les citoyens. Alors ceus 5r°
qui estoient curieus de telles nouveautés peurent voir ce que j'avois premierement ordonné pour l'entrée, suivant d'assés près l'antiquité admirée d'un chacun, et aucunement recherchée par moy, tant en tous mes autres ouvrages qu'en ces miennes petites inventions. Qui premierement estoient telles: que dedans une grande Arcade, sus le portail de l'hostel, j'avois fait peindre force trophées à l'antique, des armes, et enseignes ennemies, et au meileu d'eus tirer une fort longue et spatieuse ovalle entourée de laurier à l'un des costés de laquelle estoit le portrait de Calais, et à l'autre le portrait de Guignes,[32] et au dedans d'icelle ceste longue inscription.

32 See figs. 23–4. These 'portraits' published in 1558 were no doubt similar to, if not identical with, those used by Jodelle. The 'portrait' is neither a topographical plan nor an exact architectural elevation but something approaching an artistic bird's-eye view.

D D.
VIRTVTI ET VICTORIÆ
S.[33]

D. HENRICO REGI PRÆCLARISSIMAR. RERVM IN VNIVERSA TVM GALL. TVM ITAL. TERRA MARIQ. BENE AC FELICITER GESTARVM ERGO TRIVMPHVM PVBL. DIGNAMQ. SVIS FACTIS ET LAVREAM ET MEMORIAM MERENTI RENVENTI SED IN POSTERVM EXPECTANTI. OB FORTISS. ET VETVTISS. NOSTRORVM CALETVM CIVITATEM NVPER A FRANCISCO LOTHARINGO GVISIORVM PRINCIPE GLORIOSISS. OMNI INGENIO OBSESSAM MOX OMNI MARTE EXPVGNATAM AC

33 To the gods Courage and Victory, greeting:
To the divine King Henry, who by his glorious deeds, crowned with success by land and by sea in all France and in all Italy hath earned a public triumph together with a laurel wreath and memorial inscription worthy of his achievements; who yet hath declined this, but must look to receiving the same in time to come; by reason of the late restoration to France, her own country, of our mighty and ancient city of Calais at the hands of the most glorious Prince of Guise, François de Lorraine, who besieged it with every military craft and presently stormed it with all the arts of war, in accordance with its undying hope, after the endurance of two hundred and ten years of slavery to the Briton. Also by reason of the capture and razing to the ground, by every assault of might, of the fortress of Guignes; and likewise for the recapture of the village of Hammes, which had been abandoned in terror of the foe; and finally for the liberation of France from all vestiges of English rule, as a first and provisional tribute to the unlooked-for Success, and for your favour's sake, ye gods Courage and Victory, this monument is dedicated, in due discharge of vows undertaken, by a decree of the City of Paris. It was composed by Estienne Jodelle, and is set up at the public expense.

PERENNI VOTO CVM A CC ET X AN. BRI-
TANNORVM SERVITVTEM PATERETVR SVÆ
GALL. RESTITVTAM. OB GVINAS OMNIB.
ET VI ET VIRIB. CAPTAS, SOLOQ. ADÆQVA-
TAS. OB HAMMENSEM PAGVM QVI HOSTI-
VM METV DERELICTVS FVERAT RECEPTVM.
OB LIBERATAM DENIQVE AB OMNIB. BRI-
TAN. GALL. HOC INTERIM AD PRIMAM IL-
LAM INSPERATÆ REI COMMENDATIONEM
ET IN VOSTRVM O DD VIRTVS ET VICTO-
RIA FAVOREM EX VOTO ET DEBITO
VRBS.
PD CONS.
ST. IODELIVS PAR. P P P.

Au dessous de l'Arcade, dessus la grande frize du portail que j'avois fait si proprement couvrir, qu'il sembloit que ce feust un marbre noir nouvellement ajousteé, estoient escripts ces trois vers en letres d'or.

NON POMPA, NON ROMVLEIS TE CVRRIBVS ALTVM
ACCIPIMVS, FACTIS CVM SIT SPES REGIA MAIOR,
SPE QVOQVE MAIORES, QVORVM EST TVA LAVREA, DIVI.[34]

L'inscription de ces trois vers estoit REGI PIISS. PII CIVES.[35] Aus deus costés de l'Arcade sont deus grandes colonnes Doriques, dont les deus pieds costoyent les deus bouts de la corniche du portail; en chacune d'icelles colonnes estoient ces deus lettres d'or, H H et au meilleu des deus escrit en lettres d'argent

34 We do not receive you in a triumphal procession or raised aloft upon a Roman chariot; for the King's promise exceeds his performance, and the gods, to whom your laurel wreath belongs, are greater even than your promise.

35 To a most dutiful king, his dutiful subjects.

6r° HOC HERCVLE DIGNÆ.[36] J'avois ordonné qu'on feist mouler deus grands croissants argentés pour planter le haut de ces colonnes au lieu que l'Empereur y plante ses aigles:[37] mais la brieveté du tens, et la diversité des occupations, fit qu'ils demeurerent. Je ne parle point ici de l'enrichissement du lierre qui embellissoit ceste entrée, ni de tout autre ornement d'entre les deus portes, un

36 Worthy of this Hercules. (Presumably *columnæ* is understood, to justify *dignæ* in fem. plural.) The two columns denote *Pietas* and *Iustitia.* Cf. Jodelle, *Desseins pour la Croix de Gastines*, 1569, reprinted in Etienne Jodelle, *Œuvres complètes*, ed. Balmas, I, p. 302: 'il semble . . . que . . . tout l'œuvre convienne le mieux qu'il est possible à la devise quc le Roy a tousjours portée, qui est de la Piété et de la Justice dénotée par ses deux colonnes.' The two columns are an excellent example for the consideration of the 'spawning' of devices among the rival Habsburg and Valois houses by mutual appropriation and deformation. While Jodelle had replaced the eagles of Charles V with the crescents of Henry II, a later Caron drawing from the *Histoire Françoyse de nostre temps*, Louvre, Inv. RF 29752[18] (fig. 14) shows the columns surmounted by imperial crowns – a reference to Charles IX's marriage with Elisabeth of Austria. The received forms are then particularized by the banderoles with his ordinary device PIETATE ET IVSTITIA, the left column referring to the Mosaic Tablets and the right one to the *Lex duodecim tabularum.* Here the inscription being placed on additional tablets DELICTA POPVLI PIETATE DELEO refers to the Massacre of Saint Bartholomew's (24 August 1572), further witness to the extension and circumstantial assimilation of iconographical *lieux communs.* The caparison of the horse bears the 'K' cipher of Charles IX rather than the 'ꓘK' of Catherine de' Medici with which it is occasionally confused. (Cf. fig. 19.)

37 Jodelle here follows a direct precedent reported in Guillaume Paradin's *Continuation de l'histoire de nostre temps, depuis l'an mil cinq cens cinquante, jusques à l'an mil cinq cens cinquante six*, Paris, 1555[1], pp. 46–7: 'Avant l'entrée du Roy avoyent ceux de Metz erigé en trophée aux voutes du grand autel en l'eglise cathedrale, une table d'attente, avec un grand aigle, et les devises de l'Empereur, en lieu desquelles firent peindre les croissans, avec ce tiltre triomphal en lettres d'or, HENRICVS GALLIARVM REX, SANCTI IMPERII PROTECTOR. Qui monstroit bien la grandeur du Roy: et à en juger veritablement, depuis Charlemaigne ne fut veu à Metz, si grand, ny si puissant Roy de France.'

peu mieus devisé que mis en œuvre, voulant courir toutes telles choses le plus legierement que je pourray. Si ne veus-je pas pourtant aller si fort que je ne m'arreste ici pour dire que si les Princes estoient autant amoureus des choses qui les perpetuent, comme ils sont desireus de se perpetuer, ils tiendroient bien autant de conte de telles nouvelles antiquités, voire de tous autres labeurs dont les hommes doctes supportent leur gloire, que des chars, des images, et pompes inacoustumées. Car de ceus ci les uns se rompent, les autres s'enfument, le autres s'oublient, lors que l'honeste curiosité des doctes et des bien nourris, envoyant de main en main ces vifs instruments de la memoire, les fait demeurer entre les mains de l'eternité. Je ne veus pas dire que ce peu que j'ay deja decrit, et tout ce que je decriray ci après, aproche en rien de cela, car on sçait bien que la haste, et la foiblesse de mon esprit ne me le pouvoient permetre. Mais je diray que decouvrant dedans l'inscription les merites, dedans les trois vers l'excuse du triomphe, dedans les colonnes l'esperance future, j'ay taché de donner quelque merque à la souvenance des hommes: comme doivent faire 6v°
tous ceus qui ont quelque pouvoir sur la memoire, qui sans avoir aucun egard ou à la louange, ou à la faveur, ou à la recompanse, me semblant estre naturellement obligés envers leurs Princes, de garder alors plus soingneusement l'honneur des beaus actes, qu'ils voyent les Princes s'en soucier le moins. Or passons outre sans plus nous arrester de telle sorte. Sur la seconde porte enrichie de tapisserie, et de festons de lierre, dedans un grand compartiment entouré de son chapeau de triomphe, estoit peinte une Deesse tenant une couronne de laurier en l'une des mains, et une chaisne de fer en l'autre, ayant le Soleil et la Lune aus deus costés d'elle, et poussant une sphere du pié.[38] Sur la teste d'icelle, dedans une espace que faisoit le compartiment, estoit escrit, VICISSITVDO,[39] et au bas dedans une autre plus grand espace ces trois vers.

38 Undoubtedly Nemesis with her bridle, who could be either distributive or retributive in nature and whose identity is assured by the motto VICISSITUDO; often confused with Fortune, for which see E. Panofsky, '*Virgo and Victrix*: A Note on Dürer's *Nemesis*,' *Prints*, ed. C. Zigrosser (New York, 1962), pp. 15–38.

39 i.e. Change of Fortune. For the theme of vicissitude, on which the whole of Jodelle's play *Cléopâtre captive* (1553) is constructed, cf. the sonnet 'Mon Roy, sçait-il pas bien qui les destins

NE PROPERA, NVMENQVE VIDE, VISVMQVE VERERE,
AC GENIVM METIRE TVVM, NAMQVE OMNIA LEGI
SVPPOSVIT NOSTRÆ, NOSTRA QVI LEGE SOLVTVS.[40]

Ce qui estoit dans la montée suivoit assés bien ceste figure de Vicissitude, qui après toutes ces premieres louanges, et trophées, avertissoit de ne se fier que de bonne sorte à la felicité. Car là dedans outre l'ornement de la tapisserie, des festons, et des armes tant du Roy, que de la ville, on lisoit trois ou quatre fois ceste devise, GRADATIM, escrite tousjours dedans une ovalle couchée, et
7r° entourée d'un compartiment semé de couronnes, montrant qu'on ne va point autrement aus victoires que par degrez, et qu'en les voulant trop haster on se precipite soymesme. Au hault de la montée, sur la porte de la salle, estoit une autre figure enrichie de mesme sorte que la premiere et ainsi qu'estoient mesme toutes les autres que je diray, en laquelle estoit peinte une France armée, et triomphante,[41] ayant sous ses piés des trophées, des coulonnes brisées, et des

ont fait' (*Jodelle, Œuvres* ed. Balmas I, p. 164).

Le vice et la victoire ont bien peu d'alliance,
Vertu, valeur, victoire, encor sont en la France,
Ne crain qu'un seul poisson retarde ton vaisseau
Ny que la nuict te puisse en ton beau jour te nuire,
Sois Tiphys, sois Phebus, et pour poursuivre et luire
La vertu soit tousjours ta voille et ton flambeau.

40 Haste not, but look to my Godhead, and having seen it, revere it; and sparingly measure out thy talent, for he who is freed from my law has placed all beneath that law (i.e. God, not subject to Fortune's sway, has placed all else beneath that sway).

41 Ordinarily identified by a mantel covered with fleurs-de-lis, as in a Caron drawing for the *Histoire Françoyse de nostre temps*, Louvre Inv. RF 29752[8] (fig. 18). The type is taken up again, curiously enough in an anti-English context, by Ronsard in 1562; A. Micha, 'Sur l'allégorie de la France dans la *Continuation du Discours des Misères de ce temps*,' *Bibliothèque d'Humanisme et Renaissance*, XX (1958), pp. 578–9. Cf. Ronsard, *Œuvres*, ed. Laumonier (STFM), XI, p. 54, vv. 319–30. Although Time here crowns France, it is difficult not to think of the rescuing action implicit in the *Veritas filia Temporis* image, if for no other reason than that it follows the VICISSITVDO compart-

enseignes et guidons où l'on voyoit les Aigles et les Leopars:[42] elle tenoit en l'une de ses mains un globe et de ce costé voloit devers elle le tens, vieillard, aus pieds de bouq, chauve par derriere, comme le depeint l'antiquité, lequel apportoit une couronne de laurier sur la teste de la Deesse, et une couronne d'olive sur son globe, qui n'estoit qu'un souhait seullement pour l'avenir, comme ce mot VOTVM escrit au hault de la figure le montroit, et au bas ces trois vers./SIC RAPIDAS AQVILAS, SIC FVLMINEOS LEOPARDOS/

ment and the GRADATIM device. Moreover, this same conceit was used by Mary Tudor as a 'personal device, for the legend on her crest, on the State seal of her reign, on her coins' and since many of the inauspicious augurs of the *Recueil* (fols. 10ᵛ *et seq.*) deal with Mary and Philip II, no doubt such iconographical insinuation was both effective and appreciated. Cf. F. Saxl, '*Veritas filia Temporis*,' *Philosophy and History. Essays presented to Ernst Cassirer*, Oxford, 1936, p. 207, who justly emphasizes the hope for a universal Catholic hegemony – and an encircled and politically impotent France.

42 Cf. 'Mopsus,' p. 112, vv. 6 and 28. The eagle traditionally represents the Empire as in the earliest sonnet directly addressed to Henry II by Jodelle (*Œuvres*, ed. Balmas I, p. 161), 'Des guerres du Roy Henry Deuxiesme contre l'empereur Charles cinquiesme, après le siège de Metz levé.'

Or' que l'Empereur, l'Aigle,
et l'Espagne font voir
Que vaut nostre grand Roy,
nostre Lys, nostre France.

Cf. also 'Ode sur la Naissance de Madame . . .' (*Œuvres*, ed. Balmas I, p. 249) and 'L'Hymenée du Roy Charles IX,' Sonnet VII, v. 7 (*Œuvres*, ed. Balmas II, p. 265).
Barthélemy Aneau's gloss on Alciati's Emb. XXXIII *Signa fortium* (ed. 1549, p. 58) reads: 'Cest Emblesme est faict en grace de l'Empereur, qui porte l'Aigle: le comparant au fort champion Aristomene, le plus hardy et vaillant de toute la Grece.'
For the leopard representing England, cf. Du Bellay, 'Prosphonematique au Roy treschrestien Henry II,' *Œuvres*, ed. Chamard (STFM), III, p. 72, vv. 181–3.

Je voy tomber soubz les fleches
Françoises[a]
Le Leopard,[b] ton antiq'ennemy,
Qui souloit bruire aux forests
Ecossoizes.

In the original edition, published by Michel Vascosan in Paris in 1549, this poem was annotated as follows by Jean Proust, Angevin: [a] Il [le roy treschrestien] porte aussi les fleches, l'arc et la trousse de Diane; [b] Ce sont les armes du Roy d'Angleterre. (This line refers to the Scottish campaign with Thermes, Montalembert. (Cf. p. 99.)

GALLIA CALCET OVANS, ILLAM QVOQVE MOBILE LAVRV/TEMPVS, ET ARMIFVGA MVNDVM DIGNETVR OLIVA.[43] Il faut maintenant venir à l'appareil de la salle[44] que j'avois tellement fait dresser, que la description en deplaira aussi peu que l'ordonnance. Premierement le fons d'enhault estoit tout fait depuis un bout jusques à l'autre de grands compartiments de lierre proprement entrelassés, et semés infiniment des armes du Roy, de la
7v° Royne, de la ville, des grands seigneurs, et des grandes dames, avecque tel enrichissement qu'il estoit requis. Depuis ce fons, tant de l'un que de l'autre costé de la salle suivoit sur le hault de la tapisserie une frize fort large, et dedans les ovalles que faisoient les entrelassements d'icelle, se voyoient peintes toutes les devises qui se portent aujourdui à la court, comme le Croissant du Roy, l'Iris de la Royne, l'Eclypse de Monsieur, le Chardon de la Royne d'Ecosse, la Gorgone de Madame seur du Roy et autres. Au dessous de la frize dedans de petits quarrés attachés sur le hault des croissants, dont je parleray à ceste heure, estoient escrits les mots de chacune devise comme, DONEC TOTVM IMPLEAT ORBEM/[45] ΦΟΩΣ ΦΕΡΟΙ ΗΔΕ ΓΑΛΗΝΗΝ/[46] INTER ECLYPSES EXORIOR/[47]

43 So may Gaul triumphantly crush the swift-striking eagles and deadly leopards; and may fast-fleeting Time grant her, too, the laurel branch (of victory), and grant to the world the olive branch of peace (lit. 'arms-shunning').

44 Our reconstitution of the iconographic elements of Jodelle's programme (fig. C) is based upon his descriptions, pp. 83–98.

45 Till it fill the whole orb. (A pun on *orbis* meaning Earth and the orb or disc of the full moon.) Presumably derived from Ovid, *Metamorphoses*, XII, 615–17: Iam cinis est, et de tam magno restat Achille / Nescio quid, parvam quod non bene compleat urnam, / At vivit totum quæ gloria compleat orbem . . . Cf. W. McAllister Johnson, 'Numismatic Propaganda in Renaissance France,' *Art Quarterly*, XXXI (1968), p. 127, n. 16 for further discussion of Henry II's device and its variants in the growing imperial and dynastic context of the years 1552–6. Such conceits were exploited even after all real hope of attaining the Holy Roman Empire had passed. (Cf. G. Zeller, 'Les Rois de France, candidats à l'Empire. Essai sur l'idéologie impériale en France.' *Revue historique*, CLXXIII (1934), pp. 273–311, 497–534.) For a rather different interpretation, cf. Claude Paradin, *Devises heroïques*, Lyon, 1557, pp. 20–1: 'La Devise à present du Treschretien et victorieus Roy

Henry II. de ce nom, est la Lune en son croissant: Es sacrées escritures donques la Lune prefigure l'Eglise, quasi en tous passages, à quoy se conforme l'histoire recitée par Paul Emil du Pape Calixte II. (au paravant apellé Guy, fils de Guillaume Conte de Bourgongne,) lequel la nuit precedent sa creacion, eut vision d'un jeune enfant qui lui aporta et mit une Lune sur le giron. La Lune aussi est sugette à mutacions, croissant et decroissant de tems en tems: Ainsi veritablement est l'Eglise militante, laquelle ne peut demourer long tems en un estat, que meintenant ne soit soutenue et defendue des Princes catholiques, et tantot persecutée des tirans et heretiques: au moyen dequoy est en perpetuel combat, auquel neanmoins la Royale Majesté, ou Roy premier fils de l'Eglise promet de tenir main de proteccion, *jusques à ce que reduite sous un Dieu, un Roy, et une Loy, aparoisse la plenitude et rotondité de sa bergerie, regie par le seul Pasteur* [italics ours].'

There are in general two major types of Henry's device: (1) a single crescent lying on its back (fig. 28); and (2) three interlaced crescents (fig. 29). A third related type (fig. 30) presents a crescent moon merging into a sun disc animated by a face, the motto being no longer DONEC TOTVM IMPLEAT ORBEM but rather its offspring CUM PLENA EST FIT ÆMVLA SOLIS. (For types 1 and 3, see the first illustrated edition of Paolo Giovio, *Dialogo dell' Imprese militari et amorose*, Lyon, G. Rouillé 1559 (Baudrier, *Bibliographie lyonnaise*, IX, p. 255 *et seq.*) Type 2 is perhaps an allusion to the arms of Clovis, first Christian King of France, whether they be *trois couronnes*, *trois crapauds*, or *trois croissants* (cf. p. 28, n. 83). One may well wonder whether it is simply because Paradin's book is a Lyonnais production that he assimilates Henry's ordinary device with that of the city of Lyon (*Un Dieu, Un Roy, Une Loy*) or whether the whole idea is rather more allied with the mystique of kingship.

46 Let it bring light and calm. The source of this motto has not been located but it probably comes from a poem in the Homeric tradition. (Proper scansion is provided by the use of archaic ΦΟΩΣ rather than standard ΦΩΣ). Claude Paradin, *Devises heroïques*, Lyon, 1557, p. 64 remarks: 'Madame Catherine, treschretienne Royne de France, ha pour Devise l'Arc celeste, ou Arc en ciel: qui est le vray sine de clere serenité, et tranquilité de Paix.' (fig. 21). The rainbow appears on several of Catherine's jetons. (Cf. F. Mazerolle, *Les Médailleurs français du XV*^{e} *siècle au milieu du XVII*^{e}, II, Paris 1902, cat. 912 and 922, but with the interpolation of the motto ΠΕΡΙ * ΑΜΗΧΑΝΙΑΣ * ΕΥΕΛΠΙΣΤΙΑ. Both Henry's and Catherine's devices appear in a Caron drawing for the *Histoire Françoyse de nostre temps*, Louvre, Inv. RF 29713 (fig. 15). (For other devices used by Catherine, see

also Edmond Bonnaffé, *Inventaire des meubles de Catherine de Médicis en 1589*, Paris 1874, pp. 121–2.)

The Greek motto is also found in Jeronimo Ruscelli, *Le Imprese Illustri*..., Venice, 1566, pp. 153–4 with the following translations: *Lucem ferat, et serenitatem; Apporti luce, et serenità.* As he had for Henry II's device (pp. 181–6), Ruscelli gives a religious connotation: 'questa Regina comminciò ad usarla essendo ancor polzella, et in casa del padre. Et si può credere, che essendosi sempre fatta conoscere per tutta spirituale, et tutta volta alla devotione, et al servigio di Dio, la levasse con animo d'intendere, che in ogni torbulenza, delle quali suol' esser quasi sempre piene questa nostra vita terrena, elle aurebbe avuto l'animo, et il cuor fermo in Dio, che fosse per liberarnela, ricordandosi della promesse del Signor nostro.'

47 I have my origin between eclipses. The Dauphin was born at Fontainebleau 19 January 1544 between an eclipse of the moon (10 January) and an eclipse of the sun (24 January). Cf. J. Fr. Schroeter, *Spezieller Kanon der Zentralen Sonnen – und Mondfinsternisse . . . von 600 bis 1800 Chr. in Europa* . . ., Dybwad, 1923, pp. 58, 146, 278.) Claude Paradin, *Devises heroïques*, Lyon, 1557, p. 74, comments: 'La grande et riche Coupe d'or, portée à present en Devise par Monseigneur le Dauphin, me sembleroit representer le Crater du Corbeau d'Apollo: qui (selon les Poëtes) fut transferé en luisant sine celeste. Et quant au mot de la Devise, se pourroit aussi referer, à l'heureuse naissance dudit Seigneur.' This seems to be a rather particular, if logical, explanation of an image which does not usually occur with the motto INTER ECLYPSES EXORIOR.

This conceit parallels certain variants of Henry II's DONEC TOTVM IMPLEAT ORBEM (fig. 30) and it is echoed in Mary Stuart's ALIAMQVE MORATVR referring to her possession of the Scottish throne (thus allowing Francis to be called Le Roi Dauphin prior to his own accession) while awaiting that of France. Henry III's MANET VLTIMA COELO infers that, already in possession of the thrones of France and Poland, only a celestial crown awaits him.

When the Dauphin succeeded Henry II as Francis II his device was extended to a pair of celestial and terrestrial spheres with the inscription VNVS NON SVFFICIT ORBIS. Cf. Caron's frontispiece for the *Histoire Françoyse de nostre temps*, Louvre, Inv. RF 29717 (fig. 12). As with Madame Marguerite, this distinction is confirmed in the jetons: H. de la Tour, *Catalogue des jetons de la Bibliothèque Nationale. Rois et reines de France*, Paris, 1897, cats. 107 and 112 (fig. 32).

RERVM SAPIENTIA CVSTOS/[48] et les autres principalles. Les grands croissants dont je veus parler, estoient de lierre, fort bien faits, et fort bien assis, qui pendoient depuis ceste frize que j'ay dite jusques bien bas,[49] entrelassés tousjours l'un dans l'autre deus à deus, estants liés à l'endroit où ils s'accouploient par le haut et par le bas, de liens de taffetas noir, sur lequel en letres d'argent estoit escrit ce mot IVNGVNTVR,[50] soit pour autant que la rencontre des deus fait un rond, ou soit pour l'alliance du Roy et du Grand seigneur, qui portent tous deus le croissant.[51] Du costé des fenestres, à l'endroit où se devoit soir le Roy, estoit une autre figure d'une deesse couronnée de roses, ayant sous les piés des roses epanchées par la place, tenant un lut en la main, au costé de 8r°
laquelle dansoient les petits Amours, et de l'autre costé venoit Bacchus, et ses Satyres: l'inscription du hault estoit, D. LETICIÆ,[52] et au dessous de la figure ces trois vers:

TV DEA, BACCHVS, AMOR, LVDISQVE, EPVLISQUE, IOCISQVE,
HEROVM MEMORES GRATA VICE MERGITE CVRAS,
PRÆLIA MNEMOSYNE NON POCVLA REGIA CVRET[53]

48 Wisdom, the guardian of wealth. (A reference to the Palladium of Minerva.) This was Madame Marguerite's ordinary device prior to her marriage, already illustrated in Claude Paradin's *Devises heroïques*, Lyon, 1557, p. 234 with the gloss: 'Madame Marguerite de France, tresillustre Duchesse de Berri, fait sa Devise de l'Olive, ensemble du Serpent, sinifiant ainsi, toutes choses estre regies, et gouvernées par sapience, ou sagesse.' In Gabriel Symeoni's *Epitalamio*, Paris, 1559, on the marriage of Claude de France and Mme Marguerite, the same elements appear with the two legends PAX ORBI TER. RESTITVTA and PRVDENTVM CONCORDIA REGUM. The first refers to the hopes for universal peace in the treaty of Cateau Cambrésis (Cf. Icon XIII, p. 156) and the other may lead to the modification of the device after marriage to RERVM PRVDENTIA CVSTOS. This distinction is maintained on the official jetons (fig. 33). Cf. P. Pradel, *Catalogue des jetons des princes et princesses de la maison de France*, Paris, 1936, cat. 260–2 and 264–5.

49 Cf. introduction, p. 50.

50 They are joined.

51 Cf. 'Mopsus,' p. 112, v. 24.

52 To the goddess Happiness.

53 Do thou, Goddess, with Wine, and Love, in pleasing variety remember

Aus deus costés de ceste figure dedans deus beaus compartiments enclos de chapeaus de triomphe, comme aus autres figures, estoient peintes deus navires semblables à celle que la ville porte en ses armes, et dedans l'espace qui faisoit le compartiment par le hault, estoit escrit, ARGO,[54] et en l'espace du dessous ceste devise, CÆLOQVE SOLOQVE SALOQVE,[55] ce qui accommodoit fort bien ceste navire Parisienne à la navire des Argonautes, laquelle a eu pouvoir au ciel, y estant encores maintenant entre les signes celestes, en la terre, par laquelle elle marcha, et se fit porter dedans la Lybie, en la mer, laquelle elle a quasi toute voiagée. On pourroit dire mille autres fatalités de ceste antique vaisseau, qui se pourroient approprier à nos armes, mais on en lira davantage dedans une des Masquarades qui suivront après.[56] Il me suffira d'ozer prononcer ce mot, que je trouve ceste devise inventée par moy assés digne d'estre gardée pour devise de la ville eternellement. On eust trouvé merveilleusement beau, qu'ainsi que ce front de salle estoit orné de ces trois
8v° figures, tout du long aussi des deus costés de la salle tous les intervalles que faisoient ces grands croissants de lierre, qui pouvoient estre huit ou dix de

to drown heroes' cares in sport and feasting and delights; and let Memory record the king's battles, not his cups.

54 Claude Paradin, *Devises heroïques*, Lyon, 1557, pp. 104–5 under the motto *En altera quæ vehat Argo* provides the following gloss: 'Les Franques, ou François (peuple jadis frequentant la marine, et gens exerçans l'art Piratique, selon Lactinus Pacatus, Sidon Apolinaris, et Beatus Rhenanus) voulurent que le lieu principal auquel ils s'estoient arrestez, qui est la Cité de Paris, capitale de France, portast perpetuellement l'enseigne de la profession et art dont ils se mesloient. Parquoy lui donnerent la Devise du Navire, qu'elle ha depuis tousjours porté jusques à present. Et n'est pas inconvenient que iceus ne participassent des Gepides lesquelz aussi auparavant se remerquoient du Navire, frequentans la mer Germanique, nacion possible Troyenne, et escartée en lointeines mers, apres la destruction de Troye, de laquelle, l'opinion commune tient, que les nobles François sont descenduz.' For the implications of Germans and French as both of Trojan descent, cf. W. McAllister Johnson, 'Numismatic Propaganda in Renaissance France,' *Art Quarterly*, XXXI (1968), pp. 141–4.

55 In heaven, on earth, and at sea.

56 Cf. p. 103.

chasque costé, eussent esté remplis de figures diverses avecque leurs devises et vers: mais chacun sçait que la main des ouvriers ne peut suivre l'abondance de mes inventions. Toutesfois ce qui fut possible d'achever y fut mis. Premierement du costé droit, au premier intervalle respondant encores sur la table du Roy, estoit la figure d'un dieu Janus, viellard comme on le peint, ayant la clef en la main dextre, et son baston en la gauche: mais n'ayant point deus visages comme on lui soulloit donner.[57] Ceste statue estoit sur un autel, dans lequel estoit escrit, IANO GALLICO,[58] la devise d'en hault estoit, IAM NON RESPEXIT VTRINQVE,[59] et les trois vers d'en bas, ceus ci.

QVI BIFRONS FVERAM, GALLIS SVM GALLICVS VNA
FRONTE DEVS, CÆLVMQVE MEA DVM CLAVE RESOLVI,
VIDI INCVMBENTEM GALLIS TOTVM ACRIBVS ANNVM.[60]

J'avois voulu montrer par ceste peinture, combien le mois de Janvier nous a esté favorable, auquel tant par la vertu de nos Princes, que par la faveur du tens, se sont faites des choses si belles et si merveilleuses, que je serois presque d'avis qu'on fist peindre un Janus en nos enseignes pour une heureuse merque de nostre bon heur.[61] La figure que l'on voyoit au prochain espace d'après suivoit d'assés bonne grace la premiere pour exprimer ceste faveur du tens. Car j'avois fait peindre au haut une petite partie du zodiaque, qui montroit 9r°
seullement le signe de Ganimede que l'on nomme Aquarius, et au dessous un jeune dieu, beau, sans barbe, courroné de fleurs, qui selon les antiques representoit le printens. A l'un des coins de la peinture souffloit un Zephire jetant

57 Barthélemy Aneau's gloss on Alciati's Emb. XVIII *Prudentes* (ed. 1549, p. 40) reads: 'La Sapience est au chef, et Pource l'homme a deux testes, represente le sage: qui ha memoire du passé, et providence de l'advenir.'

58 To the Gallic Janus.

59 He hath ceased to look both ways.

60 I who once was two-faced, am now to the Gauls a Gaulish god with but one visage; and when I opened the sky with my key, I saw the whole year bearing down on the side of the fiery Gauls.

61 Cf. pp. 89 and 123.

des fleurs par la bouche, et dedans le cham de l'ovalle voloient par ci par la quelques arondelles. Le petit espace d'en hault que faisoit le compartiment d'alentour, contenoit ceste devise, CESSIT NATVRA FAVORI,[62] et au grand espace qu'on avoit laissé au dessous de la figure, faisant une allusion à celui qu'on dit avoir esté tant heureus, qu'en une bataille les vents mesmes vindrent combatre pour lui, j'avois fait escrire trois vers comme en tous les autres.

NON CONIVRATI VENIVNT AD CLASSICA TANTVM
ÆOLIDÆ, VERVM GELIDO SOL SYDERE VERNANS
FUNDIT INASSVETOS ARVISQVE ARMISQVE CALORES.[63]

Il y a bien peu de gens comme je croy, qui n'ayent pris garde ceste année à la verité de ceste figure, et s'ils ont bien consideré le tens qu'il a fait tant durant l'entreprise que l'execution de Calais, ils n'ayent veu contre l'ordre acoustumé des années un beau Printens au meilleu de l'hyver: Quand à moy j'ose affermer estant pour lors aus chams avoir veu sortir les herbes nouvelles, et tous autres indices du renouveau. Ce qui montre assés que nos victoires ne viennent point ni par nostre seulle puissance, ni par un sort, ni par un certain ordre de la
9v° nature, mais de la seulle faveur et disposition de Dieu, qu'il les envoye en tel tens, en tel lieu, et à telles personnes qu'il lui plaist, sans la puissance duquel, tant s'en faut que nous puissions estre vaincueurs, que nous ne pouvons pas seullement estre puissans. Vis à vis de ces deus dernieres figures, dedans les deus premiers espaces que faisoient les Croissants de l'autre costé, j'en avois fait assoir deus autres, qui suivoient le mesme argument de ceste nouvelle et heureuse conqueste. Dedans la premiere se montroit un Jason hardi et courageus à arracher une toison d'or, pendue à un arbre, non obstant l'effroy que

62 Nature has vouchsafed to favour us (lit. has given in [completely] to favouring [us]).
63 Not only do the winds of Æolus come by agreement to the trumpet-call, but the sun, growing spring-like in the wintry season, pours unwonted warmth on the fields and on our battle-array.

lui pouvoit donner un horrible dragon qui estoit au pié, et qui au rebours de celui de Colchos charmé et endormi par Medée, ouvroit les yeus effroyablement et s'enfloit si fort de venin, qu'il sembloit quasi crever dans le tableau. On lisoit au dessus pour devise, ARRIPIAM VIGILET LICET,[64] et au dessous.

VELLVS AB INSOMNI LOTHARENE DRACONE TVLISTI,
CARMINIBVS NEC SVNT FERA LVMINA VICTA, NEC HERBIS,
INGENIVM, MARTEMQVE VOCES NISI CARMEN, ET HERBAS.[65]

Dedans la seconde estoit seullement figurée une vieille baniere Romaine representant une de celles de Jules Cesar, qui estant de couleur jaune estoit traversée de bihais d'une large bande noire, qui portoit ces trois letres d'or V.V.V. lesquelles comme chacun sçait assés, et comme il a esté chanté et
rechanté par nos nouveaus poëtes, qui depuis naguieres ont si bien tenu chacun 10r[c]
leur partie en la louange de ceste victoire, signifioit le VENI, VIDI, VICI,[66] de Cesar. Et pour autant que Monseigneur de Guise n'a point esté en ceci accompaigné d'un moindre bon heur, que celui là dont se vantoit le Romain, estant si opportunement venu, ayant si ingenieusement veu, ayant si vaillamment vaincu, je l'ay bien voulu avecques les autres le faire heritier de ces trois letres, lesquelles il a fait perdre en d'autres victoires (je pourrois bien alleguer Mets[67]) à ceux qui sont mesmement heritiers de Cesar. Ceste peinture

64 Though he [i.e. the dragon] be watchful, I shall seize [the prize].

65 Lorraine, you have captured the fleece from the unsleeping dragon, and its fierce eyes have not been overcome by spells or potions – unless you call genius and warlike skill 'spells and potions.'

66 I came; I saw; I conquered.

67 Rapidly publicized in such popular sources as the *Promptuaire des medalles*, Lyon, 1553, part II, pp. 222 and 246. A drawing from Caron's *Histoire Françoyse de nostre temps*, Louvre, Inv. RF 29714 (fig. 20) is considered by Guiffrey to be the taking of Boulogne by Henry II, a manifest error in that the caparisons of the horses bear the eagle *bifrons* and are thus imperial forces. The topography

avoit sa devise telle, TER HOC FELICITER ACTVM,[68] et ses trois vers tels.

CÆSARIS HOC, CÆSAR DEMAS TIBI, GVISIVS ADDAT,
NAM VENIT, VIDIT, VICIT SIMVL ISTE, TVOSQVE
DVM QVOQVE VINCEBANT, VICTO IAM CÆSARE VICIT.[69]

En escrivant ces vers ci, il me vient de naistre une assés gentille fantasie dedans l'esprit pour donner plus de grace à ceste figure, dont l'argument a esté trouvé si propre et à la chose et à la personne, c'est de metre en la devise au lieu de TER ce mot QVATER, ajoustant encore un V dedans la bande, et peignant au dessous de la baniere une fortune garrotée de chaisnes de fer, avecques ces vers changés ainsi.

HOC CÆSAR MIHI CEDE, TRIBVS SIT ET ADDITA QVARTA
LITTERA, SORS ADVERSA MEOS ET INIQVA PREMEBAT,
MOX VENI, VIDI, VICI: VINXI QVOQVE VICTAM.[70]

further coincides with contemporary relations and maps of the Siege of Metz and with the medal of François de Guise (F. Mazerolle, *Les médailleurs français du XVe siècle au milieu du XVIIe*, II, Paris (1902), cat. 408; here fig. 34), but with the avoidance of genre details (Icon XXXVI) required by the official – and thus necessarily generalized – character of an illustration intended for engraving. (Cf. pp. 36–8.) In the lower left quadrant of the medal one sees François de Guise and his men on the ramparts at the presumed moment of launching the 'Harangue que fit Monseigneur le Duc de Guise aus soudards de Mez' commemorated by Ronsard, *Œuvres complètes*, ed. Laumonier (STFM), V, pp. 202–19.

68 This was done successfully thrice.

69 This boast of Cæsar's you, Cæsar, must abandon while Guise may add it to himself; for he has likewise come, seen and conquered, and, overcoming Cæsar himself, has outdone your men while they were conquering.

70 Grant this to me, O Cæsar, that to these three letters there be added a fourth; for my men were being assailed by contrary and grievous fortune when anon I came, and saw,

J'ay ajousté ceci de gayeté de cueur, comme j'ajousteray quatre autres 10v° figures qui estoient deja toutes ordonnées, et dont les compartimens estoient faits, ainsi que me sont tesmoins ceus qui estoient avecque moy et mesmement Baptiste excellent peintre qui les faisoit,[71] et qui en avoit receu l'ordonnance dès le soir de devant: Mais l'arrivée du Roy nous pressa de si près, qu'encores que le peintre fist une admirable diligence, il fut impossible d'en faire tant: et fusmes contraints de nous contenter de ces quatres premieres, pour les intervalles des croissants, dont les deus premiers qui en estoient remplis contenoient autant d'espace de la salle, que faisoit le lieu où l'on devoit couvrir pour le Roy. Dedans la premiere donques de ces quatres figures, estoit peinte une Andromede estant deja deliée de son rocher, au pié duquel estoit son grand

and conquered; and so I conquered Fortune herself, and bound her fast in chains.

Note the alliteration in the last line. Du Bellay had also made the obvious comparison of Henry II to Cæsar. Cf. Du Bellay, 'Hymne au Roy sur la prinse de Callais' (*privilège* dated 17 January 1558 for Federic Morel), *Œuvres*, ed. Chamard VI^{1}, 17–30, vv. 96–8 'Ce que, parlant de soy, Cesar mesme disoit, / Cetuy-cy le peult dire à bon droict (ce me semble) / Je suis venu, J'ay veu, J'ay vaincu, tout-ensemble.'

71 G. Wildenstein, 'La collection de tableaux d'un amateur de Ronsard,' *Gazette des Beaux-Arts*, s. 6, LI (1958), p. 5, n. 2 first suggested an identification with a Baptiste Pellerin active in Paris in the early 1560s. This seems all the more probable considering the collaborations of the Pléiade poets with a limited number of highly specialized artists. Pellerin further illuminated prior to 1580 the *Figures et pourtraicts des sept aages de l'homme* commissioned in engravings by Nicolas Le Camus (fig. 22) and published in 1579, 1595, and 1609 and attributed, insofar as the quatrains are concerned, to Ronsard in the last two editions (Paris, BN: Réserve des imprimés; Estampes) as opposed to the first (Harvard, Houghton Library). Cf. Ronsard, *Œuvres*, ed. Laumonier (STFM), XVIII^{2}, pp. 335–8. Since the 1579 title notes that the engravings are 'sur les principaux de Feu. B.P.' it is likely the same 'Baptiste Pellerin, m^{e} peintre, d^{t} hors la porte St-Martin' whose *inventaire après décès* of 3 August 1575 is noted in G. Wildenstein, *Le goût pour la peinture dans la bourgeoisie parisienne entre 1550 et 1610*, Paris, 1962, p. 125.

monstre marin, navré deja de quelques coups, et demi estourdi, sur qui retournoit encores un Persée, ayant ses ailles au dos, volant dedans l'air, tenant le glaive dans l'un des poings, et le chef de Meduse dans l'autre, lequel il presentoit au monstre pour soudain le tourner en pierre. Et d'un autre costé se voyoit une grande compaignie de gens armés. L'escriture du dessus estoit, NOVO SVA SALVA PICARDIA PERSEO,[72] et les vers du dessous.

CAVTIBVS ANDROMEDEN PERSEVS, CETOQVE MARINO
ERIPVIT, MONSTRIS TV ME ME HENRICE MARINIS,
ESQVE TIBI, SI NOS PHINEVS PETAT, ALTERA GORGON.[73]

11r° Après ceste figure qui montroit combien la Picardie estoit heureuse d'avoir un tel Roy pour son prince, lequel ayant premierement repris Boulongne, et maintenant reconquis Calais, Guignes, et Hammes sur les Anglois, ne l'a pas seullement delivrée de son monstre marin, mais a deja resisté, et combatra en la fin le Phinée qui la veut ravir. J'avois fait faire une autre figure dedans laquelle on eust veu une Niobe deja demi tournée en pierre autour de laquelle eussent esté ses enfans, moitié fils, et moitié filles, deja presque tous morts, estant chacun d'eus navré d'une fleche d'argent. Vis à vis de ce massacre j'avois fait peindre un Phebus, et une Diane, tenant chacun un arc

72 The new Perseus is addressed by his own Picardy which he has rescued (lit. To the new Perseus, his own Picardy, saved).

An undated medal by an unidentified engraver (fig. 35) employs this conceit: F. Mazerolle, *Les médailleurs français du XVe siècle au milieu du XVIIe*, II, Paris, 1902, cat. 340. Henry seems somewhat young and without the iconographical accoutrements of the issues of 1552–3 (Ibid., cat. 89–91, figs. 42, 44 and cat. 99–101) for this medal to commemorate any event of the later 1550s, so we tentatively assign it to the capture of Boulogne because of the same parallel of English domination and French deliverance of the city.

73 Perseus snatched Andromeda from the rocks and from the sea-creature; thou, Henry, hast saved me from sea-monsters, and art to thyself a fresh Gorgon-shield (cf. p. 171) if Phineus (i.e. Philip) should assail me.

d'argent au poin, duquel ils venoient de faire telle vengeance pour l'orgueil insuportable de Niobe, qui s'osoit preferer et elle et sa race à Latone et à ses enfans. Ceste devise estoit pour le haut, DAT INIQVA SVPERBIA PŒNAS,[74] et ces trois vers pour le bas.

LATONÆ NIOBE TIBI SESE O GALLIA PRÆFERT
ANGLIA, PROLE TVMENS, PHŒBVM, PHŒBENQVE LACESSENS,
SIC SAXVM GENITRIX, FIVNTQVE CADAVERA NATI.[75]

L'orgueil d'Angleterre si bien rabaissé par ceste peinture, estoit suivi de la destinée du mesme païs, que j'avois voulu exprimer par la figure suivante, y faisant peindre un Alexandre tout tel que nous le pouvons retirer des medailles antiques, baisant et accollant une Royne figurée en Amazone, de mesme sorte
aussi que les antiques nous l'ont montré: Laquelle representoit la derniere IIv°
Royne des Amazones, qui pour le desir qu'elle eut de coucher avecques Alexandre, perdit le brave regne de ces courageuses et victorieuses femmes. L'espace du haut contenoit ceste devise, RES IMPAR SED FATA EADEM,[76] et celui du bas ces trois vers.

74 The punishment of wicked arrogance. Barthélemy Aneau's gloss on Alciati's Emb. LXVII *Superbia* (ed. 1549, p. 89) reads: 'La Royne Niobé de Thebes fut muée en pierre dure pour son orgueil. Qui signifie que les communs vices des femmes sont Orgueil, Tirannie, impitoyable durté, et faulte de sens, comme une pierre.'

75 O France, England exalts herself, like Niobe, above you as Latona; England big with offspring, challenging Phœbus and Diana; it is thus that the mother becomes a stone, her children corpses.
Cf. Ovid, *Metamorphoses* VI, 148–312.
One recalls the assimilation of Henry II and Diane de Poitiers to Phœbus and Diana, most notably in the Latin distich which surmounted the entrance portal at Anet:

PHŒBO SACRATA EST ALMÆ
DOMVS AMPLA DIANÆ,
VERVM ACCEPTA CVI CVNCTA
DIANA REFERT

Cf. P.-D. Roussel, *Histoire et description du château d'Anet*, Paris, 1875, pp. 31 and 127.

76 Different circumstances, but the same fate.

VLTIMA TE MACEDO REGINA CVPIVIT AMAZON,
ANGLICA CÆSAREVM CVPIIT REGINA PHILIPPVM
VTRAQVE SIC REGINA SVI MANET VLTIMA REGNI.[77]

Pour autant qu'on pourroit trouver quelques choses, en ceste figure qui du tout ne s'accommoderoient point, je lui ay fait porter la devise d'en haut qui est telle, que les choses estans differentes, le destin est de mesme. Car je ne voudrois point ici dire que la Royne d'Angleterre fust vaillante comme une Amazone, à laquelle on n'a point veu encore porter les armes sinon contre son peuple, ni faire autre vaillantise, sinon contre les testes des gentilz hommes de son païs. Je voudrois encores moins comparer un Roy Philippes à un Alexandre, lequel pourtant sembloit avoir un tel heur en son commencement, que s'il eust bien usé de sa fortune, et qu'en se temperant en tout, il n'eust point reculé le bras de Dieu d'avecques le sien, je croy certainement qu'il nous eust montré que les vices de nostre France, qui depuis je ne sçay combien s'est du tout depravée, crioient vengeance contre nous. Mais maintenant je voy bien
12r° (ce n'est pas la premiere fois que j'ay veu et predit) que la ballance s'abbaisse de nostre costé, et que si nous nous maintenons au chemin qu'il faut tousjours suivre, nostre bon heur se maintiendra au cours qu'il a deja commencé. Outre ce premier egard je ne feray point ce tort à ce grand Prince, et à ceste grande Princesse, qui sont conjoints par legitime mariage, d'approprier leur alliance au concubinage de ces deus: Car j'ay esté d'avis de tous tens que c'estoit le plus sotement fait qu'on sçauroit faire, d'injurier par escrit les Princes qui nous sont ennemis, principallement aus choses qui sont controuvées, ou qui touchent tellement leur honneur, que nos Princes mesmes s'en doivent facher. Quand aus legeres attaintes, aus veritables reproches, aus propheties et aus promesses qu'on se fait à soymesme, cela est permis de l'ennemi à l'ennemi.

77 O Macedonian, the last Amazon queen desired you; so also the Queen of England has desired imperial Philip; and thus each queen remains the last of her line.

C'est pourquoy je n'ay point feint de signifier par ceste peinture ce que les Anglois mesmes sçavent avoir esté prophetizé de ceste Royne cy. Ce qui me semble assés bien accommodé au destin de l'Amazone. Encore donnerois-je volontiers ceste loy, combien que je ne l'aye pas observée, que toutes telles choses se fissent par souhaits et imprecations seullement, comme je l'avois fait dans la figure suivante qui devoit estre la derniere de toutes. En laquelle j'avois fait portraire une mer, et sur icelle deus galeres, dont la premiere estoit fort richement et sumpteusement equipée, portant une Royne superbement vestue, accompaignée de ses femmes, qui paroissoit et fort triste et fort 12v°
effroyée. L'autre des galeres estoit autant bien armée qu'il estoit possible, dedans laquelle estoit un grand seigneur richement armé et accompaigné de mesme, autant triste et effroyé que la Royne que j'ay dite. Et sembloient les deus vaisseaus à force de rames fuir tant qu'ils pouvoient devers une ville, à la porte de laquelle la Deesse Nemese accompaignée d'une furie les attendoit. Le haut de la figure portoit ce mot, ET LECTI ET LETHI CONSORS,[78] et le bas ces vers ci.

IN FVRIAS FVRIATA PARES CLEOPATRA MARITVM
ISTA TRAHIT, LICET ABSIT AMOR, TIMOR ADSIT, ET HORROR,
AVGVSTIQVE MEO REDEANT SVB PRINCIPE REGNA.[79]

78 Companion both of the bed and of the deathbed (lit. of Lethe, punning with *lecti*).

79 Yon Cleopatra, driven insane, drags her husband into a like fatal madness; though love be absent, let fear and terror be present; and under my tutelage let the reign of Augustus return.

Jodelle was not the only poet to compare Philip II and Mary Tudor to Anthony and Cleopatra. (Cf. Adrien Turnèbe, *Panegyricus*, Paris, Attaignant, 1558 fol. B . . . affuetus Iberus / Delitiis qui totus hebet luxuque liquescit / Faxo sua mihi cum Cleopatra Antonius amens / Expendat pœnas, et supplex arma recondat.) Similarly, Henry II as the victor restoring peace and prosperity could be compared to Augustus after the Battle of Actium. (Cf. Du Bellay, 'Hymne au roy sur la prinse de Callais,' *Œuvres*, ed. Chamard, VI[1], p. 20, vv. 1–10.)

Chacun sçait assés qu'en la bataille navalle d'Octavien et d'Antoine, Cleopatra se fit mener dedans une gallere dont le mas estoit d'or, les voiles et les cordes d'argent, et le reste plain de pompes et delices, mais qu'aussi tost qu'elle vit que la fortune commençoit à tourner de la part ennemie, elle s'espouvanta, et se print à fuir à toute force. Ce que voyant Antoine, moitié par amour moitié par crainte la suivit, abandonnant ses forces, et se retirant miserablement avecques elle dedans Alexandrie, où depuis assiegés par Octavien furent tellement menés de furies, que par desespoir et crainte d'estre portés en triomphe, ils se tuerent tous deus l'un après l'autre. Après leur mort Octavien Cesar qui depuis fut surnommé Auguste, demeurant seul dominateur des Romains,
131r° se vit en la fin Monarque du monde. L'imprecation doncques de ceste derniere figure que j'avois fort bien ordonnée pour la fin, estoit telle que ceste Royne ci s'estant montrée fort superbe, et desireuse de la guerre, ayant sollicité plusieurs fois son Antoine (di-je son Philippes) à faire la plus cruelle guerre qu'il pourroit, ayant mesme en tout tâché d'offenser nostre Cesar,[80] jusques à lui denoncer la guerre sans aucune occasion, sente en la fin la juste vengeance de son orgueil, tellement que voulant encores accompaigner son mari soit de sa personne et de ses forces, ou bien de ses forces seullement, pour venir contre nostre Roy, que de rechef plus epovantée qu'elle n'a esté dernierement, elle soit contrainte de fuir avecque sa honte et future ruine pour trouver les furies en son païs. Et qu'elle tire après soy, non pas tant par amour que par crainte, son mari, pour estre autant participant de la furie que de la folie. Ainsi ce seroit que nostre Roy après la ruine de ces deus, qui avecques lui avoient parti la domination de l'Europe, demeureroit seul dominateur, et se faisant après Auguste metroit tout un monde sous sa monarchie, ramenant encores ici l'heureus et paisible siecle

80 The emphasis 'nostre Cesar' for Henry II is significant in that more general European usage of this epithet was restricted to the Emperor Charles V. Here it prepares the reader for the later allusion to Augustan world peace. Cf. Icon LVI, where the theme had already been publicly developed for Philip II's 1549 entry into Antwerp. Jodelle's circumstantial assimilation of Mary Tudor and Philip as Anthony and Cleopatra conveniently ignores or consciously disposes of this precedent.

d'Auguste. Voilà tout ce qu'il y avoit de figures pour ceste salle. En laquelle ne se pouvoit plus voir autre chose que l'on peust remerquer, outre tout ce que j'ay decrit, fors qu'au bas de la salle, qui estoit le costé par où l'on devoit servir, outre la tapisserie et le lierre qui le decoroient, dedans un grand et 13v°
spatieus quarre de la longueur d'une toise,[81] estoient escrits douze vers comprenans toutes les choses que le Roy a faites depuis son avenement à la couronne, le tout allant d'ordre, et le tout si bien escrit, et en si grands caracteres, qu'il se pouvoit facilement lire de la table du Roy. Ceci estoit au dessus des vers, EX D. CAROLI LOTHARINGI PYRAMIDE, A STEPH. IODELIO DESCRIPTA,[82] et les vers qui suivoient estoient tels.

SCOTIA TVTA SVIS, ACCEPTA BOLONIA, METÆ,
ET RHENI PAVOR ATTONITI, FVSVSQVE PER VMBRAS
CÆSAR, ET HINC VICTÆ TVRMIS REDEVNTIBVS VRBES,
MOX QVOQVE DEFENSÆ LOTHARENI GLORIA METÆ,
INSTAVRATÆ ACIES, VRBESQVE ÆDESQVE SORORIS
CÆSAREÆ, RENTINA TIBI PALMA ADDITA GVISI,
AC SI QVA IN BELGIS QVÆSITA TROPHŒA SVPERSVNT:
HAS INTER PALMAS PARMA, ET MIRANDVLA, SENÆ,
CORSICAQVE, ET TOTIES DECEPTVS IN ALPIBVS HOSTIS:
NVNC QVOQVE QVOD RELIQVIS POTIVS FATALE CALETVM,
QVÆQVE FEROX POTIOR FATALI GVINA CALETO,
HÆC SVNT QVÆ REGEM LAVRV RES LAVDE CORONANT.[83]

81 A *toise* was equal to 6 *pieds*. Cf. Kurt Glaser, 'Die Mass – und Gewichtsbezeichnungen des Französischen. Ein Beitrag zur Lexikographie und Bedeutungsgeschichte,' *Zeitschrift für französische Sprache und Literatur*, XXVI^{1} (1903), p. 109.

82 From the Description of the Pyramid of the Lord Charles of Lorraine, by Estienne Jodelle.

83 These are the things that crown the king with laurel and his achievements with glory: Scotland kept safe for her people, Boulogne captured, the terror of Metz and of the fear-stricken Rhine, the Emperor routed in the darkness, and the cities conquered by the squadrons returning from this engagement; presently, too, the glorious defence of Metz in Lorraine,

the battle-lines restored, and the cities and palaces of the Emperor's sister, the victory gained for you by Guise at Renty, and such other triumphs as remain among those you have pursued in Belgium; among these victories also are Parma, Mirandola, Siena, Corsica, and your many successful ruses against the enemy in the Alps; now too there is Calais, which to others had, rather, been disastrous; and warlike Guignes, which had been of more import than doomed Calais.

It was common practice for poets to give flattering lists of the king's victories. (Cf. Ronsard, *Œuvres* ed. Laumonier (STFM), VII, pp. 5–7 'Au Roy'; pp. 30–1, 'Ode au Roy' and Du Bellay, *Œuvres* ed. Chamard, VI^{I}, pp. 6–13, 'Discours au roy sur la trefve de l'an M.D.LV'). Jodelle was, however, exceptionally well informed about such matters. (Cf. *passim* V.-L. Saulnier 'L'actualité militaire dans l'*Eugène* de Jodelle' in *Revue universitaire*, LX (1951), pp. 147–53 and E. Balmas, *Etienne Jodelle*, Ch. IV).

Scotland, which had been invaded by the English after the death of James V, was successfully defended for Queen Marie of Lorraine, and her daughter Mary Stuart with the aid of French troops under Thermes in 1549–50. (Cf. Icon L, p. 185.)

Boulogne, lost during the reign of Francis I (1544), was recovered 24 March 1550 through the Treaty of Outre-Eau, which was particularly galling to Charles V.

After occupying Metz on 10 April 1552, Anne de Montmorency took Augsburg and hotly pursued Charles V, who barely had time to flee to Villac, the last German fortress on the Rhine. Other cities taken in this campaign included Verdun, Toul, Danvilliers, and Yvoy. (Cf. Francis de Crue, *Anne de Montmorency*, Paris, 1889, pp. 117–35.) On 19 October 1552, Charles V returned to lay siege to Metz, which was defended by the Duc de Guise (Cf. Ronsard, *Œuvres*, ed. Laumonier [STFM], V, pp. 203–19, 'Harangue du duc de Guise.') The siege had to be abandoned by the Emperor on 31 December despite the diversionary tactics of his sister Marie, widow of Louis II, King of Hungary and Bohemia, who was governor of the Low Countries from 1531 to 1555. Her troops attacked the frontiers of Picardy so effectively that Henry II had to send part of his army to resist them. (Cf. Gaston Zeller, *La réunion de Metz à la France*, Strasbourg, 1929.)

Charles V was defeated at Renty on 13 August 1554 by troops under the Duc de Guise. (Cf. François de Rabutin, *Commentaires*, ed. Michaud et Poujoulat VII, p. 481.)

Parma was attacked by Don Ferdinando Gonzaga for Charles V and successfully defended by Octave Farnese (1550–2). Mirandola, under the protection of the French from 1548 on, was attacked by Pope Julius III and delivered by Farnese in 1551. Siena, a republic under French

Ces vers, comme l'inscription le montre, sont tirés de la Pyramide de monseigneur le reverendissime Cardinal de Lorraine,[84] qui est un petit œuvre

protection from 26 July 1552 to 17 April 1555 finally surrendered to Cosimo de' Medici 22 April 1555. (Cf. Icon LXIV, p. 196.) Corsica, formerly under the control of Genoa, was invaded and 'liberated' by French troops in August-September 1553. The campaigns in the Alps (Piedmont, etc.) were largely under the direction of Brissac. (Cf. Icon XLIX, p. 184.)

It is interesting to note that this extract from the so-called *Pyramide* addressed to the Cardinal of Lorraine deals exclusively with the victories of Henry II and seems to have occupied the entirety of the 'bas de la salle,' i.e. directly in front of the King, across the room.

84 A reference to his personal device, as explained in Claude Paradin, *Devises heroïques*, Lyon, 1557, pp. 72–3: TE STANTE VIREBO 'Entrant dernierement Monsieur le R. Cardinal de Lorreine en son Abbaye de Cluny, estoit eslevée au portal d'icelle sa Devise, qui est une Pyramide, avec le croissant au dessus: environée du bas jusques en haut, d'un beau Lierre verdoyant. Et le tout acompagné, de l'inscription qui sensuit: Quel Memphien . . .' Ivy is usually given an unfavourable significance, as Paradin, p. 208 'IMPROBITAS SVBIGIT RECTVM: Le Lierre croissant auprès d'aucun bois droit, le gate et ruine par son entortillement. Aussi (comme l'on dit communement) le tort bien mené, peut rendre le droit inutile.' But here the ivy grows on a pyramid, which is classed as '*Principum opes, plebis adminicula.* Pyramides Phariûm monumẽta perennia Regũ, / Errãtibus circũligat hedera sequax brachiis. / Regum opibus firmis plebs sustentatur egena: / Mentisq[ue] constans firmitas viret perenniter.' *Hadriani Ivnii medici emblemata* . . . , Antwerp, 1565, Emblema XIIII, p. 20. Even this symbolism could be interpreted pejoratively as in a Protestant sonnet of about 1562 directed against the Cardinal de Lorraine. (BN ms. fr. 22560, fol. 15):

Car si nous t'entendons Lyerre tu te veux dire
Et par la Pyramide est entendu le Roy.
Jamais on ne planta Lyerre contre paroy
De luy mesme il y vient l'embrasse et s'en fait sire.
Tout ainsi on t'a veu toy-mesme t'introduire
A lier nostre prince et à luy donner loy.
Lyerre semble envahir le mur et le tenir
Mais en fin il le fait en ruine venir
S'on ne l'arrache avant que dans la pierre il mine.

que je fi dernierement d'environ six cents vers heroiques Latins, autant beau comme je croy qu'aucun qui soit encores sorti de moy, sans excepter mesmes
14r° ceus que j'ay faits d'une beaucoup plus longue alaine. J'avois esperance voyant un chacun à l'envi lui presenter ce qu'il pouvoit, de faire une arriere garde après tous les autres. Laquelle encores qu'elle me semblast trop foible pour garder son nom, et les graces dont il est pourveu contre les injures du tens, de la mort, et de l'oubliance, si prometoit elle pour l'avenir quelque chose aprochante de cela. Mais mon desastre acoustumé l'a pendue au croc, comme tous mes autres labeurs, lesquels si je ne pensois avoir bien faits, et si je ne pensois qu'ils fussent aucunement dignes de la lecture des grands seigneurs, je les brulerois et eus et mes livres. Si j'avois le loisir de discourir ici tout ce qui m'en est avenu, je ferois emerveiller ceus qui sans me connoistre bien, jugent de moy à l'avanture. Mais ce n'est pas ici où il me faut user de ces plaintes autant contre la fortune et les desastres, que contre l'ingratitude des nostres. Une occasion se presentera un jour, où telle misere deduite apprandra bon gré malgré à beaucoup de severes censeurs, qui tancent, reprennent, et conseillent, pour paroistre et non pour ayder, que la conduite de nos fortunes n'est point en nostre conduite. Ce qui ne fust point entré en mon cerveau non plus qu'au leur, si je n'eusse experimenté que contre toutes les prevoyances et pourvoyances que j'ay sceu jamais faire, j'ay tousjours senti les malheurs d'une destinée, tellement enchaisnés queue à queue, et se rencontrans tellement au point, qu'il a fallu qu'en toutes entreprises en depit de moy, la charte me soit
14v° demeurée au poin. Car quand aus letres (s'il faut encore un peu reprandre ma digression) qu'est-ce que j'ay jamais voulu faire voir de moy, qu'un affaire, une maladie, une debauche d'amis, un default ou une perte d'occasion, une

The device seems to have originated with the revival of the Ordre de St Michel in the Lyon Entry of 1548, for it appears upon the illuminated copy of the Statutes done especially for the Cardinal de Lorraine; cf. Paul Durrieu, 'Les Manuscrits des statuts de l'Ordre de Saint Michel,' *Bulletin de la Société française de reproductions de manuscrits à peintures*, I (1911), pp. 34ff. and pl. IX. In any case, it first appears in the album *La Magnificence à Lyon* . . . , Lyon, 1549, fol. D4 as the Obelisque (fig. 31).

entreprise nouvelle, ou ce qui est le pire de tous une envie n'ait empesché d'estre veu ? Je ne parle point des labeurs de ma petite jeunesse, mais de ceus où j'ay travaillé depuis quatre ou cinq ans, lesquels ay-je jamais sceu faire sortir en lumiere, encores que j'y tachasse et que je pensasse bien leur avoir donné des yeus d'aigle pour la soustenir ? Quand aus armes où j'ay tousjours senti ma nature assés encline, en quel camp, en quel voiage n'ay-je voulu aller, et quels aprests et quelles poursuites n'ay-je tâché de faire ? Mais tousjours ou quelque autre maladie, ou le deffaut present du moyen qui ne peut accorder avecque la grandeur d'un bon cueur, ou le delay de jour en jour, ou quelques autres incommodités m'ont tellement retenu, qu'il semble que ces malheurs me servans de fers, ma ville, qui m'est malheureuse le possible, me doive servir d'eternelle prison. Quand aus affaires, encores que je n'i sois ni fait ni nourri ausquels pour le moins n'estois-je point né ? Mais tant s'en faut comme me reprochent plusieurs que je les fuye, qu'ils m'ont de tout tens fui, sans qu'il y ait en rien qui m'en ait rendu incapable que le trop de malheur, ou le trop de capacité, desquels, l'un m'a peu apporter les haines et les envies, et l'autre la 15r°
presumption et fiance de moymesme, qui deplaisent merveilleusement aus grands. J'entens bien deja ce qu'on me dit sur ceci, que je suis encore fort jeune,[85] et que je ne sçaurois faire telles complaintes, sans que j'aye dedans moy une demesurée outrecuidance. Je ne respons autre chose, sinon que par le passé, et par le present je juge bien du futur. Toutesfois j'espere encores, et peut estre qu'au meilleur de mon aage, la fortune se fera meilleure pour moy. Je revien à ma Pyramide laquelle j'avois fait fort bien escrire, dorer et acoustrer pour presenter, mais s'offrant ceste occasion de festin, et pensant que toutes les choses que j'avois bien faites, estans bien executées et bien receües, lui donneroient une meilleure entrée, je luy fi garder le coffre qu'elle garde encores. Certainement j'avois assés de fois appris que le vice et la desobaissance reculoit la vertu et le service premier, mais je n'avois encore jamais oui dire, que la vertu reculast la vertu et le service le service. Or ne demeurons point si long tens en si beau chemin, et venons à ce qui a esté cause de tout le mal, qui est

85 Jodelle was 26 at the time.

la premiere des masquarades, ne nous hastant point de deduire les fautes qui y
furent commises, le retranchement que je fu contraint d'y faire, les excuses qui
à la verité me doivent absoudre, ains remetant tout cela jusques à tantost que
le lecteur l'aura toute leüe. Mon invention estoit, qu'ayant veu porter à la
ville une navire en ses armes, et me resouvenant de la navire Argon dont j'ay
15v° deja parlé, je deliberay pour les belles accommodations que l'on verra cachées
la dessous, faire ma masquarade d'Argonautes. Or pour autant qu'entre tous
autres travaus que les Argonautes ont soufferts, et auquels la pauvre Argon
mesme a esté sujete, cetui ci est un des plus memorables, que dedans la Lybie
ils furent contraints de la porter sur leurs espaules, je voulois aussi qu'en la
masquarade la rapportans au Roy pour lui estre heureuse et fatalle comme elle
leur avoit esté, et pour le conseiller et lui prophetiser ses heurs et ses malheurs,
comme elle leur avoit tousjours conseillé et prophetizé, ils la portassent sur
leurs espaulles, aussi bien qu'ils avoient fait dans la Lybie, pour montrer au
Roy qu'en tous perils et dangers il la falloit porter, ce qui à mon jugement estoit
assés propre à ceste communauté de Paris. Pour ce aussi que Minerve l'avoit
fait bâtir du bois de la forest parlante, qui est la cause qu'elle parloit, et qu'elle
estoit prophete, je voulois que Minerve les accompaignast, comme elle leur
avoit esté presente et favorable en leur voiage de la toison d'or. Davantage
sçachant que la beauté d'une masquarade est la musique, je voulois qu'Orphée
qui estoit jadis l'un des Argonautes, marchast devant eus, sonnant et chantant
une petite chanson en la louange du Roy, et que comme il souloit ancienne-
ment tirer les rochers après soy, deus rochers plains de musique le suivissent,
laquelle chantast comme si ce fust esté la vois de quelques Satyres ou quelques
16r° Nimphes cachées au dedans. Mais à cause que le reste se verra mieus par la
lecture des vers je viendray à la chanson d'Orphée, à laquelle je faisois
respondre ceus qui estoient dans les rochers.[86]

86 It is most probable that Jodelle wrote both poems to fit the melody of an extant *chanson*. All four verses have the same rhyme scheme (a b a b c c) and the same rhythm (7 7 7 7 10 10). The rhyme scheme is very common, coming perhaps from the Italian or 'Peut-être aussi ont-ils [les poètes] simplement imité quelque chanson populaire avec refrain, car *c c* est un

CHANSON D'ORPHEE

Si jamais rochers et bois
Ma force dans soy sentirent,
Si sous ma vois sous mes dois
S'arrachans ils me suivirent,
Suivés rochers, et avecq' vostre Orphée
Admirés moy d'un grand Roy le Trophée.

Si quelque Nimphe dans vous
Quelque Pan, quelque Satyre,
Pour ouir mes accords dous,
D'avanture se retire,
Chantés rochers, et avecq' vostre Orphée
Adorés moy d'un grand Roy le Trophée.

LA MUSIQUE DES ROCHERS

On nous avoit veu cacher
Pour t'ouir, aus roches creuses,
Mais avecque le rocher
Nous tirent tes mains heureuses,
Raviz, abstraits, mourants d'ouir Orphée,
Et plus encor d'ouir un tel Trophée.

refrain qui s'impose naturellement à la chanson populaire à la suite d'un quatrain.' (Philippe Martinon, *Les Strophes*, Paris, Champion, 1912, p. 289). The rhythmic pattern is more unusual and Martinon cites only one other example of its use in the sixteenth century (p. 561) in the 'Ode au Rossignol, et à l'Arondelle, d'un ennuy secret' by Pontus de Tyard (*Œuvres*, ed. Marty-Laveaux, p. 154). Tyard, however, reverses the order of masculine and feminine rhymes (*vers intercalaires*).

16v°

O heureus Roy qui as eu
Pour ton sonneur un Orphée,
Heureus sonneur qui as peu
Si bien sonner tel Trophée,
O trois trois fois trois fois heureus Orphée,
O trois trois fois trois fois heureus Trophée.

Après cete chanson, qu'expressement j'avois fait douce et en bas style, usant de vers intercalaires qui ont bonne grace en la musique, j'avois fait parler Minerve en telle sorte.

MINERVE

Voyant ainsi ô Roy dans ma main docte et forte
Branler asseurément les armes qu'elle porte,
Et voyant ma Meduse effroyer de rechef
Tous vos yeus des serpens de son horrible chef,
Me voyant mesme avoir la bourguignote[87] en teste
Qui son panache fait flotter dessus sa creste,
Ne sçay-tu pas desja que Minerve je suis
Qui seule sur les arts et sur les armes puis
Autant qu'Apollon mesme, autant que Mars mes freres?[88]
Minerve, qui laissant mes deux villes premieres
Athenes, et puis Rome (aujourdhuy seul tombeau
De ce qu'elles ont eu de bon, de grand, de beau)
Me suis de ton Paris faite la gardienne
Par ton Pere, qui seul me rend Parisienne,

87 A sort of helmet or casque. Cf. Huguet, *Dictionnaire*.

88 An allusion to the dual nature of Minerva which, in the context of Francis 1's reign, may be the very substructure of the popular *ex utroque Cæsar* conceit whose specific development depends upon a variety of texts. (Cf. Icon 1, and introduction, pp. 29–32.)

Et me rendra tousjours, si tousjours je ne voy 17r°
Fouller l'heur que je donne à ta ville et à toy,
Et sur le sçavoir saint mettre le pié barbare,
Sçavoir, qui seul les Roys des lourds bouviers separe,
Sans lequel, soit qu'un Roy le suive par autruy,
Ou qu'en soymesme il ayt sa conduitte par luy,
Il ne sçauroit guider l'espoir de plus grand gloire
Ny, estant mort, avoir de sa mort la victoire.
Mais pourquoy tout ceci puisque tes bras tu tends
Pour de ta gardienne estre garde en tout tens?
Je m'egare, et m'estant proposée autre chose
Je m'esbahi qu'ainsi sans propos je propose.
Or sache donc que c'est, et sachent tous pourquoy
Ma trouppe tant estrange arrive devant toy.
  Tu as bien leu qu'avant que la Greque jeunesse
Eust voué de laisser le repos de la Grece,
Se donnant au hazard pour premiere ramer
Et contreindre au faiz l'eau pucelle de la mer,
En suivant le conseil du cauteleus Pelie,
Qui pensoit perdre ainsi de son Neveu la vie,
S'il pouvoit envoyer ce courageus Jason
Au dangereus conquest de la riche Toison:[89]
Sur le mont Peliaque en la forest parlante
Je fei faire pour eus la Nau prophetisante[90]
Qui fut nommée Argo, et Argonautes ceus

89 According to the legend, Pelias had unlawfully usurped the throne from his brother Æson. His nephew Jason, the rightful heir, was secretly raised by the centaur Chiron in the grottos on Mt Pelion until, as a young man, he returned to assert his claim. He was then required to prove himself by obtaining the golden fleece in Colchis.

90 The boat built for the voyage at the foot of Mt Pelion had the gift of speech and hearing because of the wood given by Minerva. Cf. Apollonius I, 526.

Qui dedans elle iroient par les flots depiteus.
Ils demarent, ils vont, mille monstres ils voyent,
Souffrants cent mille maus cent fois ils se devoyent,
17v° Ils viennent en Colchos, où Medée les fait
Joüir de la Toison, et son frere deffait,[91]
Ils partent en danger, mille perils les suivent,
Et recourant leurs maus d'autre maus leur arrivent:
Mais sur tout par les bords de la seche Lybie
Furent contraints porter leur Navire affoiblie,[92]
Leur mere soulageants, qui les avoit portés,
Et du desir de l'or les avoit contentés
Sous ma guide tousjours, qui de leur navigage
M'estois faite compaigne en tout ce grand voyage,
Favorisant ma Nef, qui après par les Dieus
Tirée en hault fut faite un astre de nos cieus.[93]
  Or maintenant voyant que j'ay voulu me faire
De ton Paris peuplé Deesse tutelaire
Dès que ce grand François vint gouster nos douceurs,
Pere second de moy, pere de mes neuf Seurs:[94]
J'ay tousjours veu porter pour enseigne honorable
De la felicité de Paris admirable
La figure d'Argon, qui monstroit un destin
Que ceste mesme Argon tu aurois en la fin.

91 Jason was able to take the golden fleece with the help of the sorceress, Medea, who then accompanied him on the return journey. According to one legend she arranged to have her brother killed and his limbs scattered in the way in order to delay pursuit.

92 The ship was carried twelve days and nights across the Libyan desert.

93 The constellation Argo navis which in modern astronomy has been broken down into Carina, Puppis, and Vela. It is near Canis Major and included the star Canopus.

94 For Francis I as patron of the arts and father of the Muses, cf. vv. 10–14 above, Icon I, and pp. 159–60.

J'ay ces jours obtenu de Jupiter mon pere
Qu'elle redescendroit, pour en ce tems prospere
Te l'offrir, t'asseurant que par son grand moyen
Plus que n'est la Toison tu conquerras de bien
Emplissant tous les lieus de maint et maint trophée,
Ainsi comme le sçait ce tout divin Orphée,
Qui maintenant ton Nom dessus son Lut sonnoit,
Et qui jadis aussi les Grecs accompagnoit:[95]
Ainsi que sçait Jason et ses compagnons mesme, 18r°
Ayant bien veu là bas filer ton heur supresme
Par les fatalles mains de ces trois seurs qui font
Ou redefond sans fin l'heur que les hommes ont.[96]

JASON

Je sçay mesme, qu'un jour et la Toison dorée,
Et le sceptre, et les biens, et la race honorée,
De ceus qui vont portant en leur col la Toison[97]
Sentiront que Henry est leur fatal Jason,
Apprenants que sans fin la celeste ordonnance
Donne à ceste grand Nau sur la Toison puissance,
Ceste Nau, qui non pas seulement en Colchos,
Mais aus deus bouts du monde emportera ton los.
Elle est encor parlante, elle est encore prophete,[98]

95 Orpheus was one of the Argonauts. The classical lyre is replaced here as usual in the sixteenth century by the lute. Cf. p. 86.

96 The three fates who spin, weave, and cut the threads of life.

97 A reference to the Spanish order of the Golden Fleece established 'En mémoire de l'expédition fabuleuse des Argonautes' by Philippe le Bon, Duke of Burgundy, on the occasion of his marriage to Isabella of Portugal in 1429.

98 Cf. p. 103.

Ce te sera des Dieus une seure interprete,
Elle te donnera mouvement et conseil,
Et voguera tousjours d'un superbe appareil.
Aumoins si tu fais tant que l'envie contraire,
Ainsi que mille ventz ne luy puissent mal faire.
Si tu gardes aussi qu'Ignorance qui suit
Bien souvent les Vertus aus quelles elle nuit,
Face sans y penser, tort aus hommes louables,
Aus hommes vertueus, aus hommes proffitables,
Comme, sans y penser, je tuay quelquefois
Cyzique nostre amy, le meilleur Roy des Roys.[99]
Si tu sçais bien sauver en un tel navigage
18v° Tout le peuple qui fait avec toy son voiage
De Geans monstrueux, horribles, affamés,
Sans cesse sur le sang des petis enflammés,
Ou bien dessus leurs biens, comme nous nous sauvasmes
Ce jour là qu'Amycus Cyclop nous tuasmes:[100]
Si tu veus delivrer les pauvres affligés,
Ayder aus souffretteus, venger les outragés,
Ainsi que Calaïs et Zethes, qui tuerent
Ces grands Oyseaus infaits, qui long tens tourmenterent
Phinée le prophete:[101] ou comme Hercule fit
Alors que Promethée en franchise il remit.

99 Cyzikos, king of the Dolions on the island of Cyzicus was accidentally killed by Jason when he and his party were mistaken for enemies.

100 The giant Amycus, king of the Bebrycians, was actually overcome and killed by Pollux. He was not really a cyclops but was compared to one by Valerius Flaccus IV, 104.

101 Jodelle seems to confuse two episodes here. On the island of Aretias the Argonauts were attacked by monstrous birds called Stymphalides, but the prophet Phineus was tormented by the winged Harpies. After they were chased off by Calaïs and Zethes, in gratitude he showed the Argonauts the road to Colchis. (Cf. Apollonius II, 179–436.)

Si par autre moien que par poisons horribles,
Et par meurdres villains, ct trahisons terribles,
La riche Toison d'or tu t'attens d'aquester,
Plus vertueus que moy qu'il ne faut imiter
En tout, et qui fu fin et faus de telle sorte,
Qu'est encores ici cil qui ma toison porte.
Si jamais tu ne veus, ô toy fidele Roy
Rompre ni faire rompre aucunement la foy,
Ainsi qu'on la rompit à Medée insensée
Quand elle fut par moy pour une autre laissée.[102]
Si tu te peus garder, toy qui es Roy prudent,
De maint flateur subtil, maint flateur impudent,
Qui courtizan de riz, de façon, de harangue,
Couvre mille venins du dous miel de sa langue,
Et qui, si tu n'estois un bon Prince avisé,
Rendroit sur la Vertu le Vice autorisé,
Plus trompeur quc n'estoient les Serenes flatantes,
Dont j'echappay les vois doucement attrayantes 19r
Qui pour le beau loyer du son qu'ils accordoient,
Et ma vie et la vie à tous nous demandoient.[103]
Brief si en toutes peurs, tous perils, tous orages,
Argon ta pouvre Nef tu portes et soulages,
Comme dans la Lybie elle se fit porter,
Et comme tu la vois devers toy r'apporter
Dessus le dos courbé des Argonautes mesmes,
Qui paroistroicnt tous tels que sont les ombres blesmes
Des chams Elysiens, où nous dès long tens morts

102 Jason finally abandoned Medea for Glauké or Créuse, daughter of King Creon.

103 The Argonauts were saved from the Sirens by the protection of Juno and the songs of Orpheus.

Habitons maintenant, et n'auroient point de corps
Si Minerve n'avoit à vostre humaine veüe
Accommodé la chose. Estant donc ainsi veüe
Si vivement, croiés que tous vous nous voyés
Sans phantausme, tous tels que voir vous nous croyés:
Tout ainsi par la mer quelquefois nous vogasmes,
Tout ainsi quelquefois ce vaisseau nous portasmes:
Et si on ne le croit qu'on oye le vaisseau
Parler au vieil Jason, et au Jason nouveau.

ARGON[104]

Jason mon plus cher fils, et la gloire indontée
Quand j'estois sur les eaus de toute ma portée:
Si jusques aus enfers descend l'affection,
Et si les Ombres ont aucune passion,
Pren un peu de pityé de moy qui suis venue
Du ciel, où je me suis par si long tens tenue
19v° En aise et en repos: et il faut maintenant
Qu'on me voye cent maus et cent maus soustenant:
Toutesfois puisque c'est pour porter de tels Princes
Jusqu'aus dernieres mers aus derniers provinces
Je veus bien supporter encore ce labeur.
Mais Mopsus qui soulois predire le malheur
Et l'heur de mes enfans, je te pri prophetise
A mon second Jason l'heur de son entreprise.

104 The form 'Argon' was also used by Du Bellay (*Deffence*, p. vii) and Ronsard, *Œuvres*, ed. Laumonier (STFM), VIII, p. 257, v. 47).

MOPSUS[105]

De ceste peine en bref je te dechargeray
Mere, et au lieu de toy je prophetizeray
Ce qu'ont desja predit quelques Prophetes sages,
Ce qu'ont desja montré mille et mille presages:
Que les François bien tost loing du monde à l'escart
Mettront au joug le col de l'Aanglois Leopard,[106]
Et de l'autre costé rabbatront l'arrogance,
De ceus qui se font grands par ruze et alliance,
Faisant en fin la fin de l'Empire Romain,
Duquel le nom mourra sous leur fatale main.
Et qui ne le croira que la raison il croye,
Apprenant que le ciel de terre en terre envoye
L'Empire des humains, et que quand il permet
Vos humaines grandeurs croistre jusqu'au sommet,
Ce n'est sinon à fin qu'aussi tost il les baisse,
Comme monter en haut lentement il les laisse:
Cetui là des long tens est deja renversé,
Semblable au pauvre oiseau qui sur terre blessé, 20r°
Allors que dedans l'aer s'ebranler il s'essaye,
Ne fait plus que trainer et son sang et sa playe.
Et si tu crains, ô Roy, que le François prochain
De la grandeur qu'avoit jadis le nom Romain,
Ne soit point heritier de la grand Monarchie,
Et que ton Croissant cede au Croissant de Turquie,

105 The prophet, Mopsus, one of the Argonauts, died in the Libyan desert. Cf. Apollonius I, 65, 101–4. Jodelle here is concerned mainly with Henry II's aspirations to become emperor of the Holy Roman Empire, and, ultimately, a Universal Christian Empire.

106 Cf. p. 82.

Tellement que l'on vist un grand Lion couché
Après avoir long tems sur le ventre marché
Pour épier sa proye, en s'elançant deffaire
L'Aigle et le brave Coq l'un à l'autre contraire:[107]
Asseure toy par moy que les Turcs mesme tiennent,
Que les frains de l'Empire entre les mains reviennent
Des grans Roys indontés heritiers de Francus,
Par qui doivent un jour eus mesme estre vaincus.[108]
Mesmes qui te peut plus asseurer de ces choses
Que si devant tes yeus Calais tu te proposes,
Et les derniers Lauriers dont après un malheur
Ce grand Prince Lorrain couronne ta grandeur?[109]
Car cela seul deja te promet l'Angleterre
Où les destins sont faus, l'Angleterre et ta terre
Avecq l'Escoce aussi, feront que chacun Roy
De l'Europe sera contraint flechir sous toy.
Et mesme en ce discord qu'on verra bien tost naistre
Pour l'Empire, il faudra que toy le plus grand maistre,
Si tous les tiens au moins sçavent bien leur mestier,
Taches de ce grand rond avoir le tiers entier:

107 Cf. Mellin de St Gelais, *Dixain* LXXV (*Œuvres*, ed. Blanchemain II, p. 137).

108 The sense is that if Henry fears that the Turks might take advantage of the conflict between France (le brave Coq) and Charles v (l'Aigle) in order to gain their ends (like a lion attacking two birds preoccupied with their own struggles), he should rest easy because they (les Turcs) in fact want him to win even though ultimately he may conquer them!

This entire passage (vv. 21–32) is a patchwork made more difficult by the insertion in vv. 25–8 of a metaphor based upon Alciati, Emb. CXXV *Ex damno alterius, alterius utilitas* which employs the combat of a lioness and wild boar overseen by a vulture to express the Turkish threat to all Europe and disrupts the proposition 'Si tu crains . . .' and its resolution 'Asseure toy . . .' (Cf. H. Green, *Andrea Alciati and His Books of Emblems*, London, 1872, pp. 44–5.)

109 François, duc de Guise.

Si l'Europe tu as, les deus autres parties,
Veu qu'au pris de l'Europe elles sont abruties 20v
Et barbares, en fin par force et par moyens
Peu à peu couleront dessous la main des tiens:
Tant que si seul tu n'as toute la terre basse,
Tu te peus asseurer qu'un jour l'aura ta race.
Voilà ce que Calais et le cueur ajousté
Aus tiens, peut ajouster à telle Majesté.

JASON

Argon s'enrejouit, Argon parmi la voye
En murmuroit tantost un long Io de joye,
Oyant le bruit meslé de toute la cité
Qui la porte en signal de sa felicité.
Croy doncq' qu'elle est jà preste aus premieres conquestes,
Qui des vieus ennemis doivent briser les testes.
Ne crain doncq' point, tu as des Deesses et Dieus
Comme nous, pour ta guide et faveur en tous lieus,
Ta femme est ta Junon, ta seur est ta Minerve,[110]
Qui le droit de la nostre à bon droit se reserve:
Et bien que nous n'eussions autre support sinon
Que celui de Pallas, et celui de Junon,
Tu as outre ces deus une tierce Deesse,
Une Diane archere, et chaste, et chasseresse.[111]
Ce bon Roy Navarrois son jeune frere encor[112]

110 Catherine de' Medici and Madame Marguerite. Both Juno and Minerva (Pallas) guided the Argonauts on their journey.

111 Diane de Poitiers.

112 Antoine de Bourbon, king of Navarre, and his younger brother, Louis Ier de Bourbon, prince of Condé. The latter, raised at court, was a favourite of Henry II and had a distinguished military career (Metz, Renty, Piedmont, etc.).

Te pourront bien servir de Pollux et Castor,
Ce grand vaincueur de Guise est ore ton Hercule,[113]
Qui sous toy, l'Espaignol outrepassant recule,
21r° Calaïs et Zethes sont deus freres qu'il a,[114]
De deus freres encor un chacun choisira
Le nom qu'il lui est propre,[115] et l'autre divin frere
Qui d'un double conseil les affaires modere
Avecq la pieté, sera ton grand Typhis
Gouverneur de la nef.[116] Mesme je voy ton fils,
Et d'autres jeunes Dieus, et tant d'autres Deesses,
Qui leurs faveurs rendront de tous malheurs maîtresses.
Voici nos rames, li dedans elles nos noms,
Et vien accommoder les noms des bons aus bons,
Nous les allons porter ensemble et leur navire
Là dedans, pour tousjours t'attendre, et te conduire
Par tout où il plaira à ta grand Majesté
Singler d'un voile plain de la prosperité.

Voilà qui estoit si mal fait, que je dirois volontiers que tous ceus qui ont pris l'occasion au poil[117] pour me peindre de toutes les couleurs qu'ils ont peu, devroient plus tost apprandre en telles choses qu'y reprandre, n'estoit que je me commande la modestie plus que jamais. Et aussi à la verité que je ne

113 François, duc de Guise. Cf. Icon XXXVI.

114 Claude de Lorraine, duc d'Aumale et grand véneur de la France, b. 1526, and Louis de Lorraine, Cardinal de Guise, b. 1527.

115 François de Lorraine, grand prieur et général des galères de France, b. 1534, and René de Lorraine, marquis d'Elbœuf, b. 1536.

116 Charles, Cardinal de Lorraine. Cf. pp. 176–7. Typhis was the steersman during the first part of the voyage of the Argonauts. (Unfortunately, he was later killed by a wild boar!)

117 A figurative expression derived from a common iconographical image, wherein *Occasio* is seized by her forelock in passing, but once past, is irretrievable since the rest of her scalp is bald.

l'estime point pareil à mes autres œuvres que j'ay faits à loisir, mais ayant eu si peu de tens, et en ce peu de tens tant d'occupations, je m'ebahi moymesme comme je l'ay fait de telle sorte, et où j'ay peu derober les heures pour le faire. Car j'ay cent tesmoins qui sçavent, que de ce que j'ay decrit, il m'a fallu soucier entierement de tout jusques à faire assoir la moindre feuille de lierre, tellement 21v^c
que tout ce que j'avois à reciter en ceste masquarade sous la personne de Jason, je le composay mesme ce jeudi au matin, et encores avois-je assés de tens pour en venir à bout,[118] n'estoit qu'on ne cessa tout ce jour là de me rompre la teste depuis le matin jusques au soir. Tant pour la nonchalance, mespris, ou ignorance que sembloient avoir ces Parisiens de ce qui leur pouvoit apporter honneur, que pour le continuel empeschement que de moment en moment les maneuvres me venoient donner. Qui pourroit croire en quel depit me mettoient quelques uns de ces messieurs, qui pensans comme je croy tout ce que je faisois estre des fariboles, sembloient ne se soucier que des choses dont leur cerveau se rend capable? Je sçay bien que l'on dira que je ne devois point entreprandre tant de choses, et que je me devois contenter de bien faire et mener à meilleure issue ce qu'on pouvoit principallement attendre de moy. Ceus qui parlent ainsi montrent bien le deffaut de nostre siecle, qui se contente seullement de sa simple apparence, comme si l'on devoit recueillir la feuille ou l'escorce pour le fruit ou pour le suc. Car qui est celui qui ait si peu de jugement, qui ne rie toutes les fois qu'il orra dire qu'on s'est si criminellement attaché à moy, en une chose qui n'estoit faite que pour plaisir et risée, et au rebours qu'on a laissé passer si legerement toutes le choses qui emportoient une durable memoire? Combien de fois aye-je veu bailler de main en main avecques cere- 22r^c
monie, reciter avecques admiration, recueillir avecques un soin nompareil, et louer avecques une affection extreme, des inscriptions qui peut estre estoient moindres que celles que j'ay dites, n'eust esté l'authorité qu'elles empruntoient de quelque vieille ruine? Toutesfois, tant la France est curieuse de ce qui est bon, chacun comme je croy les a passées sans les lire, et moitié par ignorance, moitié par malice, ceus qui n'ont esté que trop plains de parolles en ma faute, se

118 Cf. introduction, p. 6.

sont trouvés tous muets en mon merite. Mais prenons que ceste masquarade que j'avois faite toute telle que vous l'avés leüe, ayt esté la plus mal recitée qu'on sçauroit imaginer, en quoy peut-on avoir occasion de m'accuser? Si l'on me respond maintenant, pour ce qu'elle estoit mal faite, certainement je seray contraint de quiter ma cause, moyennant qu'on produise de quoy, mais encore que le monde soit aujourdhui autant impudent qu'il est possible, je croy que je ne trouveray point de telles impudences. Si l'on me dit, pour ce qu'elle estoit mal acoustrée, je tien deja mon proces pour tout gaigné, veu que chacun sçait bien que la juste colere de voir ce que j'avois ordonné si mal mis en œuvre, me mit à bon droit hors de moy. Car me sentant autheur, sentant l'expectation qu'on avoit de moy, et voir qu'on m'avoit fait au lieu de rochers des clochers,[119] qu'on m'avoit mequaniquement mesnagé les habits, qu'à l'heure mesme qu'il
22v° fallut partir plusieurs choses deffailloient, que peut-on penser que je devinse, si l'on connoist le grand cueur que j'ay, sinon furieus et demi mort, voyant apertement que j'estois contraint d'aller en un lieu, dont je ne pouvois rapporter pour toute recompanse, que ma courte honte et ma repentance eternelle? Si l'on dit, pourautant que les acteurs estoient mal choisis, quelle faute eut-on apercu en leur prolation naturelle, si l'asseurance et la memoire eussent esté de mesme? Et comment bon Dieu eussé-je cherché de bons acteurs, veu que les trois jours que j'avois d'espace se fussent coulés à les chercher? Mesmement comment eust-il esté possible que je les eusse peu façonner, veu que je ne les sceu seullement faire repeter ce qu'ils avoient à dire fors le jour mesme, et

119 This example has often been quoted with amusement. (Cf. Chamard, *Histoire de la Pléiade*, II, p. 295.) Since, however, the *rochers* obviously were completed in time and used (cf. below, p. 118), Balmas argues convincingly that Jodelle did not mean the remark to be taken literally, but rather as an ironic aside on the general incomprehension and poor technical realization of his conceptions by the executants. (Cf. E. Balmas, *Etienne Jodelle*, pp. 369–72.) Note that this comment is restricted to the 'machinery' and costumes relating to the mascarade; Jodelle has only the highest praise for the paintings and decorations executed by Me Baptiste (cf. above, p. 92) which formed the basis of the *Recueil des inscriptions*.

encore à demi, voire une seulle heure devant le souper ? Et lors de quel remede n'usay-je ? Ne retranchay-je pas tous leurs rooles de tout cela où je les voyois hesiter ? Que restoit-il donc de mon devoir, fors que d'estre Dieu et de commander à leur nature ? Si l'on dit que je me devois garder pour les conduire, sans faire moymesme l'une des personnes et sans m'abaisser jusques là, combien que j'y confesse avoir une grande faute, quelles raisonnables excuses n'ay-je point ? Premierement qui est celui qui eust appris la personne de Jason le jour mesme, comme le jour mesme je fu contraint de la faire ? Secondement sçait-on pas bien que pour ceste seulle cause que je m'y mettois, cinq ou six
gentils hommes miens amis furent des Argonautes muets, qui autrement n'en 23r°
eussent point esté, desquels je pensois decorer mon affaire, si un desastre incroyable ne l'eust empesché de se bien porter ? Tiercement qui doute que recitant moymesme avecques les autres, je ne peusse de beaucoup les soulager, si le desordre et l'extreme colere ne m'eussent fait du tout perdre ? Et qui est celui qui ignore combien de plus grands que moy se sont mis en France sur le theatre devant sa mesme majesté ? Si l'on dit, que combien que la multitude et le desordre fust si grand, qu'on ne pouvoit quasi se remuer dedans la salle, si est ce que je n'avois pas preveu que je ferois croistre le desordre, faisant porter deus rochers et une grande navire avecques son mas bien fort long, par une entrée assés estroite, et dedans une salle qui n'est pas des plus spatieuses, qui seront ceus qui m'escoutans un peu, ne seront aussi tost contraints de m'absoudre à bon droit, comme en ceci ils m'auront voulu condamner à tort ? Car quand à l'entrée j'y avois si bien preveu et pourveu, que les rochers n'estoient point plus longs qu'il falloit, et que le mas de la navire s'ostoit et se replantoit aussi soudain qu'on vouloit. Quand à la salle on m'avoit asseuré que les napes estants levées, les tables des deus costés s'abbatroient, et que le Roy avecques sa compaignie tenant tout ce hault qu'on avoit fait plancheyer pour eus, tout le reste se rangeroit des deus costés devers le hault,
tellement que la moitié presque de la salle me demeureroit tout vuide. Ainsi 23v°
chacun eust veu à son aise toute la masquarade, sans qu'elle eust esté comme elle fut demi cachée dedans la troupe, mesme ceus qui avoient à prononcer, estant là comme dedans un theatre, ne se fussent pas si tost troublés, comme

ils firent, estans quasi comme perdus dedans ceste multitude, et parlans jusques contre la face du Roy. Si l'on me dit qu'encore que tous les autres se deussent troubler, et mal faire leur devoir, que je devois pour le moins moy qui estois l'autheur, demeurer constant, et en bien faisant reparer aucunement la faute des autres: je respondray deus choses, premierement qu'il estoit impossible que je le fisse, secondement si je l'eusse fait, que j'eusse mal fait. Car quand au premier, comment se pourroit-il faire qu'un homme s'estant tourmenté par quatre jours, ayant quasi perdu le repos de toutes les nuits, s'estant mille fois extremement faché de ne voir son entreprise aller selon son desir, ayant la memoire enbrouillée d'une meslange et confusion de choses qui toutes se tiroient d'un mesme tonneau, appellé à l'execution de son affaire avant quasi que d'estre à demi prest, hasté par l'importune cririe et par la necessité sans aucun ordre et consideration, renversé et voyant renverser ses gens l'un sus l'autre à l'entrée du lieu où il falloit aller, ayant esté fort malade environ une heure devant et se trouvant encore fort mal dedans le lieu mesme,
24r° estant contraint d'attendre ses gents un à un, et voyant tous ses appareils rompus avant que d'en rien faire, voyant demeurer des choses necessaires par le desordre, ne trouvant presque point de place pour le reste, voyant dès le commencement par la faute d'une musique se naistre une rizée, voyant mesme qui est le pire du jeu les premiers interlocuteurs qu'il avoit soulagés et asseurés faillir outre son esperance, eust peu tellement se commander à soymesme, que de donter le courrous, l'apprehension, et la honte, et au lieu de crever et desirer d'estre cent piés sous terre, montrer un visage impudent et une vois de meurdrier entre tant de fautes, qui n'eussent pas laissé pour tout cela de lui estre imputées? Il me semble, pour venir au second point, que s'il fust avenu ainsi que je vien de dire, que j'eusse esté mille fois plus coupable que je ne suis, veu que chacun eust pensé que demeurant paisible et asseuré, je n'eusse point connu les fautes: et quand à moy j'ay esté tousjours de ce naturel, de recevoir plus tost sur moy tous les blames du monde, que l'ignorance ou la crainte. Mesme je fay juges tous ceus qui me virent en telle pene, s'il n'estoit pas facile de connoistre à ma morte contenance, qu'il n'i avoit rien qui me reserrast tous les sens, que le juste depit, qui eut pour lors telle force sur moy, que je ne

sçavois si j'estois moy. Mais qui seroit bon Dieu celui là qui m'ayant connu le moins du monde, et m'ayant veu en tout autant asseuré qu'on sçauroit estre, pourroit penser que c'eust esté par un estonnement que les grands me pou- 24v°
voient donner, veu que je suis tous les jours entre eus, et que devant eus j'ay autrefois tant asseurement recité? Se pourroit-il encore trouver quelcun, qui en accusast la memoire et ma trop grande fiance en icelle, veu que je ne fay jamais vers, que je ne sçache aussi tost par cueur que je les ay faits?[120] Je deduirois encore plusieurs autres points, qui feroient autant tourner le tout en ma louange, comme quelques uns ont tâché de le faire tourner en mon vitupere, n'estoit qu'il me semble, que j'ay deja passé toutes les bornes de raison en ceste mienne forme d'apologie, que je ne me suis sceu tenir d'entrelasser ici: et qu'en estant si long je ferois penser à un chacun que la faute auroit esté beaucoup plus grande, et de plus grand deshonneur à moy qu'elle n'a esté. Or sçachent donq' tant les nostres que les estrangers, si ceci vient jusques en leurs mains, que combien que ceste masquarade ne fust point ni conduite ni recitée, comme je le desirois, si est-ce toutesfois, affin qu'on ne pense point que du tout nous demeurasmes, qu'elle fut entirement prononcée, excepté ce que j'en avois retranché paravant, tellement que le deffault seroit le plus petit qu'on sçauroit dire, n'estoit que par l'extreme apprehension que j'en ay eüe, je me le suis moymesmes agrandi, tant la presence d'un Roy m'est sainte, et tant la moindre faute que je puisse faire, m'a semblé grande et prejudiciable de tout tens. Qu'on sçache aussi, que quand on se fust du tout arresté, sans en pro- 25r°
noncer un seul vers, que la chose n'eust pas esté moins louable à cause de l'invention, veu que coustumierement toutes telles mascarades sont muetes, qui pourtant n'ont point moins de grace: et qui plus est quand elle n'eust rien valu, ni quand à l'invention, ni quand à l'action, que je ne m'en deusse aucunement soucier, ni penser que la gloire de mes autres inventions en fust amoindrie, veu que c'est une chose qui ne fait seullement que passer pour un leger plaisir, et de laquelle on ne se doit soucier qu'à l'heure presente. Mais qu'on sçache aussi, que pour autant que Dieu m'a donné le cueur tel, que j'endurerois aussi tost un elephant en mon œil qu'une tache en mon honneur, il m'a

120 Cf. introduction, p. 6.

esté impossible de me garder d'user de beaucoup de parolles en ceci, veu que ni ma raison ni les raisons de tous mes amis ne m'ont persuadé qu'à grand peine que ce desastre fust peu de chose. Aussi que j'ay bien voulu en alongeant mon propos montrer la pure verité du fait, affin qu'usant de longue confutation en une faute petite, je face aussi reconnoistre à toute la France sa faute acoustumée, qui en ce siecle se montrant et ingrate et envieuse tout ensemble, au lieu de supporter les bons esprits qui l'honorent, ouvre les yeus le plus severement qu'elle peut sur leurs moindres vices, et s'aveugle incessamment en toutes leurs vertus. Après que nous eusmes tellement quellement achevé ceste masquarade qui estoit environ de quatorze personnes, à sçavoir celles
25v° qui ont parlé avecq' dix autres Argonautes tous habillés à la matelote antique de blanc et de noir, qui sont les couleurs du Roy,[121] nous en fismes entrer une autre qui ne parloit point, que j'avois devisée en telle sorte que la premiere ayant esté des couleurs du Roy, ceste ci seroit des couleurs de la Royne qui sont blanc et verd,[122] ce qui fut assés bien executé selon mon vouloir. Les personnes estoient, la Vertu, la seconde la Victoire, la troisiesme la deesse Mnemosyne, qui signifie la Memoire: desquelles la Vertu fort richement acoustrée à l'antique de mesme sorte que les deus autres, avoit son acoustrement semé d'estoilles, la Victoire de trophées, et la Memoire de serpens mordans leur queue. Avecques elles devoient estre trois enfans nuds, comme si ce fussent

121 The colours black and white were chosen by Henry II to compliment Diane de Poitiers, who never wore anything else after the death of her husband, Louis de Brézé, in 1531; they were later adopted by Catherine de' Medici after Henry's own death in 1559, despite the fact that court etiquette prescribed white mourning for the Queen of France. Cf. Icones XLV–XLVI. However, Henry's penchant for black may originally have been a result of the captivity in Spain after Pavia.

122 Both colour combinations are documented at least as early as the Lyon Entry of 23–4 September 1548. Barthélemy Aneau's gloss on Alciati's Emb. CXVIII *In colores* (ed. 1549, p. 145) comments: 'Les devises, et signifiances des couleurs sont à plaisir selon les affections des personnes. Mais toutesfois les meilleurs sont celles, qui le plus pres approchent du naturel. Comme le blanc de innocence, le rouge de honte, le noir, de dueil, ou mort, le verd d'esperance, et aultres telles.'

esté de petits Amours ou de petits Jesus, dont les deus portoient deus paniers à l'antique façon, plains de toutes fleurs et parfuns meslés ensemble, avecques des eufs vuidés et remplis de toutes bonnes eaus de senteurs pour jeter deça dela pesle mesle et parfumer toute la compaignie. Le tiers devoit avoir son panier plain de couronnes arrangées l'une sur l'autre, selon l'ordre de ceus et celles à qui l'on les devoit presenter, et ausquels chacune couronne estoit propre: comme au Roy la couronne de laurier, tant pour ce que nous le faisons aujourdui le Phebus de la terre, que pource qu'après tant de victoires nous le voyons de rechef si bravement vaincre: à la Royne une couronne de palme, laquelle elle porte mesme en l'une de ses devises: à Madame seur du 26r°
Roy une couronne d'olive, pour ce que nous la pouvons justement nommer nostre Pallas, à qui l'olive a esté anciennement sacrée, et pour ce qu'elle mesme en a pris la devise, portant dedans une targue Palladienne le chef de Gorgonne: à monseigneur de Guise la couronne de peuplier, qui est celle dont Hercule se couronnoit après ses combats, et que prenoient mesme les anciens vaincueurs après avoir gaigné le pris dessus Olympe: à monseigneur le reverendissime Cardinal de Lorraine une couronne de lierre, pour ce que luimesme en sa devise se fait le lierre embrassant tout à lentour ceste grande Pyramide des François, qui commence deja de porter et son chef et sa renommée jusques dedans le ciel: à madame la duchesse de Valentinois la couronne ou de laurier ou de fleurs, l'une pour ce que Diane se peut bien couronner de la couronne de son frere, et que le laurier est tousjours appellé chaste à cause de Daphné, l'autre que ses nimphes lui peuvent faire dedans les bois lors qu'elle va chasser: à Monsieur, à monsieur de Lorraine, à la Royne d'Escoce, à Mesdames, des couronnes de mirte, qui sont les couronnes de l'Amour. Toutes ces couronnes devoient estre prises par la Vertu dedans le panier de l'enfant, et presentées par elle mesme de la sorte que j'ay dite, en la presence de la Victoire et de la Memoire, dont la premiere pour nous avoir esté tant favorable, estoit la cause 26v°
d'un tel present, et la seconde estoit pour en rendre perpetuel tesmoignage à la posterité. Ce present fait la Vertu avecques une harangue convenable à cela, devoit prier le Roy de la mener dancer, et les deus autres Deesses deus autres Princes, tellement que la dance commenceant devoit faire passer le reste de

l'après-soupée en telle rejouissance, qui est la fin coustumiere de tous les festins. Ceste derniere masquarade eust merveilleusement pleu, si l'on eust fait tout ainsi que je vien de dire, et ainsi qu'on sçait que je l'avois arresté, mais au lieu d'enfans nuds, les Parisiens mirent de leurs enfans vestus et bien peu deguisés, tellement que les ailes et les trousses que devoient avoir ces Amours, demeurerent au peintre. Quand aus couronnes encore que j'eusse dit que si l'on n'en trouvoit de naturelles, qu'on en fist contrefaire de toutes les sortes, on n'en recouvra pas une, fors celle de laurier pour le Roy encore qui fut apportée bien tard. On ne scauroit dire combien je fu marri de ceste negligence, tant pour ce que ce present eust esté merveilleusement agreable, que pour autant que j'avois deliberé de faire escrire le plus proprement que l'on eust peu, dedans un lien de tafetas qui eust lié les couronnes, un vers ou deus vers au plus, accommodés à tel present. Et me souvient que j'avois deja fait ces deus pour la couronne du Roy.

Magna tIbI Capto ConCessIt CVra CaLeto,
CINGE COMAS, SIMILES IANVS ET ANNVS ERVNT,[123]

27r° Le premier de ces deus vers est numeraire, et pour autant que le second contient, que toute ceste année sera autant heureuse qu'en a esté le premier mois, tant que le Roy se doit à bon droit couronner, j'ay compris dedans les

123 With Calais captured, a great care has left you, so crown your hair; the whole year's course shall be like its opening month.

In this numerical distichon, the letters IVLCM in the first line when re-arranged give MCCCCCLVIII (1558), the year of the capture of Calais. There are many examples of poems of this kind but Jodelle was undoubtedly inspired by a gold medal struck during the reign of Charles VII. (See fig. 36.) On the obverse side is the legend DOR.FIN.SVIS. EXTRAIT.DE.DVCAS.ET.FV.FAIT. PESANT.VIII.CARAS.EN.L'AN. QVE.VERRAS.MOI.TOVRNANT.LES. LETTRES.DE.NOMBRE.PRENANT. When one adds up the same letters extracted from the legend on the reverse side (QVANT.IE.FV.FAIT. SANS.DIFERANCE.AV.PRVDENT. ROI.AMI.DE.DIEU.ON.OBEISSOIT. PAR.TOUT.EN.FRANCE.FORS.A. CALAIS.QUI.EST.FORT.LIEV.), they give the year 1451. (This medal also

letres numeraires du premier ce nombre mil cinq cens cinquante huit, qui est le nombre de nostre année. Tous les autres vers qui devoient estre dedans les autres couronnes demeurerent à faire comme les couronnes à recouvrer. Le reste de la masquerade se porta tellement que je croy que la compaignie ne s'en mescontanta point. Voila comme je pense, tout ce qui se peut recueillir de tout le labeur que j'avois pris pour penser me montrer, en une si belle occasion, curieus de l'honneur de mon païs, et affectionné au service de mon Prince. Il ne me reste plus rien maintenant, fors de m'adresser avecques toute l'affection que je puis, aus majestés, hautesses, et excellences, des Princes, Princesses, grands seigneurs, et grands dames de ce Royaume, pour les suplier tres-humblement, puisque ayans esté tous spectateurs de mon œuvre ils en pourront bien aussi s'en faire lecteurs, de me faire droit en ceste cause: et après avoir à l'imitation des dieus, receu la volonté pour le fait, et l'ordonnance pour l'execution, ne souffrir plus dore en avant, que les calomnies des envieus tachent à me faire demeurer sus la teste ce que je ne meritay jamais. Les as-
seurant, que toutes les fois qu'ils voudront user de mon labeur en plus grandes 27v°
choses, et que le juste espace du tens me permetra, de faire aussi bien que j'y auray de pouvoir et de vouloir, je feray paroistre à tous ceus, qui dernierement ont si bien demasqué leurs fausses volontés encontre moy, que l'envie qu'on a sur la Vertu, ne raporte point d'autre fin, ni d'autre loyer à son homme, fors que le contraire de son attente, et la perpetuelle rage de sa vie. Je chastirois bien autrement ces messieurs, en la fin de ce recueil, n'estoit que je ne veus point irriter les grands par cela, ni donner la moindre occasion à ces escumeurs des œuvres vertueuses, de faire par ce moyen trouver mauvais ce qui ne peut deplaire qu'à trois sortes de gens: à ceus qui sont si stupides qu'ils ne peuvent rien sentir: à ceus qui sont si degoustés qu'ils ne peuvent rien savourer: à ceus qui sont si malins qu'ils tachent de faire perdre le sentiment et le goust des autres. Si ne les laisseray-je point si tost echaper, sans leur protester par

exists in a slightly different, smaller module with the legend PESANT.III. CARAS.) Cf. F. Mazerolle, *Les médailleurs français du XVe siècle au milieu du XVIIe*, II, Paris, 1902, cat. 1–2.

le vray Dieu, que si jamais ils s'attaquent injustement à moy, je hazarderay plus tost et l'esprit, et le cors, et les fortunes, que je ne leur face connoistre, que l'homme de bien doit aussi tost mourir de mille morts, que d'estre une seulle fois trahistre à sa vertu. Ce qui me garde aussi de me piquer davantage contre eus, c'est que je croy certainement que toutes telles gens ne m'ont aucunement connu. Car qui est celui si mal né, qui me voyant franc et sincere en toute chose, et sans aucune envie, ambition, dissimulation, ou tromperie
28r° me vendre et me dependre moymesme pour l'ami, ait peu tellement forcer sa conscience que tâcher de me nuire? Qui est celui aussi, qui sçachant que j'ay tousjours fait, et que je feray tant que je vivray, un bouclier de ma vie pour sauver mon honneur, mesme qu'ayant receu de Dieu plus d'un moyen pour faire repantir ceus qui me feront tort, j'aymeray tousjours mieus crever que de ne prandre vengeance de telles injustices, ayt esté tant ennemi de soymesme, que de me vouloir estre ennemi sans raison? Quand à quelques bestes et quelques imposteurs que je sçay, qui ont à ce coup decouvert leur venin, pour autant que je decouvrois par tout leur maladie, qu'ils attendent pour tout certain de moy, ce qu'ils ont ordinairement connu en ma nature: c'est que j'ay tousjours tant aymé ma nation, que je ne la souffriray jamais deshonorer par je ne sçay quels fatras dont on brouille le papier, et encores moins piper par impostures: Et pour autant qu'en poursuivant trop hastivement un vice, on en encourt le plus souvent un autre j'attendray que leur honte et confusion se meurisse. Je reserveray aussi à dire de bouche, au tens et au lieu qu'il faudra, les indignités premierement, et secondement l'ingratitude, desquelles ceus mesme pour qui je faisois, ont usé envers moy, ne voulant point faire part aus estrangers de la barbarie des nostres. Je supliray seullement de tout mon cueur ma ville dont je vien de parler, ou plus tost au lieu de ma ville toute la France, de n'estre plus tant ennemie de soymesme, qu'on lui puisse à bon droit reprocher qu'elle abuse ordinairement de tous ses meilleurs
28v° esprits. Je jure Dieu, que la resouvenance des pitiés que j'en ay veües, me fait presque venir la larme à l'œil, et me semble que j'oy les plaintes, et les execrations de nos bons vieus peres, que Dieu a retirés de ce monde, qui n'ayans point eu en leur siecle la felicité que nous avons, detestent la meconnoissance et la

perversité du nostre. Que l'on reconnoisse donques si nous ne sommes du tout aveuglés, ce bon heur que Dieu nous donne, que l'on acquiere ce thresor, que l'on jouisse de ceste volupté, qu'on reçoive et qu'on gouste ce qu'on cherche et qu'on desire, qui est le moyen de se perpetuer: et si tu voulus jamais rien faire pour toy ô France, je te prie et reprie de rechef, que tu faces aus letres et à la vertu le traitement, dont toymesme tu les confesses estres dignes. Et allors encore que je fusse le plus miserable de tous, un si heureus changement me servant d'assés suffisante recompanse, m'encouragera de telle sorte et moy et mes semblables, que la bonté de tes Princes, ne doit esperer de nous une moindre recompanse, que l'accroissement de leur gloire, la commodité de leur vie, et l'immortalité de leur renommée.

FIN

CHRISTIANORVM NOSTRI TEMPORIS HEROVM, ET HEROINARVM ICONES.

Ad D. Margaritam Francicam. Avthore Steph. Iodelio Parisio.[124]

LECTORI[125]

Hic nondum absolutus Iconum libellus, hac ratione Typographo dandus esse videbatur, ut hæ aliquot quas nuper incœperam, Heroïcarum imaginum inscriptiones, prioribus quas legisti inscriptionibus adderentur. Maxime cum singulos Icones, sicut et inscriptiones alias, tribus versibus comprehenderim. Nec mireris quod in hoc toto libello, Latina Gallicis coniunxerim: id enim in quibusdam aliis libris data opera facere volui, ut et ea quæ Gallice scribo, pure ut arbitror latinitati commixta, tandem aliquando, quod paucis adhuc contigit, ad exteras nationes transire possint. Minus etiam te mirari velim, quod paucis istis imaginibus, tot versus ad hanc illustrissimam Principem scriptos præposuerim: cum hi non in istas imagines tantummodo, sed in integrum opus, dum erit perfectum, præfationis vice scripti sint. Si nostrum hoc qualecunque

124 The images of the Christian heroes and heroines of our age; to the Lady Marguerite of France. By Estienne Jodelle; Parisian.

125 See pp. 128–9 for the translation.

est Iconum initium, gratissimum tibi, ac Principibus nostris acceptissimum esse sensero, nommodo cæteros clarissimorum nostri temporis Heroum Icones, verum innumeros, et qui vix a me sperari potuissent ingenii mei labores, quam citissime fieri poterit, emittam, ne tuam illam, quam sustinere videor expectatione, simul ac futuram nostri fortasse nominis gloriam, tardius quam oporteat differens uno et eodem obitu me et opera mea sentiam interire. Tu interim si quis in te est candor, candidissimum tuum poetam, semper ut debes ama, huic bene imprecare, et ita vale.

TO THE READER.

It seemed that I ought to hand over this still unfinished book of Icones to the printer, in order that to the former 'inscriptions,' which you have read, there should be added those few 'inscriptions' upon the portraits of heroes which I had lately begun; especially since I have confined each single Icon, like the other inscriptions, within a limit of three lines. Nor should you be surprised that within the compass of this book as a whole I have combined Latin with French items; for I have deliberately done this in certain other books, so that even those things which I write in French, being mixed up with good Latin – as I believe – may at length penetrate to foreign nations, which is something that so far has happened to but few. Also, I would not wish you to be surprised that to these few Icones, I have prefixed so many verses written to this famed Princess of ours, since these verses have been penned as a preface not merely to the Icones in question but to the entire work, pending its completion. If I come to feel that this my beginning of the Icones, such as it is, is fully acceptable to you and quite favourably received by our rulers, I shall publish as quickly as possible not only the remaining Icones of the most famous heroes of our time but also countless products of my talent, such as could hardly have been looked for from me, in order that I may not delay more than necessary your expectations of me – expectations I seem to detect, together with the future renown, it may be, of my own name – and so feel that I and my works are perishing in a common demise. For the present, if you have any fair and friendly feeling in you, be ever kindly, as you should, to your honest poet, and wish him good fortune; and so farewell.

AD D. MARGARITAM FRANCICAM[126]

Quo me grande meæ numenque decusque iuventæ
Margari, quo præceps, varios ubi carmina fluctus
Nostra mihi movere, furor vertitque rapitque,
Damnatum toties repetens opus? Ergo potentes
Spernentemque aulas, spretumque potentibus aulis,
Torpentem merito, æternumque incœpta prementem,
Tangat honos, angatque labor, spes fallat alatque
Improba, ut emeritus tandem, studioque tenaci
Turpe trahens senium, curis corrodar, et omnis
Nomine ditatum censu sensuque carentem,
Cum desperanda fugiat mercede voluptas,
Libertasque, quiesque aulis regalibus exul?
Sic lætos Aquilo nautas, Bellona quietos
Agricolas, tutosque lues agit horrida cives
Ut ratis, ut labor, ut pereat deserta supellex.
Quin potius me ruris honos, urbisque moretur
30v° Mollities, et lætus Amor, et lætior Evan:
Quin placeant lætæque domus, choreæque, salesque,
Balnea, confusæque dapes, pila, discus, et arcus,
Ac buxo simulata ducum certamina, tali,
Saltatorque recens, et quæ spectanda theatris
Scena placet: Quin et placeant agrestia Fauni

126 For a translation of this poem see p. 134. For a detailed commentary cf. E. Balmas, *Etienne Jodelle*, pp. 387–91.

Numina, Pan, Driades, et Naiades amnibus udæ,
Flava Ceres, viridisque Pales, variataque Flora,
Et Pomona rubens, et candida Cynthia sylvis,
Sylvarumque meis gratæ venatibus umbræ,
Fontesque fluviique, pecusque et rustica dona.
Hic aderunt sociique pares, superique faventes,
Quæque renascentem perimunt in limine curam
Transactæ simul et venturæ oblivia sortis,
Ac grandes imo ducti de splene cachinni,
Queis mihi Regales populorum fabula luxus,
Queis vanescentis vilescant somnia vitæ.
Aut potius si deses et hæc ingloria vita
Crimen habet, si sera parit satiata voluptas
Tedia, si Nemesin, Furias, Epimethida, secum
Accelerata trahit luxu instigante senectus:
Arma meos (nam legiferum sic stamen et ardor
Nativus iubet) arma meos stimulantia cogant
Exodisse lares, ac me mihi dulcis Enio
In flammas, in tela vocet, placidumque cruorem:
Nec litui tantum sonus aut stips Regia tantum,
Sed me magnarum accendant exordia rerum,
Quo fortasse vocor, ubi me fortasse morantem
Tardior expectat positis fortuna flagellis. 31r°
Thracius hic aderit pater, et Tritonia belli
Præses, et arma licet non curet Athlanteus Hermes,
Hi linguam, reget ille manus, ut natus utrique
Palladi, Diis ducibus faciam mihi nomen utraque.
Vel si semper honos, et opes, et laurea diro
Carmine devotum fugiant, cum Martis in arte
Magnanimo sit vita brevis, miseroque perire
Dulce sit, hic aderit quæ me iuvet Atropos, et quæ
Blanda necis cupidum necet, iniustamque sororum

Sævitiam, crimenque indignum munere penset
Æqua suo, fatoque brevi fata impia vincat.
Est in Morte salus, Mortem fecere dolores
Esse malum, dolor omnis abest si morbus et absit,
Non patitur qui felle tumens, qui sanguine fervens,
Dum fera pugna placet, totusque cupidine laudis
Uritur, atrocique nihil dum lumine cernit,
Pectore nil timet, accenso nil corpore sentit,
Aut misso furtim plombo, aut stridente sagitta,
Incautus cadit: at patitur qui dæmone frætus
Dexteriore, suis nativa laboribus auctus
Munera, Musarumque potens, sollersque sagaxque,
Dum sacras videt irrideri Regibus artes,
Pauperiemque, suoque horret in limine Diras,
Semotus lento præcordia roditur igne,
Mille sub ingratis referens recidiva Camœnis
Vulnera, et insani videat cum damna laboris
In pœnas semper ruit excruciandus easdem,
31v° Consultusque trahit sua fata, sciensque, cavensque.
Sic ego: namque videns discrimina certa, ruensque
In meliora, feror, feror ad consueta coactus,
Quæ quoque nunc inter tot gaudia ruris et urbis,
Inter et arma sequi dulcis nunc cogeret error.
Quid facerem? Deus ecce Deus, quam magna Deum vis,
Invitum ruit in pectus, concussa tremiscunt
Membra, fugit color, et rigidi stant vertice crines,
Erumpit quo tota tument mea viscera Phœbus:
Danda via est, mora nulla, rudis ludibria vulgi,
Et fastus procerum, et Regum fastidia, vati
Sustinuisse dolor gravis: at sacra munera divum
Fallere, torquerique mora, nec Numine rumpi,
Ter tria legitimum poscant ceu sydera partum,

Et dolor et scelus est. Sed cum mihi Numen abundet
Margari, quod maiora inter sacraria Galli
Ac magni Elysia stupeant in valle Quirites,
Materies nos ipsa fugit, fluviumque fugacem
Nequicquam sequor in medio ceu Tantalus amne,
Meque ea pœna manet nova. Nam quid Regibus istis
Quid contemptrici sanum meditabimur aulæ?
Iamque monet Deus. Extremis ubi dives ab Indis
Mercator rediens, patrias rate rupit arenas,
Quas circunfusis merces in littore primum
Civibus, e gravida laudator nave recludat,
Nescit adhuc, sic turba ruens, sic ardor ementum
Impedit. Hic Tyrio saturatas murice lanas,
Et peregrina suæ petit ornamenta puellæ:
Huic adamas, huic chrisolitus, viridisque smaragdus 32r°
Gemmificaque placent vulsi de rupe lapilli:
Ille Sabea Deum gratissima munera templis
Thura petit, Tmolique petit flaventis odores,
Et dives quæ metit Arabs felicibus arvis:
Hi variis quæsit a petunt animalia terris,
Pellesve, unguesve, aut niveis cum dentibus ossa:
Hic quoque non uno natos e semine fœtus,
Ac dulces succos simul, arboreamque medullam,
Salubres et Apollineis cupit artibus herbas.
Hic merces, hic damnat iter, probat alter utrumque,
Ille premit, ferit ille ferox, petulantior alter
Irruit: hic totum simulans verbosus Eoum
Velle sibi, redit ad vacuas sine mercibus ædes,
Qui loculos vacuus prius ad commercia venit:
Hic coniunx amplexa virum sobolesque parentem,
Et grati comitem revocant a plebe sodales.
Fit strepitus fit pugna virum, ferit æthera clamor

Nauticus, et variæ turbant nova gaudia rixæ.
Quid faciat? Iam thura capit, navemque relinquens,
Vota soluturum se se prius indicat, ullas
Quam populo vendat spreto sic Numine merces.
Civibus hæc pietas placet, et discedente caterva
Ingreditur sacra templa pius, supplexque memorque
Auspicibus dat thura Deis. Mihi plurima Graium
Romuleumque gravi quæsita labore per æquor
Munera, Francigenæ properant ad littora gentis.
Iamque Notos faciles, afflataque carbasa, Galli,
32v° Fecundæque procul insignia læta carinæ,
Ex alta videre Pharo: sed noxius ardor,
Qui solo saturat ferventia pectora visu,
Vulgus iners, et Livor iter qui culpet opesque,
Et voces variæ, et rerum variata cupido,
Rixæque, clamorque ingens, cæcique tumultus,
Ingrato miserum expectant in littore nautam.
Iamque hic Meoniæ turgentia carmina Clius,
Et grandes petet Iliadas: cui triste theatrum,
Funestæque placent regum infortunia clades,
Horribiles monitus volet, aptandumque cothurnis
Carmen atrox, dignumque hirci mercede salacis.
Hic servos, iuvenumque faces, matresque patresque,
Hic Satyram et fixos sibi quæret acumine mores,
Ille lyram, petet ille leves ab arundine versus,
Ille elegos et dulce leget sibi carmen amorum.
Omniaque illa petent nonnulli forsitan, ex his
Qui nil vel cupiant, vel emant, laudentve, legantve.
Seu quod torpor eos, rudis aut inscitia ledat.
Omnia sunt mihi, sique mihi nunc omnia desint,
Numen adest, quo cuncta calens agitante cœgi:
Sed dare thura iubet, mercesque recludere nostras,

Donec placatis commercia prospera Divis
Agrediar, pro muneribus venalibus olim
Dum laudem populus, dum reddet et aula favorem.
En igitur mea thura, meis en fumat acerra
Numinibus. Vos o pavido bona Numina Vati,
Si qua Deos pietas movet et libamen, adeste
Magnanimi heroes. Tuque o cui prima sororum 33r°
Calliope, cui legipotens cum Pallade Virgo
Concessere, tuo cui fas dare iura poëtæ,
Diva fave, facilesque Deos mihi redde litanti:
Ut te te duce, post aliquot Regumque Ducumque
Eiconas, tot divitiis tua Gallia partis,
Seque suosque beet: nec iam de versibus, aula,
Phœboque gratisque queam post sæva Camœnis
Damna queri: sed laude ferar sublimior et re,
Iconemque meum claris Iconibus addam.

TO THE LADY MARGUERITE OF FRANCE.

O Margaret – potent godhead and glory of my youth – whither does the poetic frenzy whirl and guide me headlong, even when my poems have aroused diverse storms about me, returning to the work so often condemned before? And am I to be touched by honour, I who spurn the courts of potentates and by these courts am shunned in my turn; who deservedly lie in listless languor and endlessly suppress the task I have begun; and is toil to pain me, then, and restless hope deceive and nourish me, so that, having finished my task at length and by my dogged toil brought distasteful old age upon myself, I may be eaten up by cares and so from me – enriched with all honour but lacking wealth and my bodily senses, – every pleasure may depart, together with the reward I must despair of, and also freedom, and that peace of mind which is a stranger to royal courts? So does the North Wind harry successful mariners, and the

War-God upset men of peace at their farming, and so does dire disease harry secure citizens; to the ruin and loss of the ship, the farmer's toil, and the property abandoned in a plague. Nay, rather let the honour of the countryside and the soft ease of city life detain me; and joyous love, and Bacchus more joyous still; let prosperous houses please me, and dances and witty jests; baths, and rich banquets, the ball, the discus and the bow, and the reproduction upon the boxwood pipe of the quarrels of men of war; the dice, and the lively dances, and the scene that gives pleasure when acted in the theatre. Yet, too, let the country's gods give me pleasure – the Fauns, Pan, the Dryads, and Naiads dripping from their streams, yellow Ceres, green Pales, and Flora in her many colours, with Pomona glowing apple-red, and Diana moon-white in the glades, and the forest-shades that please me in the chase; and the springs and the rivers, flocks and herds, and the country's gifts. Here shall we have equal-minded companions and the favour of gods above, and such things as abolish care on the very threshold at the moment of its re-birth; and forgetfulness of our past lot, together with oblivion towards that which is to come; and loud laughter drawn from the very bottom of the spleen, by which I shall consider as trivial the luxury of kings, whereof men tell foolish tales, and all the dreams of this transient life. But if it be rather this idle and inglorious life of mine that is reproachable, if sated pleasure begets tardy loathing for itself, if old age brings with it Nemesis, the Furies, and Epimetheus' daughter[127] at a quickened pace, prompted by luxury; then let arms – for this is what I am bidden, both by the thread of my destiny and by my inborn high spirit – let arms, I say, prompt and command me to loathe my home, and Enyo,[128] which is sweet to me, must call me to fire and sword and to delight in bloodshed; and I would not that the mere sound of the trumpet, or the King's pay alone, should inspire me, but rather the outset of mighty deeds, to which perchance I am summoned, and where perchance delayed good fortune awaits me, having put aside her whips of chastisement. Here shall I be accompanied by the Thracian father,[129] and

127 Pyrrha? Cf. Ovid, *Metamorphoses* I, 390.

128 The horrors of war, assimilated to Bellona by the Romans. Cf. Ronsard, *Œuvres* (STFM), V, p. 175, V. I.

129 Orpheus.

Triton's daughter who presides over war,[130] and Hermes, grandson of Atlas, though he care not for arms; these latter shall guide my tongue, and the first of them shall guide my hand, so that, as son of both, I may make myself a name in either way[131] with Pallas and the two gods to lead me. Or if, cursed by an evil spell, I am to be shunned by honour and wealth and the laurel crown, then since in the pursuit of war a brave man's life is short and to the unhappy man to die is pleasant, Atropos[132] will be at hand to help me and of her kindness to slay me when I wish to be slain; and may she compensate for the cruel savagery and wicked crime of her sisters by justly exercising her function, and so overcome an unkind fate by the swiftness of my death. In death there is salvation; for it is pain that causes death to be an evil, and all pain is absent if disease also be absent. He who does not feel the swelling growth of poison, who is glowing with healthy blood while the fierce fight pleases and he is entirely consumed with the desire for glory, and sees nothing with a darkened eye; he it is who fears nothing in his heart, and feels nothing in his excited body; whether he falls from the leaden bullet stealthily aimed, or the whistling arrow, he falls unheeding; while that man suffers indeed who, relying on a happier fate, increased in Nature's gifts by his own exertions and endowed with the arts of the Muses, and being both clever and wise, is tortured in his heart by a slow fire, alone and in isolation, when he sees the holy Arts scorned by kings; he trembles at poverty and the onset of the Furies within his own home; he receives a thousand recurring wounds from the Muses' ingratitude, and though he sees the losses occasioned by mad toil he ever rushes into the same punishments to be tortured again; and thus, purposely and knowingly and with foresight, he brings his own fate upon himself. So it is with me: for, seeing the dangers clearly marked, and rushing on to better things, I am borne ahead; borne by compulsive force towards my familiar occupations, which even now among so many joys of town and country life, and even now among the clash of arms, my cherished folly would oblige me to pursue. What was I

130 Minerva (Pallas Athene).

131 i.e. by performance or original composition.

132 The Fate who cuts the thread of life.

to do? Lo, it is a god, even a god – how great is the power of gods! – who rushes into my unwilling heart, and causes my limbs to shake and tremble; my cheeks grow pale, and upon my head the hairs stand upright; Apollo rushes out where all my entrails swell; a way must be opened – no delay! –; I am the laughing-stock of the untutored mob, and the scorn of the lordly; a pain, this, hard for a poet to endure; but to cheat the holy functions of gods, and to be tortured by delay and not broken by the god, as if the nine stars were demanding to be born in regular fashion, is both painful and a crime. Yet since I have godhead enough, O Margaret, for the Gauls to wonder at, among their exalted shrines, and for the mighty Romans to gape at in the vale of Elysium, my very subject itself eludes me, and in vain do I seek to follow the fleeing river, like Tantalus in mid-stream, wherein consists a new punishment that awaits me. For what true note shall I rehearse for yonder kings or their sneering courtiers? And now 'tis a god that prompts me. When the merchant, returning rich from the furthest Indies, touches his ancestral shore again, he still knows not which part of the merchandise from his laden ship he shall first open upon the shore for the citizens who throng about him, so hampered is he by the crowd's rush and the fierce eagerness of the buyers. One man is seeking woollen cloth dyed in Tyrian purple and foreign adornments for his mistress; some delight in diamonds, some in chrysolite and the green emerald, and stones plucked from the gem-bearing cliff-face; another one asks for Gabæan frankincense, gifts most welcome to churches,[133] and the perfumes of golden Tmolus,[134] and those things which the rich Arab harvests in his fertile fields; others look for animals, sought out in divers lands, or for hide or horn or bones and snow-white tusks; another again desires the produce of not merely a single seed – he wants at once sweet juices, and the heart of a tree, and the health-giving herbs of the medical art. One condemns the produce, another the journey, while yet another approves of both; one is pressing, another rages in anger, while another's onset is more of a peevish kind; one, who pretends with many words to covet the entire East, goes back to an empty house without

133 Lit. to the temples of the gods.

134 In Lydia.

any goods, since he has first come to the trading-place with empty purse. Here is a wife embracing her husband, and children their parent, and glad companions calling their comrade from the throng. There is an uproar; men fight; the noise of the sailors ascends to heaven, and diverse quarrels upset the new-found pleasures. What should he do? Now he takes his incense and, quitting the ship, announces that he will first discharge his vows[135] before he sells any merchandise to the people in so impious an atmosphere. This show of piety pleases his fellow-citizens, and as the crowd disperses he piously enters the church and, with a pleading and grateful mien, offers incense to the saints[136] who have blessed his voyage.

For me, many gifts of the Greeks and Romans, sought out with hard toil across the sea, rush to the shores of the French-born race. And now from their high watch-tower the Gauls have seen afar off the favouring breezes and the ship borne in, and the joyous signs of a productive vessel; but harmful passion, which with its very look appals ardent hearts, and the idle mob, and Envy who blames the voyage as well as the riches earned, and a diversity of voices, and the varied lust of possessions, and quarrels, and mighty uproar, and blind unrest, await the unhappy sailor upon the ungrateful strand. And now this one will look for the swelling songs of Mæonian Clio[137] and enormous Iliads; while he who is pleased by the tragic theatre and dire disasters, the misfortunes of kings, will want dread admonitions and the grim songs fit for the buskined stage, such as merit the prize of a wanton goat;[138] another will look for (the appearance on the stage of) slaves, and the passions of young men, and mothers and fathers;[139] while another will look for satire, and the habits of men transfixed by the satirist's dart; and another again will seek the lyre, and still another shall seek light verse from the flute;[140] another will choose for himself elegy

135 i.e. religious vows, in church.

136 Lit. the gods.

137 The muse of history. Mæonian is Lydian, i.e. Homeric.

138 Traditionally the ancient prize for tragedy (Tragœdia = goat-song.) Cf. A.E. Haigh, *The Attic Theatre*, III, p. 39.

139 i.e. the characters of ancient comedy.

140 The instrument of light verse in elegiac and other metres.

and the sweet song of loves. And some perchance will look for all of these, even among such as neither desire nor buy nor praise nor read any of them: because either an idle nature, or untutored ignorance, is their bane. All these I have; and even if at this moment I should lack them all, I have a god at whose instigation I was fired to begin all of them; but she bids me offer incense and open my bales of merchandise, until, once I have appeased the gods, I may begin my profitable trafficking, or until the people give me due praise for the gifts I have lately put to sale, and the Court gives due favour too. So here, then, are my offerings of incense; lo, my censer smokes for the gods. (I call upon you), deities kind to the trembling Bard, if any piety and any offering move the gods at all, assist me, ye great-souled heroes. And do thou to whom Calliope, foremost among her sisters, and the Maiden who presides over law,[141] together with Pallas, yield place; thou who mayest rightly rule thy devoted poet, favour me, goddess, and do thou render the gods benign to me as I offer sacrifice, so that beneath thy sway, after some Images of kings and leaders, thy Gaul, having acquired so much of riches, may make herself prosperous and her children too; and that I may no longer be able to complain to the grateful Muses, after my cruel losses, about my verses, about the Courts and about Apollo, but may (instead) be borne up higher in reputation and in fortune, and add my image to the Images of the famous.

LVGENTIS ET LACERÆ EVROPÆ[142]

ADSPICITE REGES ET PELLEGITE.

VOSTRA EGO ILLA TERRAR. QVONDAM
OMNIVM FORTVNATISS. EVROPA DVAB. OL-
LIS POTENTISS. GENTIB. GRÆCIS PRIMVM

141 Astræa, personifying Justice.
142 For the translation, see p. 141. For commentary, cf. E. Balmas, *Etienne Jodelle*, p. 391 *et seq.*

DEINDE ROMAN. IMPERANTIB. VNIVERSI
TERRAR. ORBIS BIS DOMINATRIX NON
IAM CORNVTO VT FINGITVR IOVI SED DEO
OPT. MAX. RESTITVTÆQ. SALVT. AVTHORI
FILIO ÆTERNIS COÆTERNÆ AMBOR. SAPI-
ENTIÆ CONSILIIS DELECTA SANCTIORVM
VIRORVM BEATIORVMQ. DÆMONVM MINI-
STERIIS DEVOTA ET HACTENVS INTER SO-
RORES PATERNIS AMORIB. FŒLICITER DI-
LECTA NVNC VERO PROH DEVM IMMOR-
TAL. QVOD VIX POTVISSET SPERARIER MA-
TRVM OMNIVM MATER MISERR. VOS HIC
CVM LACHRVMIS ROGO FILII HOSPITES VT 33v°
IN LVGENTE LACERA ET PERTVRBATISS.
PARENTE TANQVAM IN NAVFRAGOR. TA-
BVLA VOSTRÆ ILLIVS TAM EGREGIÆ LAV-
DIS TRIVMPHORVMQ. AMPLISSIMOR. FI-
GVRAM SPECTETIS MISERABILEM QVÆ SI
NON A MEIS SED AB ALIENIS SI NON A CHRI-
STIAN. SED A BARBARIS SI NON A CON-
IVNCTIS SANGVINE FEDERE ET RELIGIONE
PRINCIPIB. SED A SEPARATIS ET IGNOTIS
INTER SE POPVLIS VEXARER ET VASTA-
RER SI NON DIVINO MVNERE AC D. FRAN-
CISCI GALLIAR. REG. OPERA OMNI PROPE-
MODVM CALIGINE LIBERATI FVISSETIS SI
NON INTER TOT ET REGNI ET RELIGIO-
NIS DISSIDIA DOMI MILITIÆQ. DESPERA-
TA PACE DESPERARETVR SALVS HAS ISTAS
LACHRYMAS ET INDIGNAM CALAMITATVM
MEAR. EFFIGIEM MINIME CERNERETIS AD-
ESSETQ. D. SPES QVÆ HAC IN IMAGINE

TVRBVLENTÆ FABVLÆ FELICIOREM EXITVM POLLICERETVR, SED CVM DESPERATA QVOQVE SPE RES OMNES IN PEIVS ABEANT VOS ADVOCO QVORVM HIC IMAGINES ADSPICIO MEORVM PIGNORVM CHARISS. PIGNORA GALLICI HEROES AC VOBISCVM DEOS IVDICES VLTRICESQVE FVRIAS AGITE VERTITE RAPITE GLADIIS IGNEM IGNIB. SANGVINEM AC SOLVM CÆLO COMMISCETE CONFVNDITE NEC PRIVS IPSIS CALAMITOSISS. MATRIS VISCERIB. PARCERE LICEAT QVAM VOSTRIS FATALIB. VICTORIIS AD III ORB. IMPERIVM TANQVAM EX FV-
34r° NERE REVOCATA DE MEIS IPSIVS ET BARBAROR. SPOLIIS TRIVMPHVM AGAM CELEBERR. HOC AD SACRAM STATVAM RITE PROMITTITE TER REPETITE ET MEMORES DISCEDITE.

MATRI MÆSTISS. PIVS FILIVS INSCRIPS.

[AN ADDRESS] OF EUROPE, MOURNING AND TORN.[143]
Kings, behold and read with care.

I, who once was your most fortunate Europe twice mistress of the whole world under the rule of those very potent nations, first the Greeks and then

143 In this address, written during the first half of 1558, Jodelle expresses his hopes for the peace of Europe. Cf. Ronsard, 'Exhortation au camp du Roy pour bien combattre' (July 1558) and 'Exhortation pour la paix' (September 1558) in *Œuvres*, ed. Laumonier (STFM), IX, pp. 3 and 15 *et seq.* For a commentary on Jodelle's composition cf. E. Balmas, *Etienne Jodelle*, p. 391.

the Romans, chosen not by the cuckold Jupiter, as the fable goes, but by God the Greatest and Best and by His Son the Author of our Salvation and by the everlasting counsels of that Wisdom Who is co-eternal with both Father and Son; consecrated by the devotion of holy men and blessed spirits, and hitherto among my sisters happy in the cherishing love of a father, but now – ah immortal gods! scarce could it have been looked for – the unhappiest of mothers: I now do here with tears implore you, O my sons and my friends, to behold in the person of a mourning, injured, and most unhappy parent, as on the votive tablets of shipwrecked men, the desolate figure of that wondrous glory of yours and of your most ample triumphs; for if, not by my people but by others' subjects; not by Christians but by heathens; not by those princes related by blood, faith, and religious practice, but by peoples cut off and mutually unknown I were harassed and laid waste; if you had not been freed from almost all the shadows by Heaven's aid and the assistance of my lord Francis, king of France; if among so many divisions in the kingdom and in its religion the despair of salvation itself had not followed the despair of peace at home and abroad; then you would in no wise now behold these tears and my grievous appearance in distress, but the Divine Hope would be at hand and amid this picture of a tale of unrest would promise a happier outcome; but since now even hope is despaired of, and all goes from bad to worse, I appeal to you whose Images I behold here, dearest pledges of all my pledges, heroes of France; and with you I appeal to the gods as judges and to the avenging Furies: drive, pursue, smite; mingle and confound fire with sword, blood with fire, earth with heaven, and let it not be possible to spare the vitals of myself the most distressful of mothers, until by your decisive victories I am recalled as if from the funeral pyre to a third empire of the world,[144] and may celebrate a splendid triumph out of my own spoils and those of the heathen. Promise this solemnly at the holy image, repeat it thrice, and mindful thereof depart.

Dedicated to a very sorrowful mother by her dutiful son.

144 i.e. the universal Christian empire which will succeed those of the Greeks and the Romans.

GALLICORVM HEROVM.

Quibus D. illius Francisci, duarum eius uxorum, sororis unius, duorum natorum, alteriusque filæ, licet omnes obierint, Eiconas adiunximus.

The Icones of the heroes of France; to which we have appended the Icones of the famous Lord Francis, his two wives, one sister, two sons, and one of his daughters, though all of these are deceased.

Among the children of Francis I, Jodelle omits the two daughters, Louise and Charlotte, who died in infancy.

I
D. FRANCISCI
Galliar. Reg. Augustiss.

GALLIA CVI CVRÆ, MARS, MVSA, DEVSQVE FVERVNT,
HVNC POST FATA NOVVM VENERETVR GALLIA NVMEN,
MARSQVE DVCEM, MVSÆQVE PATREM, SVPERIQVE COLONVM.

Lord Francis, most august King of the Gauls.
He who devoted himself to Gaul, to Mars, to the Muses, and to God, should be venerated after death as a new deity by Gaul, as a commander by Mars, as a father by the Muses, and by the gods as a new settler among them.

Francis I (1494–1547) founded the Valois-Angoulême house when he acceded to the throne in 1515. He immediately initiated an exceptionally well-balanced patronage whose character is adequately conveyed by the first line of the tristich and which was at its most brilliant from c. 1527–40. (Cf. Jean Adhémar, 'Le mécénat de François Ier,' *Revue de l'Université de Bruxelles*, VIII (1955–6), pp. 244–53.

His military encounters were scarcely memorable even if he was granted the epithet *Invictissimus* after his two major victories – at Marignan (1515), which led to the capture of Milan and Cérisoles (1544), which provided an advantage against the Imperials which was not exploited. His captivity after the disaster at Pavia in 1525 may have resulted in a change of orientation inspired by the direct example of the Emperor Charles V.

Perhaps as a result of the influence of his sister, Marguerite de Navarre (Icon IV, p. 147), Francis was interested in the early reformers such as Briçonnet and Lefèvre d'Etaples, and Calvin's *Institutio religionis christianæ* (1536) is dedicated to him. He further encouraged artists, writers, and translators and founded the Collège de France.

The reference to the Muses no doubt refers directly to his own poetic efforts (cf. A. Champollion-Figeac, *Poésies du roi François Ier . . .*, Paris, 1847), but he is generally referred to as 'père des arts et lettres' and this task of restitution becomes the iconographical touchstone of his reign. Only shortly after his death, for example, the deified Francis has his portrait painted by Pallas (the theological category of the emblem being indicated since its prototype is St Luke painting the Virgin) as Symbol xxiiii of Book I (fig. 6) of *Achillis Bocchii Bonon. Symbolicarum quæstionum libri quinque* (Bologna, 1555). Such references appear prominently in Minerva's speech in the present *Recueil's* Mascarade of the Argonauts (pp. 105–8).

Henry II therefore fell heir with his descendance to Francis' presumably unceasing combat against 'le vil monstre Ignorance,' a position alluded to in 'La Renaissance des Arts et Lettres' (fig. 19), one of the Caron drawings for the *Histoire françoyse de nostre temps*, Louvre, Inv. RF 29752[19], in the flattering prologue of Jodelle's *Cléopâtre captive* (1553) where he is called 'père et maistre des muses,' and even unto the funerary urn intended to enclose his heart. (Cf. V.L. Goldberg, 'Graces, Muses and Arts: The Funerary Urns of Henry II and Francis I,' *Journal of the Warburg and Courtauld Institutes*, XXIX (1966), pp. 206–18.)

All this is but part of the more elaborate *ex utroque Cæsar* epithet, for which see the introduction, pp. 29–32.

II
D. CLAVDIÆ
Galliar. Reginæ D. Francis. uxoris I.

IAMQVE ORBI PEPERISSE FACES VT TROICA MATER
DICAR EGO, SED NON MISERO QVIBVS ARDEAT IGNE,
AT QVIBVS VT PHŒBI FVLGET FACE FVLGEAT ORBIS.

Lady Claudia, Queen of the Gauls, first wife of Lord Francis.
Now shall I be said, like the Trojan mother, to have given birth to torches for the world; not, however, torches whereby it may burn with fires of unhappiness, but torches whereby the world may shine with Phœbus' light.

Claude de France (1499–1524), eldest daughter of Louis XII and Anne de Bretagne, married Francis I in 1514 while he was still Dauphin, bringing in her dowry, besides Brittany, Blois, Coucy, Montfort, and Etampes. She was lauded for her virtue and affectionately called *la bonne reine* by her subjects. Her device was the moon with the motto *Candida candidis*.

The epithet *Troica mater* may refer to Rhea-Cybele, mother of the gods; by extension, of Francis' descendants, who are all referred to in like manner (i.e. D. HENRICI). M. Jean Guillaume kindly informed us of the Ovidian source (*Heroides*, XVI, vv. 43–50). If the epithet were taken literally, Claude would be assimilated to Hecuba, the notably fruitful second wife of Priam and mother of numerous children including Hector, Paris, and Cassandra. Whichever identification one accepts, the metaphor children / torches refers not only to life but also to the destruction resulting from the deeds of the former's brood as opposed to the 'light-giving' powers of Claude's own descendance.

The legitimacy and continuity of the dynastic succession is emphasized by the inclusion of the predeceased, the Dauphin François and Charles d' Orléans (Icon V) and Madeleine (Icon VI); and by the exceptionally banal Icon

(III) of Eleanor of Austria, who had no children by Francis I. Thus only Henry II (Icones VII–XIII) and Mme Marguerite (Icones XXVIII–XXX) survived from the first marriage bed.

III

D. LEONORÆ 34v[c]

Caroli V. Imperat. Roman. sororis ac Francis.
Galliar. Regis uxoris II

VTRAQVE VIVA FVI, BVRGVNDA, ET GALLICA, FRATER
HOC MIHI, VIR DEDIT HOC, DEMPTO MIHI CONIVGE, TOTA
FRATRIS ERAM, NVNC CVM RELIQVIS SVM GALLICA DIVIS.

Lady Eleonora, sister of Charles V, Emperor of the Romans, and second wife of Francis, King of the Gauls.
In life I was both a Burgundian and a Frenchwoman; my brother gave me one nationality, my husband the other. When my husband was taken from me I was entirely my brother's; now, I am French, with the other gods.

Eleanor of Austria (1498–1558), elder sister of Charles V, married first Emmanuel of Portugal who died in 1521, leaving her with two children, and then, by the treaties of Madrid and Cambrai in 1530, Francis I. She had no other children and after the death of Francis in 1547 she first went to the Low Countries and then in 1556 to Spain where she died within a few months of her brother.

Both Eleanor and Charles V could claim to be Burgundian since their father, Archduke Philip of Austria, was the son of Maximilian I and Marie de Bourgogne. Their mother was Joanna the Mad, daughter of Ferdinand and Isabella. In 1517 Charles V succeeded both to the crown of Spain and to the house of Burgundy.

IV
D. MARGARITÆ
Navarror. Reginæ ac Francisci Reg. sororis.

EST ALIQVIS GENITOR DIVVS MIHI, DIVAQVE MATER,
ET FRATER DEVS EST, ET SVM QVOQVE DIVA, PAREMQVE
HVIC PIETAS, HVIC CORPVS, ET HVIC FECERE CAMŒNÆ.

Lady Margaret, Queen of Navarre and sister to King Francis.
I have a god for sire, a goddess for mother, and my brother is a god; and I too am a goddess, and piety has made me equal to the first, beauty to the next, and the Muses to the last.

Marguerite de Navarre (1492–1549) was the daughter of Charles d'Orléans, duc d'Angoulême and Louise de Savoie. Known first as Marguerite d'Angoulême and then as Marguerite d'Alençon after her marriage to the Duc d'Alençon, who died in 1525, she became Queen of Navarre by her marriage to Henri d'Albret in 1527. She was, of course, well known for her interest in the Reform (Briçonnet, Lefèvre d'Etaples, etc.) and for her considerable talents in diplomacy (Treaty of Madrid, 1525) and literature (*Le Miroir de l'âme pécheresse*, *Les Marguerites de la Marguerite des Princesses*, *l'Heptaméron*, etc.). Cf. P. Jourda, *Marguerite d'Angoulême, duchesse d'Alençon, reine de Navarre*, Paris, Champion, 1930, 2 vols.

V
D. D. FRANCISCI ET CAROLI,
alterius Galliar. Delphini, alterius Aurelior. Ducis, D. Francis. Reg. filiorum I. et III.

FRATRIBVS INVIDISSE LIQVET DIVOSQVE DVCESQVE,
NVNC HOS DVM REQVIE, FACIE DVM VINCIMVS ILLOS,
INVIDIAM DVCIBVS LIQVIT, DIIS ATROPOS AVXIT.

The Lords Francis and Charles: one the Dauphin of France, one the Duke of Orleans: the eldest and youngest of three sons of Lord Francis the King. 'Tis clear that the gods and the generals alike envied us, the brothers; now that we surpass the gods in peace of mind, the heroes in beauty of looks, Atropos has ceased to envy our generalship but has increased envy for our godhead.

The Dauphin, Francis (1517–36), was supposedly poisoned by Sebastien, comte de Montecuculi, who accused the Seigneur de Dinteville. Sebastien, was, however, tried by the Grand Conseil, found guilty, and sentenced to death. Cf. V.-L. Saulnier, 'La mort du Dauphin François et son tombeau poétique,' *Bibliothèque d'Humanisme et Renaissance*, VI (1945), pp. 50–97.

Charles, duc d'Angoulême and later duc d'Orléans (1522–45), was the third son of Francis I and his favourite. Impulsive and rash, he took the part of the Duchesse d'Etampes against the future Henry II and Diane de Poitiers. Despite his early death, either of plague or poison administered by a partisan of Henry II, he had taken part in a number of successful military campaigns including Luxembourg, where he commanded the French army in 1542 against Charles V.

R.E. Giesey, *The Royal Funeral Ceremony in Renaissance France*, Geneva, 1960, p. 8, remarks the unprecedented triple burials of Francis I and his two predeceased sons in 1547 and the resultant 'forceful display of the dynastic principle in the spectacle of the quondam potential inheritors of the sovereignty of France being accorded funeral honours in company with the King their father.'

VI

D. MAGDALENÆ

Scotorum Reginæ D. Francis. Reg. Filiæ.

TRES SOLES GEMINAMQVE PATI MEA GALLIA PHŒBEN
NON POTVIT, TRAXIT ME SCOTIA, SYDERA DEINDE,
SOLAQVE CVM SOLO SPLENDES SOROR INCLYTA SOLE.

Lady Magdalena, Queen of Scots, daughter of Lord Francis the King.
My own Gaul could not endure three suns and two moons; Scotland first drew me away, and then Heaven; and thus, my famed sister, you now shine alone save for the sun.

Madeleine de France (1520–36) married James v of Scotland on 1 January 1536 but died six months later. James v then married Marie de Lorraine, by whom he had one daughter, Mary Stuart. (Cf. pp. 99 and 162.)

Of Francis i's three sons and four daughters, only Henry ii and Madame Marguerite were still alive at this time.

VII
D. HENRICI
Galliar. Reg. augustiss. fœliciss.

CVI FRATRES CESSERE, DECVS CVI CEDIT AVITVM,
HVIC MAVORS, HVIC SI NOCEAT SORS DIRA, CADAT MARS
MARTE NOVO, ET SORTIS DOMINA VIRTVTE CADAT SORS.

Lord Henry, most august and happy King of the Gauls.
To him to whom his brothers gave place; to him to whom ancestral glory deferred, Mars also yields. If any dire fate should harm him, let Mars fall in a new battle; and let Fate herself also succumb, under the sway of Virtue.

Henry ii (1518–59) was Duc d'Orléans until he became Dauphin on the death of his elder brother Francis in 1536. His younger brother Charles, who then succeeded him as Duc d'Orléans, died in 1545, two years before Henry became king. (Cf. p. 148.)

It was traditional to refer to the king's military exploits (cf. pp. 98 and 156) and the dominance of Virtue. (Cf. Du Bellay, 'Hymne au Roy sur la prinse de Callais,' *Œuvres*, ed. Chamard vi¹, p. 21, v. 29 and Adrien Turnèbe, *Panegyricus de Calipso capto*, Paris, Attaignant, 1558, f. Aij.)

The tone of the last sentence is almost foreboding, recalling the famous prophecy of Nostradamus (1556–8) which, however, was only interpreted retrospectively as an indication of the manner of Henry's tragic death.

VIII
HENRICI 35r°
ad militiam armati.

ARMORVM SCELERVMQVE TREMOR SIC GALLICVS ARMIS
FVLMINAT ALCIDES, RHENI SEV TYBRIDIS VNDAS,
SEV GANGEM, VICTOQVE AFFECTET SYDERA MVNDO.

Henry, armed for military service.
Terror of arms and of crime, so does the Gallic Hercules shine like lightning in arms, whether it be the waves of the Rhine or the Tiber that he claims or – having conquered the whole world – the Ganges and the heavens.

For the legend of the kings of France as descendants of Hercules, cf. Ronsard, 'Harangue du duc de Guise,' *Œuvres*, ed. Laumonier (STFM), V, p. 209, V. 115–20.

The Gallic Hercules is normally depicted as leading representative types by the power of his eloquence, symbolized by slackened chains proceeding from his tongue to their ears. (Cf. Jodelle's 'A Monseigneur le Duc,' *Œuvres*, ed. Balmas, I, p. 255. and M.-R. Jung, *Hercule dans la littérature française du XVIe siècle*, Geneva, Droz, 1966.) Here only a question of nationality is implied, while the references to conquests evoke once again the notion of the universal Christian empire. (Cf. p. 142.) The precedent for this is most likely in the Parisian entry of 1549 (Paris, J. Roffet, 1549) where a Gallic Hercules with the traits of Francis I appeared at the Porte Saint-Denis with verses inviting the populace to follow Francis' successor, Henry II. Cf. V.-L. Saulnier, 'L'entrée de Henri II à Paris et la révolution poétique de 1550,' *Les Fêtes de la Renaissance*, ed. J. Jacquot, Paris, CNRS, 1956, pp. 46–7.

Barthélemy Aneau's gloss on Alciati (Emb. CLXXX *Eloquentia fortitudine præstantior*, pp. 221–2 in the edition of 1549), provides an interesting parallel to the entry: 'C'est la description Lucianicque de Hercules le François, Par laquelle estoit figuré, que Hercules avoit tant de peuples mis en son obeissance, et tant de monstres, et tyrans surmontez par vive eloquence, et savoir legitime, et constitution de justes loix, Toutes lesquelles choses les Græcz hont depuys deguisées en faictz d'armes, et appropriées à leur Hercules Græc, filz d'Alcmena.' But Aneau's last two lines of verse preceding maintain: 'Armes font place aux lettres. Car des cœurs (Tant soient ilz durs) Eloquens sont vinqueurs.' Again, a reference to the *ex utroque Cæsar* symbol (cf. p. 28).

IX
HENRICI
equitantis domi sic nuper à Ianetio pictore Paris. excellentis. in maiore tabula depicti.

SIC SVPERVM GENVS HENRICVS, POST PONDERA RERVM
LIBER EQVIS DAT IVRA SVIS, QVEIS RVRSVS IN ARMA,
QVEIS ARMIS RVRSVS SE MITTAT IN ASTRA SVBACTIS.

[Equestrian portrait of] Henry, riding at home, as lately depicted in a large portrait by Janet, a most excellent Parisian painter.
Thus does Henry, of divine ancestry, being at leisure after the burden of affairs, control his horses; horses on which he may either return to his wars or, when wars are won, return once more to Heaven.

This Icon has, perhaps, the greatest profusion of versions, whether single or composite, attributed or anonymous, deriving from a single *known* prototype of any in this album. Its interpretation depends less directly upon the tristich than the subtitle immediately preceding, where it is identified as a work of François Clouet dit Janet (c. 1516/20–1572 and *peintre du roi* since 1541), who is celebrated in Ronsard's *Elegie* 'Pein moi Janet, pein moi je te supplie' of 1555 (*Œuvres*, ed. Laumonier (STFM), VI, pp. 152–60) for his qualities as a painter of portrait likenesses.

This painting of Henry '*equitantis domi*' is related to a series of illuminated miniatures and drawings evidently based upon a work (fig. 37) by Janet's father, Jean Clouet (c. 1475/80–c. 1541) presently in the Cabinet des Dessins of the Louvre (Inv. MI 1092); cf. Charles Sterling et Hélène Adhémar, *Musée National du Louvre. Peintures. Ecole Française. XIVe, XVe et XVIe siècles*, Paris, 1965, cat. 60. This model was to become commercially vulgarized, with only the portrait heads being individually studied, for a series of kings and princes of France; cf. Louis Dimier, *Histoire de la Peinture de portrait en France au seizième siècle*, Paris, Van Oest, 1924–6, I, p. 184 and II, cat. 1589–95. The Louvre miniature is reproduced in reverse as Henry II (fig. 38) in a drawing of the Musée Condé, Chantilly (Inv. 334) which retains the same background and introduces only changes of detail while a companion type also at Chantilly utilizes a head separately taken which appears in the 1553 *Promptuaire des Medalles;* L. Dimier, *op. cit.*, II, cat. 1307–8. A panel of Francis I (fig. 39) in the Uffizi, Inv. 667, returns to the original type, but includes a distant and low-lying landscape while modifying the architecture to one with a niche and two engaged columns. The pattern, this time as Charles IX and without background, is preserved at Chantilly as Inv. 396; L. Dimier, *op. cit.*, II, cats. 145 and 1309.

The equestrian stance eventually resulted in a monument when Catherine de' Medici asked Michelangelo (who refused, in favour of Daniele da Volterra) for a commemorative statue of her recently deceased husband, a cast of whose horse was placed in the courtyard at Fontainebleau later to bear its name; Jean Adhémar, 'Le cheval blanc de Fontainebleau,' *Gazette des Beaux-Arts*, s. 6, XXXVI (1949), pp. 297–300. It is noteworthy that Antonio Tempesta's engraving (Bartsch, *Le peintre-graveur*, XVII, 149.635) of the entire monument (fig. 41) bears a dedication to Charles Cardinal de Lorraine, further emphasizing the ascendance of this house with the reigning Valois.

The iconography of the second Henry is thus remarkable for the restrained number and combination of types largely derived from his father, but none of these may be considered '*in maiore tabula depicti.*' Edmond Bonnaffé, *Inventaire des meubles de Cathérine de Médicis en 1589* (Paris, Aubry, 1874, p. 126, n. 1) suggested that item 613 'Ung autre grand portraict du feu roy Henry à cheval peint sur toile' could be that suggested in this Icon by adducing a version in oil formerly in the possession of the marquis de Biencourt at Azay-le-Rideau. This identification has been accepted by Balmas (cf. Jodelle, *Œuvres complètes*, I, p. 472) who derived his information from Ch. Maumené et L. d'Harcourt, *Iconographie des rois de France, 1re partie: de Louis IX à Louis XIII* (Paris, Colin, 1928), cat. 198, i.e. cat. 35 of Henry II. A timely comment by Mr Charles C. Hill led to the confirmation that the Biencourt picture had entered the Metropolitan Museum of Art (Inv. 45.128.12); cf. Charles Sterling, *A Catalogue of French Paintings, XV–XVIII Centuries*, Cambridge (Mass.), 1955, pp. 54–7. The painting, now some 156.2 × 134.6 cm. in dimension, shows signs of having been tampered with and was transferred from panel to canvas prior to Bonnaffé's mention of it; it is then not the painting on canvas mentioned in Catherine's inventory.

If the background of this picture (fig. 40) employs the two columns, here cannelated and without niche, of the Uffizi Francis I and extends the drafted stone into a wall, effectively dispensing with any landscape save patches of flowers, the rider's skirt provides connections with both the Louvre Francis I and Antoine Caron's later revision of the subject as Henry II's monument (fig. 13). Cf. p. 157. Maumené and d'Harcourt justly consider the Biencourt picture as 'en grand costume civil,' that is with a riding switch substituted for the baton of authority and armour requisite in a military scene. L. Dimier, *op. cit.*, II, cat. 508 considers '*domi*' to mean 'en temps de paix, signifiant que le roi n'est pas armé,' which is inacceptable in that the explanatory tristich requires the interpretation of 'POST PONDERA RERVM' as applying to that time left for leisurely recreation after daily routines.

There is still *no real assurance* that this is actually the work mentioned in Icon IX, and the very quality of the painting would mitigate against such an identity. Unless, as an extant painting, it were simply inserted into the prepared decor, most paintings specially executed for like circumstances were rather summarily executed in an *alla prima* technique and would not long have survived as physical objects. It further seems unlikely that such a complex panel would have been executed for this occasion in the time specified.

X
HENRICI

in aulæo variis floribus compositio ambulantis, sic nuper ab alio quodam artifice ad vivum expressi.

PANDE SINVM, PEDIBSQVE ROSAS ET LILIA TELLVS
FVNDE MEIS, NE MONSTRA ONERI TIBI SINT TVA, VINDEX
EN TIBI REX ONVS EST, CVI TOTA ONVS ESSE IVBERIS.

Henry, shown walking upon a tapestry of many-coloured flowers; lately executed from the life by some other artist.
Open your lap, O earth, and pour forth roses and lilies at my feet, lest your own marvels be a burden to you: lo, your burden is the avenging King, for whom you in your entirety are bidden to be a burden [of care].

There is a certain ambiguity in this description of Henry II which seems, however, to refer to a full-length portrait of the monarch standing on the ground with roses and lilies at his feet rather than on an actual tapestry. The allusion is undoubtedly to the spring-like weather which helped permit the recapture of Calais (cf. p. 89), although the epithet 'VINDEX' may also refer to Henry's campaigns in France and Italy in 1552 since it is seen in Marc Bechot's 'Libertas' medallic issue (fig. 42); cf. F. Mazerolle, *Les médailleurs français du XVᵉ siècle au milieu du XVIIᵉ*, II, Paris, 1902, cat. 91 (see also Icon XV). This premise is borne out by a line in Icon XI, 'FORS ILLVM SEV BELLA PREMANT, ATROXVE TYRANNVS.' See W. McAllister Johnson, 'Numismatic Propaganda in Renaissance France,' *Art Quarterly*, XXXI (1968), pp. 134–41.

XI
HENRICI
in maiori numismate.

SENTIAT ET NVMEN, NOMEN QVI SPECTAT IN AVRO,
FORS ILLVM SEV BELLA PREMANT, ATROXVE TYRANNVS,
NOSTRÆ NAMQVE OPIS EST VT IMAGINIS OMNIBVS VSVS.

Henry, upon a great coin.
Let him who looks for the name in gold perceive the godhead also, whether Fate or wars or a dread tyrant oppress him; for all men have need of our aid, as they do of our image.

The pun in Latin is between *nomen* (the name inscribed on the coin) and *numen* (the godhead represented by a portrait). *Opis* is also ambiguous since it may refer to aid or wealth (represented by the gold).

Despite the rather imprecise distinctions between coins and medals in the Renaissance, we are surely dealing with a coin because of the prohibitive cost of precious metal, and because of the new and distinctive types of gold coinage introduced under the second Henry; cf. Jean Lafaurie et Pierre Prieur, *Les Monnaies des rois de France*, II, Paris, 1956, cats. 807–18. Of these, three types are the most likely if we take the formula *in maiori numismate* to mean the largest module and the heaviest legal weight: the *écu d'or à l'effigie* introduced 6 August 1548 (cat. 807 and pl. XLI); the two varieties of the *Double Henri d'or* introduced 14 January 1550 (cats. 809 and 812 and pl. XLI); and the *Double Henri d'or à la Gallia* (cat. 816 and pl. XLII). The obverses of these coins are similar to the type found in the *Promptuaire des medalles* (fig. 9).

XII

HENRICI

inter trophœa.

SCOTIA TVTA SVIS, ACCEPTA BOLONIA, METÆ,
ET RHENI PAVOR ATTONITI FVSVSQVE PER VMBRAS CÆSAR
et quæ sequuntur in
duodecim illis versibus ex Pyramide sumptis, quibus et 35v°
alios versus addemus ubi sese nova facta
factis addiderint.

Henry, between his trophies.
Scotland kept safe for her people, Boulogne and Metz captured, and the terror of the awestruck Rhine, and the Emperor routed in the dark. – *and what follows in these twelve lines taken from the 'Pyramid,' to which we shall also add other verses when new exploits have been added to his deeds.*
Cf. p. 98.
If we take literally the transitional phrase 'et quæ sequuntur,' then Jodelle has not kept to his word (p. 127) that the Icones would be restricted to tristich form; otherwise we have simply an acceptable excerpt from the passage referred to.

XIII

HENRICI

æternæ memoriæ, ut hoc aliquando regali
tumulo insculpatur.

CÆSAR ALEXANDRI QVOD FLEVIT IMAGINE VISA,
HOC TANTVM IVBET ELATOS MEA FLERE NEPOTES,
QVÆ VEL ALEXANDRO GEMITVM EXTORSISSET IMAGO.

Henry of everlasting memory, to the end that this may at some time be inscribed upon the royal tomb.

Only as Cæsar wept on seeing the picture of Alexander does my image bid our grandchildren be moved to weep; an image which would have drawn a sigh from Alexander himself.

A drawing from the *Histoire Françoyse de nostre temps*, Louvre, Inv. RF 29752[14] (fig. 13) is typical of the thematic frontispieces based upon the royal emblems. The equestrian Henry (cf. Icon IX) most obviously derives from the Clouet miniature even to its scale, and indicates that the artists of the mécène Nicolas Houel had access to the collections of Catherine de' Medici. Detailed comparison is conclusive since the interlace pattern of the caparison of the Clouet horse has been here transformed to Henry's cipher (figs. 37, 40). In our drawing, Alexander the Great appears at upper left and Cæsar at upper right, while the sestet on the recto reads:

Il ne fault point, Henry, ny qu'Alexandre,
Ne que Cesar, vueille rien entreprendre
Sus tes lauriers doublement meritez,
Car filz se font tes egaulx quand aux armes,
Par ta vertu tu les as surmontez,
Estant sans vice, et toy, et tes gendarmes.

The conceit is comprehensible only when one considers Alexander and Cæsar as the previous possessors of world empire, the implication being that the *Roi treschrestien* Henry II will inherit or create a revivified Holy Roman Empire; cf. above, pp. 83 and 112. This symbolism is further specified in a frontispiece (Louvre, Inv. RF 29752[1]) for *Les figures des deux premiers livres de l'histoire de la Royne Arthémise* which, while establishing the parallel Catherine / Arthémise, Henry / Mausolus includes in the last tercet of what would have been a sonnet were its first quatrain not missing, the verses:

La terre le pleura, avec le ciel, et l'unde
Comme celuy qui peut devant son partement,
Par la paix asseurer l'estat de tout le Monde.

XIV

D. CATHARINÆ

Galliar. Reginæ Henrici Reg. uxoris.

ME CIVEMQVE DECVSQVE SVVM FLORENTIA MATER,
GALLIA ME MATREM, DOMINAM PENE ASSERET ORBIS
ALTERA CVM MEA SINT, SVNT ALTERA IVRA MARITI.

Lady Catherine, wife of Henry, King of the Gauls.
Let Florence, which bore me, claim me as her citizen and as her glory; Gaul, as a mother; the whole world nearly, as a ruling lady. Some bow to my law, and some to my husband's.

Catherine de' Medici (1519–89) was the daughter of Lorenzo de' Medici and the niece of Pope Clement VII. Her choice as a bride for Henry II in 1533 was criticized at the time but her rich dowry brought to France funds which were badly needed by Francis I. She remained childless for ten years but then between 1544 and 1554 produced ten children, three of whom died in infancy. (Cf. J.H. Mariéjol, *Cathérine de Médicis*, Paris, Hachette, 1920.)

The construction of this Icon is almost certainly one of *double emploi*, referring not only to Catherine's own child-bearing in France (and her actual position as mother of the dynasty) but also figuratively to Gaul as Catherine's ancestress through her mother, Madeleine de La Tour d'Auvergne. Cf. Gustave Cohen, *Geoffroy Tory and Catherine de' Medici. An Unpublished Manuscript of Geoffroy Tory of the Genealogy of the Counts of Boulogne Concerning the French Ancestry of Catherine de' Medici, Queen of France*. New York: H.P. Kraus, 1944.

Du Bellay's inscription in her honour is similar in sentiments but less specific. (Cf. *Poésies françaises et latines*, ed. Courbet, II, p. 454.)

XV
EIVSDEM.

DAT NEPTVNVS EQVVM, DAT OLIVAM PALLAS ATHENIS
PACEM ET BELLA, MEIS VT DETVR VTRVMQVE, DEORVM
EN NATI ET NATÆ SIMILES, TREMOR ORBIS, AMORQVE.

The Same.
Neptune gives to Athens the horse, Pallas the olive-tree, that is, war and peace; so that both should be given to my people, lo, my sons and daughters are like gods – the world's terror and its love.

The contest of Neptune and Pallas is usually meant as a reference to the *sui generis* destructive qualities of the male and the rather more constructive female aspirations. Here it is certainly a reprise of Catherine's entry into Lyon on 24 September 1548 when she, as Henry the day previous, passed by the Perspective du Change (fig. 43), there to witness the contest before the city of Troy(!). Of the two figurants before the perspective, 'Pallas poursuyvit, après avoir premièrement faict convertir sa lance en arbre de paix. "La France alors commenceant à aymer, / Muay pour vous. Princesse sage et bonne, / La guerre en paix, comme le Ciel s'adonne / A voz vertus haultement consommer."' Cf. *La Magnificence de la superbe et triumphante entrée* . . . , ed. G. Guigue, Lyon, 1927, pp. 47–8, 66.

The remainder of the passage 'meis ut detur utrumque . . . ' implies the succession of Catherine's male and female descendants to one or the other of these qualities, both of which are rather more to be assigned to Henry II as reigning monarch. Thus one of the several obverse-reverse combinations of a celebrated medal 'struck' by Marc Bechot to commemorate the Italian and German campaigns (fig. 44) pictures Henry as a composite deity with the legend ET.PACE.ET.BELLO.ARMA.MOVET.1552. (Cf. F. Mazerolle, *Les médailleurs français du XVe siècle au milieu du XVIIe*, II, Paris, 1902, cat. 89–90.) Even this is taken from an earlier miniature prototype, cf. Françoise

Bardon, 'Sur un portrait de François 1er,' *L'Information d'histoire de l'art*, VIII (1963) pp. 1–7, but under no circumstances may Henry's image be applied to Catherine's own Icon. Are we then to assume that, unless in possession of descriptive information to the contrary, Catherine's image from the preceding Icon was simply repeated (and the same for the remaining EIVSDEM) or was simply an inscription as, indeed, could have been generally the case?

XVI
D. FRANCISCI
Galliar. Delphini.

NOMEN AVI, MENTEMQVE PATRIS, MATRISQVE REFERRE
ORA IVVAT, DABIT OMEN AVVS CVM NOMINE, MARTEM
VT MENTEM PATER, ET MORES PIA MATER VT ORA.

Lord Francis, Dauphin of the Gauls.
It pleases me to recall my grandfather's name, my father's nature, and my mother's looks. With the name, my grandsire shall give an omen; with his nature, my father shall give warlike skill; and my good mother shall give me character as well as looks.

The pun on *nomen*, *omen* is hardly to be reproduced in English. There are also weak puns on *Martem*, *mentem* and *mores*, *ora*.

Francis II (1544–60), eldest son of Henry II and Catherine de' Medici, was named after Francis I. Following his marriage to Mary Stuart on 24 April 1558 he was called Le Roi Dauphin. (Cf. p. 85, n. 47).

Du Bellay's inscription in his honour resembles Jodelle's very closely. Cf. *Poésies françaises et latines* ed. Courbet, II, 456–7:

> Comme le nom il a de son grand pere,
> De son esprit heritier il sera,
> Et à son pere en vertu semblera,
> Comme de face il ressemble à sa mere.

XVII

36r° EIVSDEM.

HAS INTER TENEBRAS, INTER BELLA HORRIDA PHŒBE
SOLA MICAT, SED FATA DIEM SVB PATRE REDVCENT,
PACATVMQVE MEVS CVRRV SOL AMBIENT ORBEM.

The same.
Amidst this darkness and amidst dreadful wars Phœbe [i.e. the moon] shines alone; but the fates will bring back Day, under the father's reign; and my own Sun in his chariot shall circle a world at peace.

Cf. p. 85.
This Icon obviously refers to the Dauphin's motto, INTER ECLYPSES EXORIOR, suggesting that Henry's crescent moon will wax full (DONEC TOTVM IMPLEAT ORBEM) so that when Francis succeeds him, his sun (a globe of another kind) shall encircle a peaceful world.

Further, the closing line 'PACATVMQVE MEVS CVRRV SOL AMBIET ORBEM' is clearly a reminiscence of the motto *pacatum ipse regam avitis virtutibus orbem* occurring in emblem books and perhaps medals and which is derived from the illustration (fig. 45) to Gabriello Symeoni's *Interpretation Grecque, Latine, Tuscane et Françoise, du Monstre, ou Enigme d'Italie* (Lyon, A. Voulant, 1555). Cf. W. McAllister Johnson, 'A "Biface" Medal of Henry II?,' *Journal of the Warburg and Courtauld Institutes*, XXX (1967), pp. 401–3. Symeoni's creation, as well as the sense of Jodelle's Icon, is but an intentionally transparent paraphrase of vv. 4–17 of Virgil's Fourth or Messianic Eclogue:

Ultima Cumæi venit iam carminis ætas;
Magnus ab integro sæclorum nascitur ordo.
Iam redit et Virgo, redeunt Saturnia regna,
Iam nova progenies cælo demittitur alto.
Tu modo nascenti puero, quo ferrea primum

Desinet ac toto surget gens aurea mundo,
Casta, fave, Lucina: tuus iam regnat Apollo.
Teque adeo decus hoc ævi, te consule, inibit,
Pollio, et incipient magni procedere menses,
Te duce. Si qua manent sceleris vestigia nostri,
Irrita perpetua solvent formidine terras.
Ille deum vitam accipiet divisque videbit
Permixtos heroas et ipse videbitur illis;
Pacatumque reget patriis virtutibus orbem.

(Cf. J. Carcopino, *Virgile et le mystère de la IVe églogue*, Paris, 1930, and W. McAllister Johnson, 'Numismatic Propaganda in Renaissance France,' *Art Quarterly*, XXXI (1968), p. 127, n. 15 for the Imperial symbolism of this phrasing.) The reference to Justice descending is echoed in Mme Marguerite's Icon XXIX and enjoyed special currency in the context of sixteenth-century dynastic and political preoccupations. Cf. Frances A. Yates, 'Queen Elizabeth as Astræa,' *Journal of the Warburg and Courtauld Institutes*, X (1947), pp. 27–82.

XVIII
D. MARIÆ
Scotorum Reginæ.

SCOTIA REGINAM PRIMIS ME SPECTAT AB ANNIS,
GALLIA REGINAM PRIMIS ME SPERAT AB ANNIS,
HOC DAT VTERQVE PATER, DET VIR DET PLVRAQVE VIRTVS.

Lady Mary, Queen of Scots.
Scotland beholds me as her Queen from my earliest years; Gaul hopes for me as her Queen from my earliest years; this is the gift of both my fathers; let my hero-sire give it, but let Heroism itself [who is my other sire] give more.
Mary Stuart (1542–87), daughter of James V of Scotland and Marie de Lorraine,

married the Dauphin on 24 April 1558. (Cf. pp. 85 and 149.) She became queen of Scotland on the death of her father when she was only a few months old, but she moved to the French court in 1548 and received her upbringing there. (Cf. A. de Ruble, *La première jeunesse de Marie Stuart*, Paris, Huard et Guillemin, 1891.)

XIX
EIVSDEM.

QVID NATVRA MANV, GENIVS QVID FLAMINE POSSIT,
QVID FORTVNA FAVORE, BREVIS TRIA NVMINA VITÆ,
EN CORPVSQVE ANIMVSQVE PROBANT VENTVRAQVE REGNA.

The Same.
What Nature can do by her [shaping] hand, and my guardian spirit by its breath, and Fortune by her favour – these three being the guiding deities of our brief life – lo, these things my beauteous form, and my mind, and my coming reign do show forth in turn.

XX
D. CAROLI MAXIMILIANI
Aureliorum Ducis.

MARTIS AMOR, VIVAXQVE ANIMVS, VENERANDAQVE DIVVM
FORMA MIHI EST: QVI SIC PVERVM PVERILIBVS ANNIS
PELIDEM REFERO, REFERAM IVVENEMQVE VIRVMQVE.

Lord Charles Maximilian, Duke of Orleans.
A love of war, and the majestic beauty of the gods – these gifts do I possess; and I who thus in my boyish years recall the boyhood of Peleus' son [Achilles],

shall recall him as a youth and a full-grown man as well.
The future Charles IX (1550–74) was only eight years old at the time, although he ascended the throne a scant two years later under the regency of Catherine de' Medici. His preceptor was Amyot and apparently he was already showing signs of his later passionate interest in hunting and jousting. (Cf. Jodelle, 'Ode de la chasse au Roy,' *Œuvres*, ed. Balmas I, p. 210.)

The words 'PVERILIBVS ANNIS PELIDEM REFERO' would surely represent an allusion to Achilles' education under Chiron the centaur, cf. Alciati, Emb. CLXV *Consiliarii Principum* (ed. 1549, p. 179). It had in any case been previously used in a fresco by Rosso Fiorentino at Fontainebleau which presumably represents Francis I and the Dauphin Francis (†1536); cf. D. and E. Panofsky, 'The Iconography of the *Galerie François Ier* at Fontainebleau,' *Gazette des Beaux-Arts*, s. 6, LII (1958), pp. 150–4.

XXI
D. EDOARDI
Angolismentium Ducis.

ORE LEPOS, GENIO GRAVITAS, ET MORIBVS EXIT
ANTE SVVM MIHI TEMPVS HONOS, VTRIVSQVE MINERVÆ
HIS EGO CEV IVSTA LIBRO DVO MVNERA LANCE.

Lord Edward, Duke of Angoulême.
Charm proceeds from his looks, earnestness from his spirit, and uprightness from his character, in advance methinks of his age; and with these I balance, in an equally-poised scale as it were, the two gifts belonging to the two Minervas [i.e. warlike and peaceful skills].

The future Henry III (1551–89) was christened Edouard-Alexandre and used these names until 1566 when he received the duchy of Anjou as his apanage.

XXII

36v° D. HERCVLIS

Andium Ducis.

HERCVLIS EST NOMEN MIHI, MAIORI HERCVLE NATO
QVAM QVI NATVS ERAT IOVE, SIC IMITABOR VTRVMQVE,
HVC ME ME GENVS, HVC HOMEN ME GRANDIVS VRGET.

Lord Hercule, Duke of Anjou.
My name is Hercules, son of a greater Hercules than he who was son of Jove: so shall I imitate both of them; to this am I urged both by my descent and by my august name.

There seems to be some confusion about the names and titles given to the youngest son of Henry II and Catherine de' Medici. Born in 1554, he was first called Hercule but in 1564 took the name François. Cf. Jodelle, *Œuvres*, ed. Balmas I, p. 256:

> Hercule on te nomma peu après ta naissance,
> Depuis nommé François quand tu sortois d'enfance,
> En ce nom tu changeas un nom de haut renom,
> Mais des deux noms je fay la difference nulle,
> Car puis qu'en tous effets François estoit Hercule,
> Suivant François tu prens d'Hercule encor le nom.

Similarly, in his early years François-Hercule was called Duc d'Anjou (cf. Thevet, Rasse des Nœux, etc.) even though he later became Duc d'Alençon and only reverted to his former title after the accession of Henry III, who was called Duke of Anjou in the intervening years. (Laumonier erroneously identifies the recipient of one of Ronsard's sonnets as Charles d'Orléans when it evidently should be François-Hercule for this very reason. Cf. *Œuvres* (STFM), VII, p. 299.) For the formalities relating to the name change, cf. *Registres des délibérations du Bureau de l'Hôtel de Ville de Paris*, t. V, p. 553 *et seq.*

XXIII
D. ELISABEÆ
Henrici Reg. filiæ oliva coronatæ.

PALLADIA CVR SIT CINCTVM CAPVT HOSPES OLIVA
DISCE MEVM, VEL MARGARIDIS POST TEMPORA PALLAS
HIC ERO, VEL VETEREM PER ME FERET ORBIS OLIVAM.

Lady Elisabeth, daughter of King Henry, garlanded with the olive.
Learn, stranger, why my head is bound with Pallas' olive bough: either I shall be Pallas here on earth after Marguerite's day, or the world shall produce its ancient olive [the emblem of peace] by my aid.

Elisabeth de Valois (1546–68) became Queen of Spain by her marriage to Philip II on 22 June 1559. Both her marriage and that of Madame Marguerite to the Duc de Savoie were results of the Treaty of Câteau Cambrésis. Jodelle later wrote a series of poems on the death of Elisabeth de Valois. (Cf. *Œuvres complètes*, ed. Balmas, I, pp. 208–10.) Her device was inappropriately enough *Iam feliciter omnia* and an appropriate florilegia from the Spanish point of view may be found in *Le Imprese Illustri . . . del Sor Ieronimo Ruscelli*, Venice, 1566, pp. 313 ff.

XXIV
D. CLAVDIÆ
eiusdem Reg. fil.

GALLICA ME GENVIT DOMVS, ET LOTHARENA MARITAM
ACCIPIET, SIC CVM DOMVI DOMVS OMNIS VTRIQVE
NVNC CEDAT, LVCINA MIHI BENE CESSIT HYMENQVE.

Lady Claudia, daughter of the same King.

A French house bore me, and Lorraine shall receive me in matrimony: thus since every house now yields to these two houses, my birth and marriage have alike been fortunate.

Claude de France (1547–74) married Charles III, duc de Lorraine on 22 January 1559. Cf. M.R. de Magnienville, *Claude de France, duchesse de Lorraine*, Paris, Perrin, 1885.

XXV
D. MARGARITÆ
eiusdem Reg. fil.

ME GRATÆ CHARITES, ME ME VENVS AVREA FOVIT
PVRPVREO BLANDITA SINV, LICET ILLIVS HOSTIS,
CYPRIDA TV COMITEM NE DEDIGNARE MINERVA.

Lady Marguerite, daughter of the same King.
The grateful Graces, and golden Venus who embraced me in her rosy bosom, have nurtured me. O thou Minerva, though thou be a foe to Cypris [i.e. Venus], do not spurn Cypris as thy companion [within my nature].

Marguerite de Valois (1553–1615) later married Henry of Navarre, the future Henry IV, in 1572. (The marriage was dissolved in 1599.) Her various romantic entanglements were the subject of much gossip, and this early reference to Venus embracing her in her rosy bosom seems almost prophetic. The *topos* is nonetheless based upon a perfectly respectable Neoplatonic assumption that these two 'opposing' natures may under certain circumstances be complementary. Cf. Edgar Wind, *Pagan Mysteries in the Renaissance*, New York, 1968[2], p. 71.

XXVI
EARVNDEM D. D. D.
Elisabeæ, Claudiæ et Margaritæ.

PRIMA CANES ET EQVOS, OPTATQVE VT DELIA SYLVAS
VT PALLASQVE ARTES, CHOREASQVE VT CYPRIA, ET OLLI
VTRAQVE IVNCTA SOROR FIT NIMPHA, CAMŒNA, CHARISQVE.

The same Ladies, Elisabeth, Claudia and Marguerite.
The first of these longs for dogs and horses and, like Delia [i.e. Diana], the wild woods; and, like Pallas, the arts; and like Venus, the dance, and each of her two sisters, joined with her, becomes a nymph, a Muse, a Grace.

It was only natural that poets should address the three sisters comparing them to nymphs, three of the Muses or the three Graces. Cf. Ronsard, 'A mes Dames,' *Œuvres*, ed. Laumonier (STFM), VII, pp. 75–80. Cf. Icon I, p. 144, for a less generalized usage of these conceits.

XXVII
SEPTEM ILLORVM REGIS 37r°
Natorum in eadem tabula expressorum: Per imprecationem.

CONCORDES ANIMI, FELICIA SCEPTRA, BEATVM
CONNVBIVM, VIRTVTIS AMOR, NOMENQVE PERENNE,
ANTE OBITVM VOS ORBE BEENT, POST FVNERA CŒLO.

These seven children of the King, depicted in a single portrait: a prayer.
May hearts united, happy reigns, blest marriages, the love of virtue, and lasting

fame, bless you with the gift of the world in life, and of Heaven in death. A Caron drawing for the *Histoire françoyse de nostre temps*, Louvre, Inv. RF 29724 (fig. 16) shows the descendance of Henry II and Catherine as they are crowned by Juno, personification of sovereign power. Henry's pose and attributes are derived from his father's title-page from the same series, Louvre, Inv. RF 29716 (fig. 11), which is a variant upon the *Ex utroque Cæsar* symbolism which became standard for French monarchs of the Renaissance. This is made explicit by the sword entwined with serpent (-basilisk) and olive, for which see Karl Giehlow, 'Die Hieroglyphenkunde des Humanismus in der Allegorie der Renaissance, besonders der Ehrenpforte Kaisers Maximilians I,' *Jahrbuch der kunsthistorischen Sammlungen des allerhöchsten Kaiserhauses*, XXXII (1915), pp. 214–15 s.v. *disciplina militari prudentia*, *immortalis ac sempiternæ famæ heros*, *pace et bello clarus*. (Cf. Icones XV and XVII.) This composite emblem, with a Greek legend derived from Homer, *Il.*, III, 179 ('For a good king and a mighty warrior'), appears as one of the marks of Fédéric I Morel from his appointment as *imprimeur royal* on 4 March 1571 (cf. J. Dumoulin, *Vie et œuvres de Fédéric Morel, imprimeur à Paris depuis* 1577 *jusqu'à 1583*, Paris, 1901, pp. 135–6) and is thus specifically linked with concepts of French royalty. See introduction, p. 29 *et seq.*

This Icon is not only restricted to the living children, but also merely a group portrait presumably in contemporary costume; the Caron drawing includes the deceased son Louis (1548–50) in diminutive scale and the twins Jeanne and Victoire († 1556) held by a nurse in the shadows – none of whom appear elsewhere in the Icones – while the rest of the family has obviously fulfilled the wish expressed in this Icon. The sonnet on the verso of the drawing fully corroborates the marriage of Elisabeth and Claude (quartered arms and closed crowns) while Marguerite still bears the arms of France awaiting 'ce brave ROY, / Qui tient le Navarois soubz sa main souveraine.' Charles IX precedes his deceased brother Francis II (closed crowns and sceptres) while his two younger brothers are at far left background.

XXVIII
D. ILLIVS MARGARITÆ
Henrici Reg. sororis unicæ.

VNICA NATA MANET REGIS, SOROR VNICA REGIS,
DAT MVSAS PATER, ET VIRES IN PRÆLIA FRATER,
VNICA SIC PERIMIT MORTEMQVE SCELVSQVE MINERVA.

That Lady Marguerite, the only sister of King Henry.
She remains the sole surviving daughter of a king, and a king's sole sister: her father's gifts to her are the Muses, her brother's are strength for battle; thus does she, as sole and single Pallas, abolish death and wickedness.

Cf. p. 86.
Marguerite de France (1523–74), daughter of Francis I and sister of Henry II was successively Duchesse de Berry (1550) and Duchesse de Savoie (1559). Scores of books were dedicated to her by the writers she protected and helped, and because of her intellectual gifts she was commonly called Minerva or Pallas. Cf. Ronsard, 'XXIV Inscriptions,' *Œuvres*, ed. Laumonier (STFM), IX, p. 198:

> La grand' Minerve et la Pallas de France
> Loing des mortels ont chassé le discord,
> A l'Olivier l'une donne naissance,
> L'autre le fait revivre après sa mort.

With her earlier motto RERVM SAPIENTIA CVSTOS, her device is 'un rameau d'Olive entortillé de deux serpents entrelassez l'un à l'autre.' (Cf. R. Peyre, *Une Princesse de la Renaissance: Marguerite de France, duchesse de Berry, duchesse de Savoie*, Paris, Emile-Paul, 1902.) With the later version RERVM PRVDENTIA CVSTOS it is 'une teste de Meduse eschevelée de serpens.' (Cf. Scévole et Louis Sainte-Marthe, *Histoire généalogique de la Maison de France*, p. 502.) The Gorgon head is identified with the shield of Pallas.

XXIX
EIVSDEM
ex mea ad illam Gorgone.

DVM CŒLVM MIHI VICTRICI, NOCTEMQVE RECLVDO
ÆTERNAM SCELERI, ET PROFVGIS VIRTVTIBVS ORBEM,
ME CŒLVM, ME TERRA DEAM, ME TARTARA NORINT.

The same, from my *Gorgon* addressed to her.
While I reveal Heaven to myself as conqueror, and to wickedness show endless night, to the exiled Virtues the orb of Earth, Heaven and Earth and Hell shall know me to be a goddess.

Like the *Pyramide* addressed to the Cardinal Charles de Lorraine (cf. p. 177), the *Gorgon* has been lost, if indeed it ever existed. The elliptical quality of this inscription makes it difficult to imagine the lines in a poetic context.

XXX
EIVSDEM PALLADIVM
semper inter meos lares habitum.

NEC DIOMEDÆIS, MANIBVS NEC CEDAT VLYSSES
EFFIGIES SACRATA TVIS, MANEATQVE SVPERSTES
PALLADIO CVSTODE, DEÆ DOMVS HVIVS ALVMNA.

The Palladium of the same, ever kept among my household gods.
The sacred image would not yield to the hands of Diomedes, or to yours, O Ulysses; and may it remain, with the Palladium to guard it, the nursling of the goddess of this house.

XXXI
D. ANTONII
Navarrorum Reg.

PATRE MEO, PATRIA, PATRIBVSQVE ET SANGVINE REGVM,
RE, REBVS, REGNO, MAGNA QVOQVE CONIVGE MAGNVS,
SPE MAIOR, CANDORE DVCES SVM MAXIMVS INTER.

The Lord Anthony, King of Navarre.
Great because of my father, my country, my ancestors, and the blood of kings; great in wealth and in achievements, in my kingdom and in my illustrious marriage; greater still in promise; I am, among princes, greatest of all by reason of my shining goodness.

Antoine de Bourbon (1518–62), by his marriage to Jeanne d'Albret in 1549, became King of Navarre. His great ambition was to reunite the Spanish and French parts of that kingdom, which no doubt influenced his vacillation between Catholicism and Protestantism. He was often an embarrassment to Henry II, who nevertheless named him governor of Picardy. Cf. A. de Ruble, *Antoine de Bourbon et Jeanne d'Albret*, Paris, Labitte, 1881–6.

XXXII
EIVSDEM. 37v°

CÆSAREIS SVA REGNA CADENS ANTONIVS ARMIS
CESSIT, AT ISTE TVIS QVI NVNC QVOQVE CÆSAR, ET ARMIS,
ET IVRE ANTONI, REGNVM TIBI CEDET ADEMPTVM.

The same.
[Mark] Anthony, as he fell, yielded his reign to Cæsar's arms; but he who now is Cæsar [i.e. Emperor] shall yield up, to your arms and on Anthony's terms, the kingdom he has taken from you.

The reference is to the part of Navarre held by the Spaniards. Jodelle suggests a reversal of the roles of Anthony (Antoine de Bourbon) and Cæsar (Charles v, later succeeded by Philip II) which did not in fact occur.

XXXIII
D. IANÆ
Navarror. Reginæ.

MATERNIQVE HÆRES STVDII, SOLIIQVE PATERNI,
CHARA VIRO, MAGE CHARA DEO, TOT DOTIBVS ADDAM,
SEMPER VT ESSE QVEAT CHARVS MIHI VIRQVE DEVSQVE.

Lady Jeanne, Queen of Navarre.
Heir of maternal devotion and of a father's throne, dear to my husband and still more dear to God, to a dowry so manifold I shall add this: that both my husband and my God will ever be able to remain dear to me.

Jeanne d'Albret (1528–72), daughter of Henri d'Albret and Marguerite de Navarre, was renowned for her piety. She became a Protestant in 1556 but remained a typical Valois in her appreciation of music and poetry. Cf. A. de Ruble, *Antoine de Bourbon et Jeanne d'Albret*, Paris, Labitte, 1881–6.

XXXIV
EIVSDEM.

ELYSIOS GENITRIX, PETIIT NEC AVVNCVLVS AGROS,
NAM GALLIS DVM MARGARIDEM, TE IANA NAVARRIS
LIQVERVNT, GEMINA GEMINI SVB IMAGINE VIVVNT.

The same.
My mother seeks not the Elysian fields, nor my uncle either, for while they left

Marguerite to the French and you, Jeanne, to the people of Navarre, they now live as twins under a twin image.

Jeanne's mother was, of course, Marguerite de Navarre and her uncle Francis I. Both have presumably become gods (cf. pp. 143 and 147) and may have been assimilated to Apollo and Diana.

XXXV
ILLVSTRISS. PRINCIP.
CAROLI *Lotharingorum Ducis.*

ME MEA MAGNA DVCEM LOTHARINGIA, IACTAT ALVMNVM
GALLIA, FORMA MIHI, GENVS EST MIHI TALE, SOCERQVE,
VT SOBOLEM GENEROSQVE IOVIS, ET ADONIDA VINCAM.

The most illustrious prince Charles, Duke of Lorraine.
My great Lorraine boasts of me as her Duke, and France boasts of me as her offspring; my good looks and high birth are such, and my father-in-law is such, that I can surpass the offspring and children-in-law of Jupiter, and also outdo Adonis.

Charles III, Duke of Lorraine (1543–1608), succeeded to the title on the death of his father, Francis II, in 1545. He was taken to the court to be raised there after the capture of Metz in 1552 despite his mother's opposition. He became an intimate of the Dauphin, Francis, and married Claude de France on 22 January 1559. This should have strengthened French influence in Lorraine but was actually used later by the young duke as a claim to the throne of France. Cf. L. Daville, *Les Prétentions de Charles III, duc de Lorraine, à la couronne de France*, Paris, 1908.

XXXVI
ILLVSTRISS. PRINCIP.
FRANCISCI *Guisiorum Ducis.*

NEC METÆ, RENTINA NEC EST MIHI PVGNA, CALETVM
DIRAQVE GVINA SATIS, RESTANT TOT MONSTRA, QVIBVS IAM
AVSPICE EGO ALCIDES HENRICO CEV IOVE FIAM.

The most illustrious prince Francis, Duke of Guise.
Not enough for me are Metz and the battle of Renty, Calais, and grim Guignes; so many monsters remain whose Hercules I am to be, with Henry, like Jupiter, as my lord of battle.

François de Guise (1519–63) was one of the ablest generals of the sixteenth century. He defended Metz against Charles v in 1552, defeated the Emperor's army at Renty in 1554 and captured Calais and Guignes in January 1558. (Cf. pp. 4 and 71.) François' relationship to Henry as *optimus princeps* and to his own ancestors (Icon XXXVII) had been set by the legends of his own medals as well as those of Henry (fig. 47) issued in gratitude for the Defence of Metz in 1552. Cf. F. Mazerolle, *Les médailleurs français du XVe siècle au milieu du XVIIe*, II, Paris, 1902, cat. 329–30.

For the Hercules comparison in connection with François de Guise, see also Belleau, 'Ode presentée à Monseigneur le duc de Guise à son retour de Calais,' *Œuvres*, ed. Marty-Laveaux, I, p. 197, vv. 17–18 and François Habert, *Le Dieugard de la ville de Paris à Monseigneur de Guise*, Paris, Attaignant, Sonnets XIII and XIV.

XXXVII
38r°
EIVSDEM.

NEC PATRES, TITVLIQVE, PATRVM NEC CANDIDA RVPES,
NEC PATRIBVS QVÆSITA MEIS FATALIS IDVME,
ME DECORANT, SED EGO PATRES, RVPEMQVE ET IDVMEN.

The same.
Neither ancestors and their monuments of honour, nor the white rock of my forebears, nor doom-ful Edom, my ancestors' goal, give honour to me; but it is I who give honour to my fathers, to the rock and to Edom.

The Guise family traced its ancestry to Godefroi de Bouillon, one of the leaders of the Second Crusade. Cf. Ronsard, 'Harangue du duc de Guise,' *Œuvres*, ed. Laumonier (STFM), v, p. 206. Their goal was the recapture of Jerusalem and Palestine, often referred to poetically as Edom (Idume or Idumæa). Cf. Ronsard 'Hymne de la Justice' (STFM), VIII, p. 47, vv. 1–12; 'L'Hymne de Charles Cardinal de Lorraine' (STFM), IX, p. 32, vv. 49–50 and 'Chant Pastoral' ibid., p. 94, v. 370.

XXXVIII
ILLVSTRISS. PRINCIP.
CAROLI *Cardinalis Lotharingi.*

REM POPVLI, REGVMQVE DOMOS, RITVSQVE DEORVM
DVM GERIT, ELOQVIO, GENIO, RE, CORPORE DIVVS,
OMNES SOLVS HABET CVMVLATO IN NVMINE DIVOS.

The most illustrious prince Charles, Cardinal of Lorraine.
While he ordains the affairs of the people and the houses of kings and the rites of the gods, divine in eloquence, talent, wealth, and beauty, he in himself alone possesses all the gods in an accumulation of divinity.

Charles, Cardinal de Lorraine (1525–74) was a younger brother of the Duc de Guise. Named Archbishop of Reims at the age of 15, it was he who crowned Henry II on 25 July 1547. Two days later he was made a cardinal and throughout the rest of his life continued to play an important role in affairs of state.

Cf. J.J. Guillemin, *Le Cardinal de Lorraine, son influence politique et religieuse au XVIe siècle*, Paris, 1847. Jodelle had special reason to be grateful to him for, as Charles de La Mothe tells us in the introduction to the posthumous edition of his works (1574), 'Charles Cardinal de Lorraine le fit premierement cognoistre au Roy Henry.'

XXXIX
EIVSDEM
ex sua Pyramide.

SVPPOSITO TALEM GENIO FERS CAROLE MOLEM,
QVALIS ATLANTÆIS COLLOQVE HVMERISQVE RECVMBIT,
NON ATHLAS TAMEN IPSE, NEPOS SED ATLANTICVS IPSE.

The same from his own Pyramid.
Charles, you bear upon your spirit the weight of so great a mass of care as would fall from the neck and shoulders of Atlas himself: but you yourself are not Atlas, but Atlas' grandson [i.e. Hermes, associated with good fortune].

Cf. pp. 98 and 171.
The pyramid or, more properly, obelisk, is used by Jodelle in his 'Desseins pour la Croix de Gastines.' Cf. *Œuvres complètes*, ed. Balmas, I, pp. 302–3 and E. Balmas, 'Un inedito di Jodelle: a proposito della "Croix de Gastines"' in *Montaigne a Padova e altri studi* (Padua, Liviana, 1962), pp. 51–107.

The *Pyramide* addressed to the Cardinal de Lorraine was probably never completed. Cf. E. Balmas, *Etienne Jodelle*, p. 363.

XL
EIVSDEM

HANC STATVAM, CEV PYGMALION, LICET ALGEAT, OMNI
SPE, LACHRIMIS, PRECE, CARMINIBVS, VOTISQVE FATIGO.
DII FACIANT, DIVI NOBIS VT IMAGO CALESCAT.

The same.
Like Pygmalion, I assail this statue, though it be cold, with every kind of hope, tears, prayers and spells and vows. May the gods cause the image of a god to grow warm for our sakes.

The *topos* is taken from Ovid, *Metamorphoses* x, and the image itself, in the absence of other indications, can be acceptably considered that of *Fortuna bona*. Those qualities enumerated in Icon XXXVIII and the indirect reference to Hermes (who was not only messenger of the gods but also patron of the artisanat) in Icon XXXIX make it possible for the Cardinal of Lorraine series to be read sequentially. This may then generally relate to Alciati, Emb. CXVII *Ars naturam adiuvans* (ed. 1549, p. 120), whose verse runs:

Sur ung boulet Fortune à tous hazardz;
Sur ung quadrangle, Hermes præside aulx ars.
Contre Fortune est faict art pour remede:
Car mauvais sort au bon art requiert ayde.
Appren bon ars (O jeunesse oportune)
Qui hont en soy redresse de fortune.

XLI
ANNÆ MOMMORANTII
præfecti militiæ, quem vulgo Connestablium appellamus.

NOMINE, CONSILIO, FACTIS, OPIBVSQVE FIDEQVE,
FVSA NVBE, ITERVM CANA HÆC FVLGESCET IMAGO,
CEV MARTIS TOT SIGNA INTER RVBET IGNIBVS ASTRVM.

Anne Montmorency, commander of the soldiery, whom we commonly call the Constable.

Mingled with the clouds already in fame, wisdom, deeds, wealth, and faith, this white-haired image shall once again shine bright, just as the planet of Mars glows fiery red among all those constellations.

Anne de Montmorency (1493–1567) was named after his godmother, Anne de Bretagne, wife of Louis XII. As a distinguished general and strategist he was closely associated with Francis I, who named him marshal in 1522 and connétable in 1538. At the time of the capture of Calais he was already in his mid fifties but he had also been taken prisoner at the defeat of the French army at St Quentin in 1557. Cf. André Du Chesne, *Histoire généalogique de la maison de Montmorency et de Laval*, Paris, Cramoisy, 1624, pp. 377–422.

38v°

XLII
EIVSDEM.

INVIDIT FORTVNA MEIS PRIVS ÆQVA TRIVMPHIS,
NAM RESTABAT ADHVC, SVPERATIS REGIBVS, ILLAM
LÆTVS VT EXTREMA POSSEM SVPERARE SENECTA.

The same.
Fortune, formerly fair, cast an envious glance upon my triumphs; for once the kings were defeated it still remained for me to be able to surpass *her* in my extreme old age.

XLIII
ODONIS
Cardinalis Castellonei.

INGENIVM, CANDORQVE, SIMVL VIX ADDITA CVIQVAM
LVMINA, PVRPVREO MIHI SIC CVM MVRICE FVLGENT,
VT PROCERES IVVET HOC, IVVET HOC MISERABILE VVLGVS.

Odo, Cardinal of Châtillon.
Talents, and goodness, and brilliance scarce given to anyone, shine so brightly in me along with my purple that both men of rank and the multitude of poor men are delighted at this [my Cardinalate].

Odet de Coligny, Cardinal de Châtillon (1517–71), was the second son of Gaspard de Coligny, maréchal de France and Louise de Montmorency, sister of Anne de Montmorency. He was made a cardinal on 4 November 1533 by Pope Clement VII, Catherine de' Medici's uncle, who wished to attach himself to powerful nobles at the court on the occasion of his niece's marriage to the future Henry II. Cf. L. Marlet, *Le Cardinal de Châtillon*, Paris, 1883 and fig. 17.

XLIV
EIVSDEM
in Castellum unde Castelloneus dictus est.

PIERVS AONIDAS IAM PENE IN TVRRE NECABAT
CVM PENNIS FVGERE NOVIS: ECCE ALTERA TVRRIS,
EXTINCTAS PROPE QVÆ RECIPIT REFICITQVE CAMŒNAS.

The same, on the castle whence he is named 'de Châtillon.'
Pierus was already half-slaying the Aonian maidens [i.e. the Muses] in the tower, when they fled away on new wings; behold here another tower, which receives and refreshes the almost expiring Muses.

The name Pierus should read Pyreneus. In Ovid, *Metamorphoses* V, two actions are described and Jodelle, unfortunately, picked the wrong referent to make this Icon incomprehensible. Pyreneus was a king of Thrace who tried to imprison the Muses, daughters of Jupiter and Mnemosyne, who could assume wings at will to make their escape. Pierus was father of the Pierides, also nine in number, who were changed from maidens into birds after unsuccessfully contesting the Muses in song.

Odet de Châtillon was born at Châtillon-sur-Loing, a small town situated on the slope of a high hill on the frontier between Burgundy and Bresse which was dominated by an impressive château with a donjon 27 metres high which still exists. Cf. Charles Fontaine, *Odes, énigmes, et épigrammes*, Lyon, Citoys, 1557, p. 49. 'A Monseigneur le Cardinal de Chastillon':

> C'est un beau nom que Chastillon:
> C'est un fort nom pareillement:
> La Muse, en ce disant ne ment,
> Chastillon est son bastillon.

The Cardinal de Châtillon was very much interested in all the arts (cf. Ronsard, 'Le temple de Messeigneurs le connestable et des Chastillons,' *Œuvres*, ed. Laumonier (STFM), VIII, pp. 72–84) and added a wing to the château with a large gallery where poets and musicians collaborated in the entertainment. Cf. M. Becquerel, *Souvenirs historiques sur l'amiral Coligny et sa famille et sa seigneurie de Châtillon-sur-Loing*, Paris, Firmin-Didot, 1876. There is no specific evidence, however, to support Becquerel's statement: 'Jean Goujon lui prêta son ciseau pour décorer cette galerie, ainsi que le peristyle du château' (p. 17. Cf. also p. 30).

XLV
DIANÆ PICTONICÆ

NEC STIRPS CLARA, MEOQVE VALENTIA IVNCTA VALORI,
NEC MIHI LVMEN ERVNT TOT OPES, NEC SPLENDOR ANETI,
A MAIORE DIANA REFERT SIBI LVMINE LVMEN.

Diane de Poitiers.
Neither my illustrious descent, and Valentia joined to my valour, nor so much wealth as this, shall be a glory to me, nor yet the fame of Anet . . . ; Diana reflects upon herself the light of a greater light.

Diane de Poitiers (1499–1566) was Duchesse de Valentinois, and Valentia is a play on words suggesting her title as well as valour. In 1512 she married Louis de Brézé, who died in 1531, after which she wore only black relieved with white. (Cf. p. 121.) Because of the name Diana, it was common to compare her to the goddess Diana both as huntress and as the moon. Cf. Françoise Bardon, *Diane de Poitiers et le mythe de Diane*, Paris, Presses Universitaires de France, 1963. Henry is, of course, the sun (cf. p. 122) and the crescent device which he used, along with all its other connotations, no doubt also suggested Diane de Poitiers. (Cf. p. 83, n. 45.)

XLVI
EIVSDEM

LVNA DIANA, HECATE, TENEBRIS, SYLVISQVE, EREBOQVE
PRÆSES ERO, MODO SIT MIHI NOX INSCITIA, SÆVÆ
CRIMINA SÆVA FERÆ, VETERVMQVE INSOMNIA MANES.

The same.
I, Diana, shall be the Moon, Hecate, a leader in the darkness and in the forest and in the underworld, so long as I have night and secrecy and the fierce crimes of a wild beast, and those Manes [i.e. spirits of the departed] which caused the ancients to lose their sleep.

Cf. Jeronimo Ruscelli, *Le Imprese Illustri . . .* , Venice, 1566, p. 181, who quotes a Latin distichon which parallels Jodelle's own *vers rapportés* to Diana:

Terret, lustrat, agit, Proserpina, Luna, Diana
Ima, superna, feras, sceptro, fulgore, sagitta

The three terms of comparison are also used by Jodelle in Sonnet II of the *Amours* (*Œuvres*, ed. Balmas, I, p. 393. Cf. also p. 396.)

Lune, Diane, Hecate, aux cieux, terre, et enfers
Ornant, questant, genant, nos Dieux, nous,
et nos ombres.

39r°

XLVII
GASPARIS COLLIGNÆI
maris præfecti qui vulgo Amiralis dicitur.

ARTE SAGAX, ET MARTE FEROX, TERRAQVE MARIQVE
MVNERA BINA GERO, PATIOR SED VTRINQVE PROCELLAS:
REX DAT AQVAS, DAT RES, REBVS DATE NVMINA PORTVM.

Gaspard de Coligny, Commander of the naval forces, commonly styled Admiral.
Proficient in my calling and spirited in war, I fulfil two functions by land and sea, but from both sides I am buffeted by storms: the King gives me the sea and the charge of affairs: grant ye gods, that those affairs may reach a safe haven.

Gaspard II, Amiral de Coligny (1519–72) was a brother of Odet de Châtillon (cf. p. 180) and a great favourite of Henry II. He was named Amiral de France in 1552. He quarrelled with the Duc de Guise in 1554 over the victory at Renty and was captured by the enemy at St Quentin in 1557. Cf. Jules Delaborde, *Gaspard de Coligny, amiral de France*, Paris, Sandoz, 1881, and L. Romier, *Les Origines politiques des guerres de religion*, Paris, Perrin, 1913–14.

Barthélemy Aneau's gloss on Alciati's Emb. XLIII, *Spes proxima* (ed. 1549, pp. 67–8) reads: 'Translation d'une nef agitée de tourmente: à une Republicque vexée. Et des feux de Castor, et Pollux: aulx defenseurs de Republicque, ou survenue de bon Prince, ou bons gouverneurs. Lesquelz feux apparoissans en tourmente signifient salut prochain: et sont appellez des mariniers, Sainct Esme, et Sainct Clair.'

XLVIII
IACOBI ALBONII
Galliar. ut dicitur Mareschali.

FORTVNÆ CHARVS, MARTI QVOQVE CHARVS, ET ACRI
CHARIOR HENRICO, TRIBVS HIS NVNC PRIVOR, AT IPSVM
REDDITE DII REGEM, FRVAR HIS IAM IAMQVE DVOBVS.

Jacques d'Albon [Marshal of the Gauls, as he is styled].
I who am dear to Fortune and to Mars also, and dearer still to fierce Henry, now am deprived of all three; but, ye gods, restore to me the king alone and I shall presently enjoy the other two as well.

Jacques d'Albon, Seigneur de Saint-André, maréchal de France (1512–62) was very closely attached to Henry II while he was dauphin and after he became king. Like Anne de Montmorency (cf. p. 178) and Gaspard de Coligny (cf. p. 183), he was taken prisoner at St Quentin in 1557, but his Icon is the only one to contain a discreet allusion to his desire to be released. Cf. L. Romier, *La Carrière d'un favori: Jacques d'Albon de Saint-André*, Paris, Perrin, 1909.

XLIX
IANI COSSÆI
Galliar. quoque mareschali, et in Gall. transalpina proregis.

ILLE EGO SVM, QVID MVTA LOQVI VIS MARMORA? FAS SIT
SOLA LOQVI TOT GESTA, QVIBVS CEV GORGONE VERTO
HESPERIOS IN SAXA, MEIS QVOS ALPIBVS ADDO.

Jean de Cossé, also Marshal of the Gauls, and Viceroy in Transalpine France.
I am he: what wouldst thou that the mute marble should utter? Let it be

possible to tell only of those many deeds, whereby I am (as it were, with a Gorgon-shield) turning the Italians into stone, adding them to the Alps which are already mine.

Jean or rather Charles de Cossé, Comte de Brissac (1506–63), was one of the most distinguished French generals. He participated in many of the Italian campaigns and was named governor of Piedmont in 1550. He was in Italy at the time of the disaster of St Quentin (1557), which made it impossible for the army to be maintained there despite Jodelle's somewhat biased interpretation of events. Nonetheless an appealing conceit ('HESPERIOS IN SAXA...') based on the transformation of Phineus and his companions and, by extension, related to Picardy's address to Henry in the *Recueil*, p. 93.

L
PAVLI THERMÆI
in Caletis proregis.

SCOTICA SERVATA EST TELLVS, ET CORSICA VICTA,
ALPINOS REXI LATIOSQVE, REGAMQVE CALETES,
IAM CEDANT MERITÆ LIVOR IVVENESQVE SENECTÆ.

Paul of Thermes, viceroy at Calais.
The Scottish earth is saved, and Corsica subdued; I have established rule over the men of the Alps and of Latium, and will do so over the men of Calais. Now shall envious young men give place to old age that has proved its worth.

Paul de La Barthe, Seigneur de Thermes (1482–1562) was relatively unknown until 1530 when he became one of Francis I's generals. The victory over the English in Scotland (1549–50) was a personal triumph for him. (See p. 99. Cf. *passim* Jan de Beaugué, *l'Histoire de la guerre d'Escosse*, Paris, G. Corrozet, 1556.) He also was victorious at Parma (1551), Siena (1552), and in the invasion of Corsica. (Cf. L. Romier, *Les Origines politiques des guerres de religion*, Paris, Perrin, 1913 I, pp. 385–90). After the siege of Calais in which he took part, Thermes was named governor of that city.

Cæteri desunt, quos omnes tam virorum, quam mulierum, suo ordine et scribemus, et edemus: nunc enim hos ipsos quos habebamus, non aliter edere potuimus, quam pluribus omissis, et confuso in plerisque ordine.

The rest of the Images of both men and women, which I shall compose and publish in due order, are lacking: for at this time I was able only to publish with several omissions, and in a confused arrangement for the most part, even those Images that I had in my possession.

39v°

EXTERORVM ALIQVOT.*

LI
D. PAVLI IIII.
Pontificis Max.

IAM PETRVS PAVLVSQVE TIBI CVM CLAVIBVS ENSEM
CONCEDVNT, PERDIS QVOTQVOT POTES ENSE REBELLES,
CLAVIBVS AVXILIVM REGVM LOCVLOSQVE RECLVDIS.

Lord Paul IV, Pontifex Maximus [the usual humanist way of referring to a Pope].
Now Peter and Paul give up to you the sword, along with the keys; you slay with the sword as many rebels as you can, and with the keys you unlock the assistance, and the treasure-chests, of kings.

Paul IV (1476–1559) was a member of a family of exiled Neopolitans, the Caraffas. He became a cardinal in 1536 and was elected Pope in 1555 at the age of 80. He was anti-Spanish and hence an ally of the French. The expedition of the Duc de Guise to Italy in 1557 was designed to protect the papal states against a threatened invasion by the Spaniards from Naples under the Duke of Alba. Henry II's imprudence in sending the bulk of the army to the south led to a counter-attack by Emmanuel Philibert and the defeat at Saint Quentin. Abandoned by the French, the Pope then made peace with Philip II.

* Several Images of Foreign Persons.

LII
D. CAROLI V.
Romanor. Imperatoris.

VIRTVTISQVE DOLIQVE POTENS, ET CÆSAR, ET INGENS
BELLATOR, VOLVI SENIORQVE ET PRÆSCIVS HOSTI
CEDERE, NE MIHI SIM PARTIS ET HONORIBVS HOSTIS.

Lord Charles v, Emperor of the Romans.
Master of bravery and of guile, both Emperor and mighty warrior, I decided – for I was too old, and foresaw the event – to yield to the enemy, lest I be enemy to my own gains and honours.

Charles v (1500–58) through his father the Archduke Philip of Austria became ruler of the Low Countries and through his mother Mary head of the House of Burgundy. He became king of Spain in 1517 and was elected emperor in 1519. On 26 October 1555 he formally ceded Germany to his brother Ferdinand and his other states to his son Philip. He then retired to Spain, where he died in 1558.

The *Cesar Renouvellé par les observations militaires du S. Gabriel Symeon*[*i*] (Paris, V. Sertenas, 1558 with *achevé d'imprimer* of 2 December 1557) was dedicated to the dauphin, later Francis II of France. It purports to be a parallel between Cæsar and Augustus and the second Henry and his son, and is set forth in a simple moralizing style with an abundance of exemplars. The following instance, appearing in ch. 45, *Il est bon de choisir une place inexpugnable, et la tenir fort contre l'ennemy pour sauver le demeurant d'une Province*, seems to be directly related to the substance of this Icon as well as to the case of Calais. Symeoni selects the Gallic hero Vercingetorix and lauds him for the things 'qu'il feit contre Cesar à l'assault de Gerguoie: après lequel le sage Empereur fut contraint se retirer pour aller remedier aux mutinations et desordres de Bourgogne; lequel exemple nous apprend aussi que le meilleur est (après avoir cogneu un lieu inexpugnable) de se retirer de bonne heure; sans y consommer en vain les bienes, l'honneur, la reputation, la vie, et les personnes: comme jadis feit l'Empereur Charles cinquieme devant Mets en Lorraine (fols. 40v–41r).'

LIII
D. FERDINANDI
nuper Imperatoris electi.

FRATERNI IAM IVRE SENEX SVSCEPIT HABENAS
IMPERII, NAM CVM DOMVS HÆC IAM IAMQVE SENESCAT,
HESPERIA ANTE DIEM TRAHERET SVA FATA IVVENTVS.

Lord Ferdinand [of Habsburg], lately Emperor-elect.
He, being the elder, has now of right undertaken the guidance of his brother's empire; for since this house is now upon the verge of old age, the youth of Italy would [else] now bring its fate upon itself prematurely.

Ferdinand I (1503–64), younger brother of Charles V, was king of Bohemia and, through his wife Anne, daughter of Ladislas VI, king of Hungary. He was elected 'Roi des Romains' at Cologne in 1531 and after the abdication of Charles V was confirmed as emperor at Frankfort.

LIV
D. PHILIPPI
Hispan. et Angl. Regis.

PRINCIPIIS HOSPES NE FIDE, HIC PACIS AMATOR,
DVM MAVORS FAVET, ALLECTVS BELLA HORRIDA IVRAT,
NVNC PACEM LICET EXHAVSTVS VELIT ÆRE REDEMPTAM.

Lord Philip, King of Spain and England.

Stranger, trust not beginnings. This lover of peace was tempted to swear dreadful war while Mars was in his favour; but now he would fain have peace bought back by money, though his resources have drained away.

Philip II of Spain (1527–98) was the son of Charles V. On 25 July 1554 he married Mary Tudor of England and in 1555 his father abdicated in his favour. Philip broke a truce with Henry II to send troops in league with the English to Saint Quentin (1557). Mary Tudor died 17 November 1558 with, as she said, the name of Calais inscribed on her heart, and on 22 June 1559, Philip married Henry's daughter Elisabeth! (Cf. p. 166.)

LV
D. MARIÆ 40r°
Angliæ Reginæ.

HVIC SI BELLA, CRVOR, FVRIÆ, CÆDESQVE SVORVM,
FŒDERA RVPTA, ODIVMQVE PLACENT, PORTENTAQVE, NVLLI
IAM PLACET, HANC NEC AMAT SED AMAT DATA REGNA MARITVS.

Lady Mary, Queen of England.
Since she loves wars, blood, vengeance, and the slaughter of her fellow-countrymen, and the breaking of pledges, and hatred, and monstrous deeds, she is loved by none any more; her very husband loves her not – he but loves the kingdom she brought him.

Jodelle echoes the commonly accepted ideas about 'Bloody Mary.' Mary Tudor (1516–58) became queen in 1553, married Philip of Spain in 1554, and died childless four years later. Cf. H.F.M. Prescott, *Mary Tudor*, London, Eyre and Spottiswoode, 1952.

LVI
D. MAXIMILIANI
Bohemiæ Regis, Philippo Regi dextram dantis, ut nuper Antverpiæ depictus est.

IVNGE MANVM MANVI, ET NVPER IVRATA PHILIPPO
IN GALLOS ODIA EX ODIO CONVERTE PRIORE,
AT TIBI VEL SATIVS FORET EXODISSE PHILIPPVM.

Lord Maximilian, King of Bohemia, giving his right hand to King Philip, as he was depicted recently at Antwerp.
Join hand with hand, and turn the hatred that Philip lately swore against the French away from the former state of enmity: but it would be even better for you to loathe Philip [himself].

Maximilian II of Hapsburg (1527–76) was a son of Ferdinand I, who actually remained king of Bohemia until 1562 when Maximilian was elected king of the Romans. The king of Bohemia is one of the seven electors of the Holy Roman Empire. (Cf. introduction, p. 14.)

The description is presumably a reminiscence of Cornelius Schrijver, *Spectaculorum in susceptione Philippi. Hisp. Prin. Divi Caroli. V. Cæs. F. An. M.D.XLIX. Antverpiæ* . . . , Antwerp, 1550, also published in French and Flemish editions. Fols. F2v–F3r (fig. 46) show the two Columns of Hercules with a Temple of Janus, but it is Charles V rather than Maximilian who offers his hand to the youthful Philip II while Augustus closes the temple at the left with his key. The inscription for this, the Spanish Portal (fol. F3v), specifies:

VT QVONDAM AVGVSTVS, NVNC CLAVSIT LIMINA IANI
CAROLVS, IN MVLTOS NON RESERANDA DIES:
SIC ET SPERAMVS (DOMITO PRIVS ORBE) PHILIPPE,
VSQVE SVB IMPERIO CLAVSA FVTVRA TVO

Yet the text refers to a common conceit, Alciati, Emb. XXXIX, *Concordia* for which Barthélemy Aneau provides the gloss (ed. 1549, p. 63) 'C'est le commun signe de la foy civile que toucher la main dextre l'ung à l'aultre.' Both in any case refer to preparations of Henry II and Charles V for the succession of their sons. Cf. pp. 160–2.

LVII
DANIELIS BRENTELII
Archiepiscopi Maguntini Romani Imperii Electoris.

SVM MAGVNTINIS PRÆSVL SACER ATQVE SACRATI
ELECTOR SACER IMPERII, SACRVMQVE SIGILLVM
GERMANÆ DO NOMOPHYLAX SVB CÆSARE GENTI.

Daniel Brentel, Archbishop of Mainz, Elector.
To the people of Mainz I am a holy prelate and holy elector of the holy Empire; and I give the holy seal to the German nation as a guardian of law under Cæsar [i.e. the Emperor].

Daniel Brendel von Homburg became Archbishop of Mainz and an Elector of the Holy Roman Empire on 18 April 1555. As such he was High Chancellor of Germany. He took over under difficult conditions and was universally respected for his integrity and his efforts to improve conditions. Cf. A. Baudrillart, *Dictionnaire d'histoire et de géographie ecclésiastiques*, Paris, Letouzey, 1938, Vol. X, col. 537.

LVIII
ADOLPHI COMITIS
Schaumburgensis Archiepiscopi Coloniensis ac Electoris.

ME DOMVS, ET TITVLIS DECORAT COLONIA NOSTRIS
ADDITA, CVI PRÆSVM, PER QVAM MIHI IVRA LEGENDI
CÆSARIS, ITALICI PER QVAM MIHI CVRA SIGILLI.

Adolf, Count of Schaumberg, Archbishop of Cologne, Elector.
My house confers honour on me, and Cologne, added to our family titles; Cologne, of which I am Lord, and on whose behalf I have the right of electing the Emperor, and for which I have the keeping of the Italian seal.

Adolf von Schauenberg was named Archbishop of Cologne in 1547 and as an Elector of the Holy Roman Empire automatically became High Chancellor for Italy. He died 20 September 1556 and was succeeded by Anton von Schauenberg, which suggests that Jodelle's inscription was likely composed between April and September 1556. (Cf. below.)

LIX
IANI A LEYEN
Archiepiscopi Treverensis ac Elect.

EN PRÆSVL TREVERENSIS, ET HVIC QVOQVE IVRE LEGVNTVR
INDVPERATORES, HVIC INCLYTA GALLIA CVRÆ,
HVIC VTINAM RELIQVISQVE FORET IAM GALLIA CORDI.

Jan van Leyen, Archibishop of Trèves, Elector.
Behold the high-priest of Trèves; and by him, too, are Emperors elected by right: famous Gaul is his charge; oh that Gaul might be dear both to this one and to the rest of them!

Johan von der Leyen was Archbishop of Trèves and an Elector of the Empire from 15 April 1556 to 9 February 1567 when he died. His official position was High Chancellor of Arles, the name sometimes given to the former Kingdom of Burgundy whose capital in the Middle Ages was Trèves.

LX
AVGVSTI SAXONIÆ
Ducis, eiusdem imper. Elect. 40v°

AVGVSTI NOMEN, STVDIO SAXONIA BELLI
ASPERA, IVSQVE INGENS PRÆSVM QVO CÆSARIS ARMIS,
PROPRIAQVE AVGVSTOS MIHI REDDENT ARMA PENATES.

Augustus of Saxony, Duke and Elector of the same Emperor.
The name of Augustus, and Saxony fierce in her love of war, and the majestic right that I have to command the Emperor's armies, and my own arms too, shall make my house 'august' indeed.

August of Saxony was a brother of Maurice, whom he succeeded in 1553. As an Elector he held the title of High Marshal, which explains the references to war and the army of the Emperor. He was France's ally and in 1558 fought with the Duc de Guise against the Spanish at Thionville. Cf. J. Falke, *Geschichte des Kurfürsten August in volkswirtschaftlicher Beziehung*, Leipzig, 1868.

LXI
IOACHIMI MARCHIONIS
Brandeburgensis ac Elect.

MAGNANIMOS PRÆFECIT AVOS VIRTVSQVE FIDESQVE
CÆSAREÆ QVONDAM CAMERÆ, HVIVS MVNERIS HÆRES,
HOC PRECOR, VT CAMERA TENEBRÆQVE DOLIQVE FVGENTVR.

Joachim, Marquis of Brandenburg, Elector.
Courage, and the confidence of the Emperor's [electoral] chamber of old time, made my great-souled ancestors into leaders of men; I, being heir to this

privilege, pray that darkness and deceit may be driven from that chamber.

Joachim II, Prince-Elector of Brandenburg, succeeded to the title in 1535. His official function was that of High Chamberlain. He became a Protestant as early as 1539 and brought about the triumph of the Reform in his states. 'Il s'associera à ses deux collègues électeurs, le comte Palatin et le marquis de Saxe, dans la démarche collective qu'ils présentent, ainsi que d'autres princes allemands, alliés traditionnels de la France, le 19 mars 1558, à Henri II, en faveur des protestants parisiens, menacés de poursuites par le pouvoir royal.' (*Calvini opera*, XVII, pp. 99–100). This action annoyed Henry, who felt that they should be dealt with severely as soon as peace was signed with Spain.

LXII
OTHONIS HENRICI,
Comitis Palatini.

IMPIETAS MIHI RELIGIO CENSETVR AVITA,
CÆSARIBVSNE FERAM DAPIFER NOVA FERCVLA? NON HIS
ISTA PLACENT, HOC IAMQVE VEL HOC DII PRODITE VIRVS.

Otto Heinrich, Count Palatine.
My ancestral religion is held to be impiety; and shall I bear new dishes for the emperors as their steward? These dishes please them not; and now, ye gods, reveal this one or that one as a poison.

Otto Heinrich von Pfalz became Count Palatine and Elector in 1556. He joined the Reform movement in 1542 and helped transform the University of Heidelberg into a Protestant institution. This led to disagreement with the emperor and explains the references to the two dishes since the Count Palatine was the Grand Seneschal or Steward. ('Palatine' refers to the intendant who had charge of the palace and the court.)

LXIII
HERCVLIS
Ducis Ferrar.

ORA DEO SIMILES, SIMILEM DIIS ATQVE DEABVS
SVSCEPI SOBOLEM, NOBISQVE EST AVREA TOTA,
TOTA SED EST HOSTI FERRARIA FERREA NOSTRO.

Hercules, Duke of Ferrara.
Like a god in looks myself, I have had offspring like gods and goddesses; and so for us Ferrara is all clad in gold, but for our enemy 'tis all clad in iron.

This is a rather laboured pun on Ferrara and *ferrea* – 'iron-clad' or 'cruel' and 'hard-hearted.'

Ercole d'Este (1508–59) was Duke of Ferrara and Modena. He was married to Renée de France, daughter of Louis XII, and his sister Anne was the wife of François, duc de Guise. In 1556 he entered into a league with the Pope and the French against the Spanish (cf. p. 187) and the following year was made a lieutenant general of the French army. Cf. L. Romier, *Les Origines politiques des guerres de religion*, Paris, Perrin, 1914, II, pp. 199–211.

LXIV
COSMI MEDICIS
Florent. Ducis.

ARTIBVS INGENVIS DVCE TE FLORENTIA FLORET,
SED NOCET HENRICO TVA DVM FLORENTIA, QVID SI
IAM TIBI NON LONGO FLORENTIA FLOREAT ÆVO?

Cosimo de' Medici, Duke of Florence.
Under your leadership Florence flourishes with liberal arts; but so long as your Florence does harm to Henry, take care lest Florence should not flourish for you much longer.

There are puns on *dux* – duke and *dux* – leader in war, as well as *Florentia* – Florence and *florere* – to flourish.

Cosimo de' Medici (1519–74) was successively Duke of Florence (1537), Duke of Siena (1555), and Grand Duke of Tuscany (1569). He was a cousin of Catherine de' Medici but he was not on friendly terms with Francis I or Henry II except early in the latter's reign when he tried to establish good relations. Cosimo was renowned for his patronage of the arts but Jodelle is warning him about his attitude toward France. Cf. L. Romier, *Les Origines politiques des guerres de religion*, Paris, Perrin, 1913, I, pp. 334–50.

CÆTERI DESVNT.

ICONVM FINIS.

The remaining Images are wanting. End of the Images.

AD CLAVD. KERQVIFINANVM, 41r°

Steph. Iodelii, in suas miserias,

ELEGIA.[1]

Inter Apollineos Claudi mea cura sodales,
 Parsque meæ miseræ non miser ipse animæ,
Qui genio forsan meliore iuvabis, et unus
 Ingenii poteris arbiter esse mei,
Ingenium mihi si, mihi si cura ulla, iuvamen
 Si desperatis rebus adesse queat:
Fare rogo, rogo dic quid agam, vivamne tot inter
 Vulnera, seu sanem vulnera dira nece?
Mene iuvet vivente, neces mihi vivere mille,
 An mihi mille neces me moriente mori?
Extenso Tityus, religato sæpe Prometheus
 Corpore, ab imissa viscera rodor ave:
Alternis mensas Phineus mihi, Tantalus undas,
 Impius Ixion cessit et ipse rotam:
Alternisque novum me pondera Sisyphon urgent:
 Et frustra nostra flumina lata manu:
Cum mihi vel superos, superumve arcana petenti,
 Cura vorax animum vulturis instar edat:
Cum quidquid didici, quidquid longa arte paravi,
 Harpyiæ possint diripuisse novæ:
Copia cum nunquam sed me me deserat usus,
 Et rerum medio torqueat amne sitis:
Cum morbis, damnisque dolisque agitatus in orbem,
 Ut redit usque lues, sic miser usque roter,

1 For the translation of the Elegy to Claude de Kerquefinen, see p. 201.

41v° Cum mala Pauperies, saxum mihi grande superbo,
Pondere me, et mentem spe fugiente premat:
Cum frustra lassæ veniant sua commoda sorti,
Semper et exhausto perfluat urna lacu,
Denique devoto capiti cum stamina Clothus
Gaudia nulla ferant, tædia nulla negent.
Quo feror heu! iam nota tenent mea limina Diræ,
Iam iuvat intrepida rumpere fila manu.
Sanguine sors nostro, nostro placetur iniquus
Sanguine, et invidia Iuppiter usque vacet,
Invidet, hoc certum est, et me me æquasse Deorum
Ingeniis, potuit pænituisse Iovem,
Penituisse meæ Numen variabile vitæ
Hoc satis, hoc mortis grande levamen erit.
Spes nulla est ubi nulla Deis fiducia, Livor
Si cadit in superos, vah valeant superi:
Quid dixi miser? haud virtus sed crimina, non Dii
Sed me me ultrices exagitant Furiæ.
Parcite bacchanti superi, furor egit et error,
Ac numeros inflant turgida verba leves.
Ergo cum fato iungam modo crimen acerbo,
Debet utrumque mea morte piare manus.
Non sum qui Geticis Naso miser exul in oris,
Fœmineo longas more traham lachrimas:
Sum fortis, patiensque pati, passusque tot annos
Pro lachrimis patiar ut mihi sanguis eat:
Vel superum risisse minas, tormentaque forti,
Vel se se solum vincere posse placet.
42r° Spem Iovis imperio totus mihi sustulit Orcus,
Cum spe ergo manes auferat ille meos.
Non frangunt tormenta, mora sed frangor, et expes
Heu video vigiles in mea damna Deos.

Non exhorrebo Minoam conscius urnam,
Quasque malis pœnas manibus esse putant:
Nam quæ pallentem populum Minoïa plectunt
Supplicia, in nostrum versa fuere caput.
Vah ego qui fueram linguaque manuque disertus,
Hæreo, et hic hæret vox, et inepta manus:
Cum nequeam quæ me toties vibrata retorquent
Fulmina, in assuetos conservisse modos.
Copia dira nocet, nec post mea funera tento
Lectorem in lachrimas sollicitare meas:
Iam fracto iugulo, et me iamque silente silebunt
In nostros superum crimina tanta lares.
Felices animæ durus quas victor, Amorve
Innumeras iussit vincere morte neces:
Ast ego iam moriens vobis fœlicior, adstant
Cui mala tot vestris heu graviora malis:
Victores duri, superum inclementia, Livor,
Tempus, et inferna turba minata face:
Victores duros victricia funera vincunt,
Mortis et in mortem fervidus urget amor:
Sic nec me superi, nec me fortuna, malorum
Nec rabies, animum sed necat hunc animus:
Nam modo quid speret? vel si quoque speret, inultam
Hanc quoque spem, nusquam numina sæva sinent:
Tot mala, totque metus cum Spes ferat, unica vitæ 42v°
Causa mihi Spes hæc deterioris erit.
Nequicquam sperat, cuius præsaga futuri
Mens videt, in peius quam sibi cuncta ruant.
Quin moriar, quin iam moriar, mutumque cadaver
Iam mihi ceu tumulus Spemque metumque premat
Quæ mora? quid trepido? tantis cur stamina verbis
Impia produco? quo rigeo ipse gelu?

Infelix quis me Genius tenet? unde trementi
 Hæc ratio, vitæ trux amor unde meæ?
Proh superum scelus! in nostram redit improba mentem
 Hospita supliciis Spes mage sæva meis,
Quæ vetet, ut gravius peream, me blanda perire,
 Et longum dempto funere funus alat.
Spero ergo, et vivo, si quisquam extinctus, et expes,
 Spem simul, et vitam posse fovere putat,
Quo vertar miser? an vivensque sciensque peribo?
 Hæc puto sunt fatis addita fata meis.
En tibi (consiliis quoniam melioribus uti
 Me iuvat) en Claudi spes mea, vita mea.
Solus utramque iuves, perimas seu solus utramque,
 Si sperare licet, spem quoque iunge meæ:
Si vita, et mœstæ prosint oblivia vitæ,
 Fac mala Lethæis iniiciantur aquis:
Ut si quid versis felix mage sydera fatis
 Adtulerint solus Claudius esse queat,
Non qui spem vitamque iuvet, sed iure vocari
 Qui mea spes unus, qui mea vita queat.

To Claude de Kerquefinen, An Elegy by Estienne Jodelle on his troubles.[2]

Claude, you are my [special] care among the close friends of Apollo, and though not unhappy yourself, are a part of my unhappy soul; you who perchance shall help me with a spirit better able than mine to guide, and who alone shall be able to judge my talent, if any talent or any care can deliver me, or if any assistance is able to rescue my desperate condition. I beseech you, speak; I

2 For Claude de Kerquefinen and his relations with Jodelle, see E. Balmas, *Etienne Jodelle*, pp. 395–428. Cf. also S.F. Baridon, *Claude de Kerquefinen, italianisant et hérétique*, Geneva, Droz, 1954 and S.F. Baridon, 'A Propos de l'élégie de Jodelle à Claude de Kerquefinen,' *Bibliothèque d'Humanisme et Renaissance*, XXII (1960), p. 199.

beseech you, say what I am to do, – am I to live among all those wounds, or to heal my dreadful wounds by dying? Would it please you that, with myself alive, a thousand deaths should live for me or that, with myself dying, a thousand deaths should die for me? Often I have my innards torn by the attacking bird, whether with my body stretched, like Tityus, or with body bound, like Prometheus; in turn Phineus has given me his tables and Tantalus his waves, and impious Ixion himself has handed over to me his wheel; in turn weights press upon me, like a new Sisyphus, and water is bought in vain by my hand;[3] while devouring Care, like a vulture, gnaws at my heart as I seek either gods or the secrets of gods; when new Harpies can tear asunder whatever I have learnt, whatever I have acquired by long practice of my art; when I am never deserted by my resources but by opportunity to exercise them, and in the middle of the stream I am tortured by thirst for material; when, harassed and driven through the world by diseases, losses and deceits, as my affliction evermore returns, so evermore I am buffeted about in my unhappy state, since miserable poverty, a huge stone for my arrogance, weighs me down, and my spirit too, with hope vanishing; since in vain do the proper comforts come to my wearied state, and the water-pot ever leaks, with water draining away; since finally, the threads of Clotho[4] bring no joy to my doomed head, and deny me no griefs whither, alas! am I being carried? Now the Furies are occupying my familiar threshold, now they delight to break, with unflinching hand, the thread of my life. Let Fate be appeased with my blood; and with my blood let unkind Jupiter be appeased, and may he ever cease to hate me. For hate me he does, 'tis sure; and Jove may have repented of making me equal to the gods in talents; and the fact that the fickle godhead should have repented of my living shall be enough; it shall be a mighty solace for my death. Where there is no hope, and no trust in gods, if Envy affects the gods themselves, then farewell to the gods! But what have I said, wretch that I am? It is not my virtue, but my misdeeds; not the gods, but avenging Furies that pursue

3 Alluding to the punishment of the Danaids, condemned to fetch water in a sieve.

4 The Fate who spins the thread of life.

me. Have mercy on my ravings, O ye gods; 'twas madness and blind delusion that drove me, and swelling words of pride that puff up my thoughtless verses. So, since I now unite wickedness to bitter fate, my hand ought to expiate both of these by my death. I am not one who, like Naso,[5] an unhappy exile on Getic[6] shores, can in womanish fashion prolong lengthy and tearful laments[7]; I am courageous and patient under suffering, and, having suffered for so many years, will suffer my blood to flow instead of tears; 'tis a brave man's will either to laugh to scorn the threats of the gods, or to be able to conquer himself by his sole strength. At Jove's command, all Hell has bereft me of hope; so let him take away, along with my hope, my spirit too. Torments break me not, but I am broken by delay; and hopelessly, alas, I see the gods attentive to my ruin. I will not guiltily blench before the urn[8] of Minos,[9] and the penalties men deem to exist for shades of departed wrongdoers: for the penalties of Minos, that harass the pale throng of the dead, have turned upon my own head. Alas for me, who once was eloquent with tongue and pen: I am in deep distress, and here my voice is silent and my pen is of no effect since I cannot in my accustomed ways forge thunderbolts such as do so often threaten and assail me. The dread armament hurts me, nor do I attempt to persuade any reader to weep for me after I am gone; when my neck is already broken, and already I am silent, then will these heavy reproaches of the heavenly gods against my house fall silent too. Happy the souls whom a stern conqueror, or love, has bidden to defeat, by dying, numberless deaths; but I, as I now die, am happier than you, inasmuch as I am threatened by so many evils that are worse, alas, than yours: stern conquerors, the cruelty of the gods above, and envy, and the age, and a mob threatening me with infernal fire. As stern conquerors are conquered by conquering death, and burning love of death it is that presses them to die; so the gods slay me not, nor fortune, nor the mad rage of evil

5 Ovid.

6 The Getæ were the people of Tomis, where Ovid was sent in exile.

7 In the *Tristia* and *Ex Ponto*, the long poems of Ovid's exile. Cf. Jodelle's 'Elegy' to his book, p. 69.

8 The judicial voting-urn, the symbol of Greek justice.

9 Judge among the dead.

men, but my spirit it is that slays this spirit of mine: for, what can it presently hope for? Or, even if it should indeed hope, nowhere will the harsh gods permit even this hope to go unpunished. Since hope brings so many evils and so many fears, this same hope will be sole cause of a worse life for me. In vain he hopes, whose foretelling mind sees how all for him goes speedily from bad to worse. Why should I not die, why should I not die now, and let my silent corpse rest heavily, like a tomb, upon my hopes and fears? What reason is there for delay? Why do I tremble? Why do I impiously prolong the threads[10] of fate with such vaunting words? With what icy chill is my body stiffened? What accursed spirit possesses me? Whence comes this reasoning as I tremble, whence comes the obstinate love of life in me? Ah, the wickedness of the gods above! Hope irrepressibly returns to my heart, a guest more cruel than my punishments, to forbid me in her kindness to die, and by taking away my present death to foster a distant death instead. So I hope, and live – if anyone ruined and hopeless believes he can cherish hope and life together. Whither shall I turn in my wretchedness? Am I to perish, living and aware? Yes, I think these dooms have indeed been added to my fate. Here, then, Claude, you have my hope, my life – since it pleases me to seek better counsel. You alone can aid both my hope and my life; or you alone may take both of them away. If it is possible to hope, then add hope also to that which I have; or, if life and the forgetfulness of a sad life are good things, then cause my troubles to be sprinkled with the waters of Lethe,[11] so that, if the stars should bring to me any happier event with a change in my destiny, Claude alone should be able to be, not merely one who *aids* hope and life, but one who alone can rightly be *called* 'my hope, my life.'

A SA MUSE.

CHAPITRE

Tu sçais o vaine Muse, o Muse solitaire
Maintenant avecq moy, que ton chant qui n'a rien 43r°

10 Of life. Cf. n. 4 above.

11 Bringing forgetfulness. Cf. p. 96.

Du vulgaire, ne plaist non plus qu'un chant vulgaire.
Tu sçais que plus je suis prodigue de ton bien,
Pour enrichir des grands l'ingrate renommée,
Et plus je pers le tens, ton espoir et le mien.
Tu sçais que seullement toute chose est aimée,
Qui fait d'un homme un singe, et que la verité
Sous les piés de l'Erreur gist ores assommée.
Tu sçais que l'on ne sçait où gist la Volupté,
Bien qu'on la cherche en tout, car la Raison sujete
Au Desir, trouve l'heur en l'infelicité.
Tu sçais que la Vertu qui seulle nous rachete
De la nuit, se retient elle mesme en sa nuit
Pour ne vivre qu'en soy sourde aveugle et muete.
Tu sçais que tous les jours celui là plus la fuit
Qui montre mieus la suivre, et que nostre visage
Se masque de ce bien à qui nostre cueur nuit.
Tu sçais que le plus fol prend bien le nom de sage
Aveuglé des flateurs, mais il semble au poisson,
Qui engloutit l'amorse et la mort au rivage.
Tu sçais que quelques vns se repaissent d'un son
Qui les flate par tout, mais helas ils dementent
La courte opinion, la gloire, et la chanson.
43v° Tu sçais que moy vivant les vivans ne te sentent,
Car l'Equité se rend esclave de faveur.
Et plus sont creus ceus-là qui plus effrontés mentent.
Tu sçais que le sçavoir n'a plus son vieil honneur,
Et qu'on ne pense plus que l'heureuse nature,
Puisse rendre un jeune homme à tout œuvre meilleur.
Tu sçais que dautant plus, me faisant mesme injure,
Je m'aide des Vertus affin de leur aider,
Et plus je suis tiré dans leur prison obscure.
Tu sçais que je ne puis si tost me commender,

Tu connois ce bon cueur, quand pour la recompanse,
Il me faut à tous coups le pardon demander.

Tu sçais comment il fault gesner ma contenance
Quand un peuple me juge, et qu'en depit de moy
J'abaisse mes sourcis sous ceus de l'Ignorance.

Tu sçais que quand un Prince auroit bien dit de toy,
Un plaisant s'en riroit, ou qu'un pipeur Stoïque
Te voudrait par sotie attacher de sa loy.

Tu sçais que tous les jours un labeur poëtique,
Apporte à son autheur ces beaus noms seullement,
De farceur, de rimeur, de fol, de fantastique.

Tu sçais que si je veus embrasser mesmement
Les affaires, l'honneur, les guerres, les voyages,
Mon merite tout seul me sert d'empeschement.

Bref tu sçais quelles sont les envieuses rages,
Qui mesme au cueur des grands peuvent avoir vertu,
Et qu'avecq' le mepris se naissent les outrages.

Mais tu sçais bien aussi, pour neant aurois-tu 44r°
Debatu si long tens, et dedans ma pensée
De toute Ambition le pouvoir combatu.

Tu sçais que la Vertu n'est point recompansée
Sinon que de soymesme, et que le vray loyer
De l'homme vertueus c'est sa Vertu passée.

Pour elle seulle donq je me veus employer,
Me deussé-je noyer moymesme dans mon fleuve,
Et de mon propre feu le chef me foudroyer.

Si donq' un changement au reste je n'epreuve,
Il fault que le seul vray me soit mon but dernier,
Et que mon bien total dedans moy seul se treuve,
Jamais l'Opinion ne sera mon colier.

FIN.

PART III

ILLUSTRATIONS

1 *Arch of the Porte aux Peintres*

2 Giulio Camillo dell'Abbate (?), *Arch of the Porte aux Peintres*

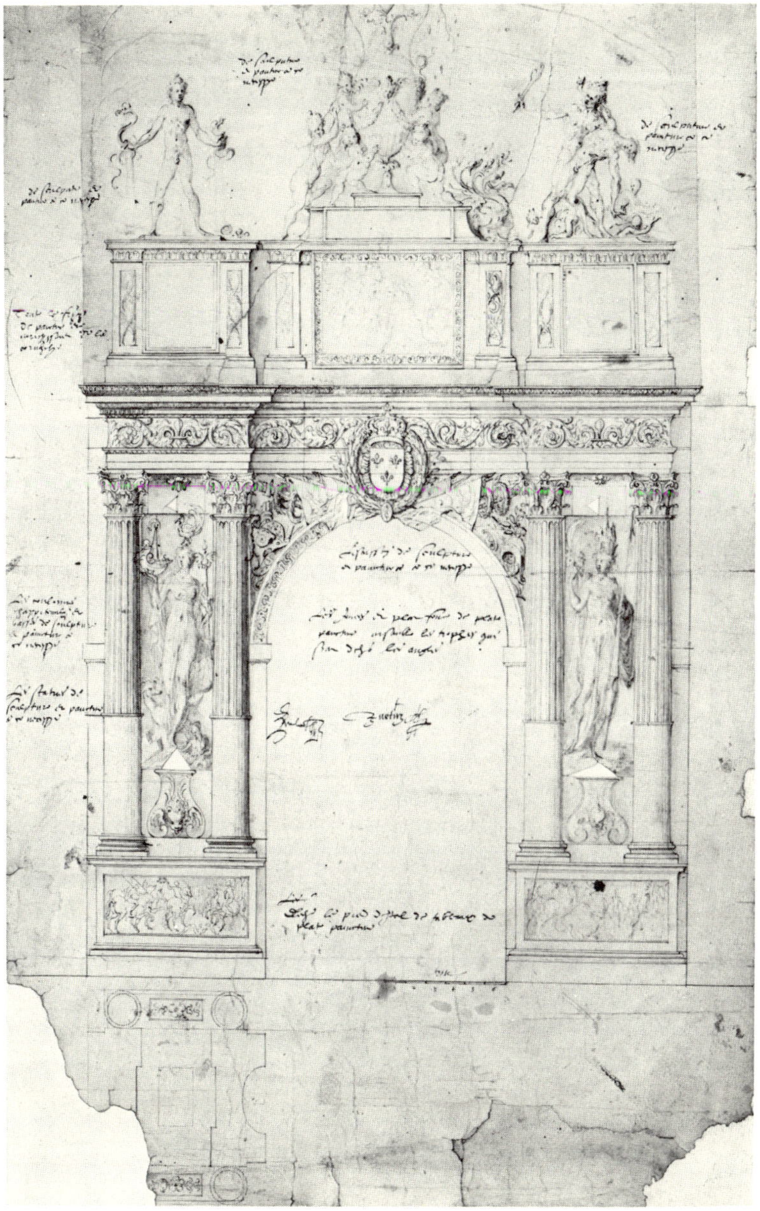

3 *SS. Denis and Rémi*

4 *The Conversion of Clovis*

5 Rosso Fiorentino, '*L'Ignorance chassée*'

6 Giulio Bonasone, '*Non vinci potis est, neq. fingi regia virtus*'

7 *'Ex utroque Cæsar'*

SEQVITVR QVODCVNQVE PETIT. *Signifiant que toute ſa vie elle ha eſté ſi heureuſe, que l'on ne luy refuſa onques choſe, de quoy elle euſt enuie.*

POVR VN GRAND SEIGNEVR.

Vn grand Seigneur me demanda vn iour, quelle Deuiſe il pourroit porter pour donner à entendre au monde qu'il auoit grande enuie, & cherchoit tous les moyens d'eſtre encore plus grãd & puiſſant que les autres. Parquoy ie luy en baillay vne d'vn Empereur armé auec ſa couronne de laurier en la teſte,

tenant

8 Gabriello Symeoni, *Cesar renouvellé* . . .

CESAR

RENOVVELLE'.

Par les obſeruations Militaires du S. Gabriel Symeon, Floren.

A Monſeigneur le Daulphin de France.

A PARIS,

Pour Iean Longis, tenant ſa boutique au Palais, en la galerie, par ou on va à la Chancellerie.

1558.

AVEC PRIVILEGE DV ROY.

9 *'In effigiem . . . Henrici secundi'*

IN EFFIGIEM CHRI-
STIANISSIMI FRAN-
CORVM REGIS, HEN-
RICI SECVNDI.

Illud honorandum populo, magnísque timendum,
Et cui iure subest Gallia tota, caput:
Henrici est Regis, rationis Regia, cui plus
Quàm linguæ est cerebri: mentis imago nota est.

10 Antoine Caron, *Histoire françoyse de nostre temps*

11 Antoine Caron, *The Reign of François Ier*

12 Antoine Caron, *The Reign of François II*

13 Antoine Caron, *The Reign of Henry II*

14 Antoine Caron, *The Reign of Charles IX*

15 Antoine Caron, *Henry II and Catherine de' Medici*

16 Antoine Caron, *The Descendance of Henry II and Catherine de' Medici*

17 Baptiste Pellerin (?), *The Elevation of the French Cardinals*

18 Antoine Caron, *The Ascendance of the Kings of France*

19 Antoine Caron, '*La Renaissance des Arts et Lettres*'

20 Antoine Caron, *The Siege of Metz*

21 ‘ΦΩΣ ΦΕΡΟΙ ΗΔΕ ΓΑΛΗΝΗΝ’

ΦΩ͂Σ ΦΈΡΟΙ ἭΔΕ ΓΑΛΉΝΗΝ.

Madame Catherine, treſchretienne Royne de France, ha pour Deuiſe l'Arc celeſte, ou Arc en ciel : qui eſt le vray ſine de clere ſerenité, & tranquilité de Paix.

22 After B. Pellerin, *Les figures et portraicts des sept aages*, *Adolessance*

23 *Le pourtraict de la ville de Calais . . .*

24 *Le vray pourtraict de la ville & Chasteau de Guines*

25 Baptiste Pellerin (?), *How Iosephe is faulselye accused by his maistresse*

26 Baptiste Pellerin (?), '*Le Char des Muses*'

27 Giovanni Antonio de Rossi, medal of the taking of Calais in 1558

HENRICVS · II · REX · CHRISTIANISS

MAIORA SEQVENTVR

28 *Impresa* of Henry II, type I

Non cede in alcuna parte alla ſudetta, quella , che di preſente porta il Figliuol ſucceſſor ſuo il magnanimo Rè Herrico; ilquale continua di portare l'impreſa, che già fece quando era Delfino, che è la Luna creſcente col brauo motto pieno di graue ſentimẽto, DONEC TOTVM IMPLEAT ORBEM. *volendo dinotare. ch'egli, fin che non arriuaua all'heredità del Regno, non poteua moſtrare il ſuo intero valore, ſi come la Luna nõ può compitamente riſplendere, ſe prima non arriua alla ſua perfetta grandezza, e di queſto ſuo generoſo penſiero n'ha già dato chiariſsimo ſaggio con la recuperatione di Bologna, & altre molte impreſe, com' ogn' vn sà in Italia.*

Per

29 *Impresa* of Henry II, type 2

Donec totum impleat orbem.

La Deuise à present du Treschretien & victorieus Roy Henri II. *de ce nom, est la Lune en son croissant: Es sacrees escritures donques la Lune prefigure l'Eglise, quasi en tous passages, à quoy se conforme l'histoire recitee par Paul Emil du Pape Calixte* II. *(au parauant apellé Guy, fils de Guillaume Conte de Bourgongne,) lequel la nuit precedent sa creacion, eut vision d'un ieune enfant qui lui aporta & mit une Lune sur le giron. La Lune aussi est sugette à mutacions, croissant & decroissant de tems en tems: ainsi veritablement est*

Paul Emil.

l'Eglise

30 *Impresa* of Henry II, type 3

DI MONS. GIOVIO. 25

Per il che gli fù da me fatta à richieſta del Signor Mortier Ambaſciator Franceſe in Roma dopò la morte del Rè Franceſco vna Luna piena di tutto tondo con vn motto di ſopra: QVVM PLENA EST, FIT AEMVLA SOLIS. *Per dimoſtrar, ch'egli haueua tanto ſplendore, che s'agguagliaua al Sole, facendo la notte chiara, com'il giorno.* DOM. *Senza fallo queſte tre impreſe di queſti tre Rè Franceſi hanno (à mio parere) tutta quella grandezza, che ſi ricerca, sì di ſoggetto e viſta, come di ſpirito e ſignificato; e non sò ſe gliargutiſſimi Spagnuoli v'aggiungeranno.* GIO. *Voi non v'ingannate certo, perche difficil coſa è il migliorare.*

d

31 *'L'Obelisque'*

32 Jeton of François II as Dauphin, 1547; jeton of François II

33 Jetons of Mme Marguerite prior to and after her marriage

34 *Hæc tibi Meta*, medal of François de Guise, 1552

35 *Perseus and Andromeda*, medal of Henry II

36 Numerary medal of the taking of Calais in 1451, larger module

37 Jean Clouet, *François Ier*

38 *Henry II*, drawing

39 François Clouet, *François Ier*

40 Workshop of François Clouet, *Henry II*

41 Antonio Tempesta, *Henry II*

42 Marc Bechot, '*Libertas*' medal of Henry II, 1552

43 *'La Perspective du Change'*

La Perspectiue
du Change.

7

44 Marc Bechot, medal of Henry II as a composite deity, 1552

45 Gabriello Symeoni, *Interpretation . . . du Monstre, ou Enigme d'Italie*

46 *'Typus hispanici huius arcus'*

47 Medals of Henry II and François de Guise for the defence of Metz, 1552

PLATE ILLUSTRATIONS

20 Antoine Caron, *The Siege of Metz*, drawing from the *Histoire françoyse de nostre temps*. Paris, Cabinet des Dessins, Inv. RF 29714

21 ‘ΦΏΣ ΦΈΡΟΙ ἭΔΕ ΓΑΛΉΝΗΝ,’ woodcut. Claude Paradin, *Les Devises héroiques*. Lyon, G. Rouillé, 1557, p. 64 Paris, BN Rés. Z 2550

22 After Baptiste Pellerin, *Les figures et portraicts des sept aages*, *Adolessance*. Paris, N. Le Camus, 1595^{2} Paris, BN Rés. G 1400 (4), fol. 96

23 *Le Pourtraict de la ville de Calais* . . . , woodcut. Paris, Bibliothèque Mazarine, 5921 F 9e/2 Rés.

24 *Le vray pourtraict de la ville & Chasteau de Guines*, woodcut. Paris, BN Est. Va 148

25 Baptiste Pellerin(?), *How Iosephe is faulselye accused by his maistresse*, woodcut. Paris, BN Est. Rés. Ed 5g, fol. 10^{v}

26 Baptiste Pellerin(?), ‘*Le char des Muses*,’ drawing from the *Suite d'Arthémise*. Paris, BN Est. Rés. Ad 105, fol. 24^{r}

27 Giovanni Antonio de Rossi. Medal of the Taking of Calais in 1558. London, British Museum

28 *Impresa* of Henry II, type I. Paolo Giovio, *Dialogo dell' Imprese militari et amorose*, Lyon, G. Rouillé, 1559^{1}, p. 24. Paris, Bibliothèque Sainte-Geneviève, Z 751

29 *Impresa* of Henry II, type 2. Claude Paradin, *Les devises héroiques*. Lyon, G. Rouillé, 1557, p. 20 Paris, BN Rés. Z 2550

30 *Impresa* of Henry II, type 3. Paolo Giovio, *Dialogo dell' Imprese militari et amorose*, Lyon, G. Rouillé, 1559^{1}, p. 25. Paris, Bibiliothèque Sainte-Geneviève, Z 751

31 ‘*L'Obelisque*,’ woodcut. *La magnificence de la superbe et triumphante entree* . . . Lyon, G. Rouillé, 1549, fol. D4 Paris, BN Rés. Lb^{31} 14

32 Jeton of François II as Dauphin, 1547 (La Tour, cat. 107). Paris, BN Cabinet des Médailles

Jeton of François II (La Tour, cat. 112). Paris BN Cabinet des Médailles

33 Jeton of Mme Marguerite prior to her marriage (Pradel, cat. 261). Paris, BN Cabinet des Médailles

Jeton of Mme Marguerite after her marriage (Pradel, cat. 264). Paris, BN Cabinet des Médailles

34 *Hæc tibi Meta*, medal of François de Guise, 1552 (Mazerolle, cat. 408). Paris, BN Cabinet des Médailles

35 *Perseus and Andromeda*, medal of Henry II (Mazerolle, cat. 340). Paris, BN Cabinet des Médailles

36 Numerary medal of the Taking of Calais in 1451, larger module. (Mazerolle, cat. I). Paris, BN Cabinet des Médailles

37 Jean Clouet, *François Ier*, miniature. Paris, Cabinet des Dessins, Inv. MI 1092

38 *Henry II*, drawing. Chantilly, Musée Condé, Inv. 334

39 François Clouet, *François Ier*, panel. Florence, Uffizi, Inv. 667

40 Workshop of François Clouet, *Henry II*, formerly panel. The Metropolitan Museum of Art, Bequest of Helen Hay Whitney, 1944, Inv. 45.128.12

FIGURES IN TEXT

SOURCES OF PHOTOGRAPHS

* Bibliothèque Nationale, Paris, figs.
1 (neg. C 36681), 3 (neg. C 41330),
4 (neg. C 41331), 6 (neg. 42333),
7 (neg. C 40261), 8 (neg. B 51440),
21 (neg. B 50343), 22 (neg. C 40451),
23 (neg. C 41052), 24 (neg. C 5214),
25 (neg. C 40322), 26 (neg. C 36138),
29 (neg. B 50341), 31 (neg. C 40262),
32 (neg. A 20048/49; 20056/57),
33 (neg. A 20058/59; 20050/51),
34 (neg. A 20354/55), 35 (neg. A 18420/21),
36 (neg. B 49612/13), 41 (neg. B 41028),
42 (neg. A 15090/91), 43 (neg. C 20231),
44 (neg. A 15086/91; 5087/88);
45 (neg. C 42350), 46 (neg. C 15525),
47 (neg. A 7737/38; 20352/53)

British Museum, London, figs. 9, 27. Reproduced by permission of the trustees of the British Museum.

Esparcieux, Fontainebleau, fig. 5

Giraudon, Paris, figs. 37 (neg. 6139), 38

Lalance, Paris, figs. 28, 30

The Metropolitan Museum of Art, Bequest of Helen Hay Whitney, 1944, fig. 40 (neg. 135386)

Musée du Louvre, Cabinet des Dessins, figs. 10, 11, 12, 13, 14, 15, 16, 17, 18, 19, 20

Nationalmuseum, Stockholm, fig. 2

Uffizi, Florence, fig. 39 (neg. 102939)

* Lettering corresponds to negative sizes, hence A is 9 × 12 cm, B is 13 × 18 cm, and C is 18 × 24 cm. All medals and jetons are reproduced in their original scale.

INDEX

This index includes proper names, both historical and mythological, but only where the references are *substantive*. (Because of their frequent recurrence, Henry II and Jodelle have been omitted entirely.)

Also listed are various devices, themes, and titles where these may prove helpful.

This book
was designed by
ANTJE LINGNER
under the direction of
ALLAN FLEMING
University of
Toronto
Press